Emotion,
Obesity,
and Crime

SOCIAL PSYCHOLOGY

A series of monographs, treatises, and texts

EDITORS

LEON FESTINGER AND STANLEY SCHACHTER

Emotion, Obesity, and Crime

Stanley Schachter

Department of Psychology
Columbia University
New York, New York

ACADEMIC PRESS
New York and London   1971

ACADEMIC PRESS, INC.
111 Fifth Avenue, New York, New York 10003

United Kingdom Edition published by
ACADEMIC PRESS, INC. (LONDON) LTD.
Berkeley Square House, London W1X 6BA

LIBRARY OF CONGRESS CATALOG CARD NUMBER: 71-137590

PRINTED IN THE UNITED STATES OF AMERICA

CONTENTS

Acknowledgments

Many of the studies presented in this book were first reported in a variety of journals and monographs published by the American Psychological Association, the University of Nebraska Press, and Academic Press. To these organizations my thanks for permission to reprint portions of the original articles.

Leon Festinger, Julian Hochberg, Dennis Kelly, and Eliot Stellar have critically read major sections of the manuscript or have been particularly generous in contributing their ideas and time to discussions of experimental design and interpretation. Lucy Friedman was most helpful in editorial work and Stephanie Sommer typed the manuscript.

Most of all, I am grateful to my graduate students and research assistants during the years that we were working together on these studies. They have been an extraordinary and imaginative group, and the extent of my debt to each of them will be evident in these pages.

The manuscript was prepared while I held a Guggenheim Fellowship. The research was supported by PHS Grants M-2584 and MH-05203 from the National Institute of Mental Health and Research Grants GS732 and G23758 from the National Science Foundation.

Part I

Emotion: Cognitive and Physiological Correlates

Chapter I

The Interaction of Cognitive and Physiological Determinants of Emotional State

Many years ago, piqued by the disorderly cataloguing of symptoms that characterized the then classic works on emotion, William James offered what was probably the first simple, integrating, theoretical statement on the nature of emotion. This well-known formulation stated simply that "the bodily changes follow directly the perception of the exciting fact, and that our feeling of the same changes as they occur *is* the emotion (James, 1890, p. 449)." Since James' proposition equates bodily changes and visceral feelings with emotion, it must follow, first, that the different emotions will be accompanied by recognizably different bodily states and, second, that the manipulation of bodily state, by drugs or surgery, will also manipulate emotional state. These implications have, directly or indirectly, guided much of the research on emotion since James' day. The results of this research, on the whole, provided little support for a purely visceral formulation of emotion, and led Cannon (1927,1929) to his brilliant and devastating critique of the James-Lange theory—a critique based on these points:

1. The total separation of the visceral from the central nervous system does not alter emotional behavior.

2. The same visceral changes occur in very different emotional states and in nonemotional states.

3. The viscera are relatively insensitive structures.

4. Visceral changes are too slow to be a source of emotional feeling.

5. The artificial induction of visceral changes that are typical of strong emotions does not produce the emotions.

Though new data have weakened the cogency of some of these points, on the whole Cannon's logic and findings make it inescapably clear that a completely peripheral or visceral formulation of emotion, such as the James-Lange theory, is simply inadequate to cope with the facts. In an effort to deal with the obvious inadequacies of a purely visceral or peripheral formulation of emotion, Ruckmick (1936), Hunt, Cole, and Reis (1958), Schachter (1959), and others have suggested that cognitive factors may be major determinants of emotional states. In this volume I shall attempt to spell out the implications of a cognitive-physiological formulation of emotion and to describe a series of experiments designed to test these implications.

To begin, let us grant, on the basis of much evidence (see Woodworth and Schlosberg, 1954, for example), that a general pattern of sympathetic discharge is characteristic of emotional states. Given such a state of arousal, it is suggested that one labels, interprets, and identifies this state in terms of the characteristics of the precipitating situation and one's apperceptive mass. This suggests, then, that an emotional state may be considered a function of a state of physiological arousal[1] and a cognition appropriate to this state of arousal. The cognition, in a sense, exerts a steering function. Cognitions arising from the immediate situation as interpreted by past experience provide the framework within which one understands and label one's feelings. It is the cognition that determines whether the state of physiological arousal will be labeled "anger," "joy," or whatever.

In order to examine the implications of this formulation, let us consider how these two elements—a state of physiological arousal and cognitive factors—would interact in a variety of situations. In most emotion-inducing situations, of course, the two factors are completely interrelated. Imagine a man walking alone down a dark alley when a figure with a gun suddenly appears. The perception-cognition "figure with a gun" in some fashion initiates a state of physiological arousal; this state of arousal is interpreted in terms of knowledge about dark alleys and guns, and the state of arousal is labeled "fear." Similarly, a student who unexpectedly learns that he has made Phi Beta Kappa may experience a state of arousal which he will label "joy."

Let us now consider circumstances in which these two elements, the physiological and the cognitive, are, to some extent, independent. First, is the state of physiological arousal alone sufficient to induce an emotion? Best evidence indicates that it is not. Marañon (1924), in a fascinating study, injected

---

[1] Though the first experiments to be described are concerned largely with the physiological changes produced by the injection of adrenaline, which appear to be primarily the result of sympathetic excitation, the term physiological arousal is used in preference to the more specific "excitement of the sympathetic nervous system" because there are indications, to be discussed later, that this formulation is applicable to a variety of bodily states.

210 of his patients with the sympathomimetic agent adrenaline and then asked them to introspect. Seventy-one percent of his subjects simply reported physical symptoms with no emotional overtone; 29% of the subjects responded in an apparently emotional fashion. Of these, the majority described their feelings in a way that Maranon labeled "cold" or "as if" emotions; that is, they made statements such as "I feel *as if* I were afraid" or "*as if* I were awaiting a great happiness." This is a sort of emotional *déjà vu* experience; these subjects are neither happy nor afraid, but only feel "as if" they were. Finally, a few cases apparently reported a genuine emotional experience. However, in order to produce this reaction in most of these few cases, Maranon points out, "one must suggest a memory with strong affective force but not so strong as to produce an emotion in the normal state. For example, in several cases, we spoke to our patients before the injection about their sick children or dead parents, and they responded calmly to this topic. The same topic presented later, during the adrenal commotion, was sufficient to trigger emotion. This adrenal commotion places the subject in a situation of 'affective imminence' (pp. 307–308)." Apparently, then, to produce a genuinely emotional reaction to adrenaline, Marañon was forced to provide such subjects with an appropriate cognition.

Though Marañon does not explicitly describe his procedure, it is clear that his subjects knew that they were receiving an injection, and in all likelihood they knew that they were receiving adrenaline and probably had some familiarity with its effects. In short, though they underwent the pattern of sympathetic discharge common to strong emotional states, at the same time they had a completely appropriate cognition or explanation of why they felt this way. This, I would suggest, is the reason so few of Marañon's subjects reported any emotional experience.

Consider next a person in a state of physiological arousal for which no immediate explanation or appropriate cognitions are available. Such a state could result were one to inject a subject with adrenaline covertly, or, unknown to him, feed him a sympathomimetic drug such as ephedrine. Under such conditions a subject would be aware of palpitations, tremor, face flushing, and most of the symptoms associated with a discharge of the sympathetic nervous system. In contrast to Marañon's subjects, he would, however, be utterly unaware of why he felt this way. What would be the consequence of such a state?

In other contexts, I (1959) have suggested that just such a state would lead to the arousal of "evaluative needs" (Festinger, 1954); that is, an individual in this state would feel pressures to understand and label his bodily feelings. His bodily state grossly resembles the condition in which it has been at times of emotional excitement. How would he label his present feelings? It is suggested, of course, that he will label his feelings in terms of his knowledge of the immediate situation.[2] Should he at the time be with a beautiful woman he might decide that he was wildly in love or sexually excited. Should he be at a gay party, he might, by comparing himself to others, decide that he was extremely happy and euphoric. Should he be arguing with his wife, he might explode in fury and hatred. Or, should the situation be completely inappropriate, he might decide that he was excited about something that had recently happened to him, or, simply, I suppose, that he was sick. In any case, it is my basic assumption that emotional states are a function of the interaction of such cognitive factors with a state of physiological arousal.

This line of thought, then, leads to the following propositions:

1. Given a state of physiological arousal for which an individual has no immediate explanation, he will "label" this state and describe his feelings in terms of the cognitions available to him. To the extent that cognitive factors are potent determiners of emotional states, one might anticipate that precisely the same state of physiological arousal could be labeled "joy," or "fury," or any of a great number of emotional labels, depending on the cognitive aspects of the situation.

2. Given a state of physiological arousal for which an individual has a completely appropriate explanation (e.g., "I feel this way because I have just received an injection of adrenaline"), no evaluative needs will arise and the individual is unlikely to label his feelings in terms of the alternative cognitions available.

Now consider a condition in which emotion-inducing cognitions are present but there is no state of physiological arousal. For example, an individual might be completely aware that he is in great danger but for some reason (drug or surgical) remain in a state of physiological quiescence. Does he experience the emotion "fear"? This formulation of emotion as a joint function of a state of physiological arousal and an appropriate cognition, would, of course, suggest that he does not; this leads to my final proposition.

3. Given the same cognitive circumstances, the individual will react emotionally or describe his feelings as emotions only to the extent that he experiences a state of physiological arousal.[3]

The experimental test of these propositions requires, first, the experimental

---

[2] This suggestion is not new. Several psychologists have suggested that situational factors should be considered the chief differentiators of the emotions. Hunt, Cole, and Reis (1958) probably make this point most explicitly in their study distinguishing among fear, anger, and sorrow in terms of situational characteristics.

[3] In his critique of the James-Lange theory of emotion, Cannon (1929) makes the point that sympathectomized animals and patients do seem to manifest emotional behavior. This criticism is, of course, as applicable to the above proposition as it was to the James-Lange formulation. The issues involved will be discussed in Chapter 4.

manipulation of a state of physiological arousal, second, the manipulation of the extent to which the subject has an appropriate or proper explanation of his bodily state and, third, the creation of situations from which explanatory cognitions may be derived.

In order to satisfy these experimental requirements, Schachter and Singer (1962) designed an experiment cast in the framework of a study of the effects of vitamin supplements on vision. As soon as a subject arrived, he was taken to a private room and told by the experimenter:

> In this experiment we would like to make various tests of your vision. We are particularly interested in how certain vitamin compounds and vitamin supplements affect the visual skills. In particular, we want to find out how the vitamin compound called "Suproxin" affects your vision.
>
> What we would like to do, with your permission, is to give you a small injection of Suproxin. The injection itself is mild and harmless; however, since some people do object to being injected we don't want to talk you into anything. Would you mind receiving a Suproxin injection?

If the subject agreed to the injection (and all but one of 185 subjects did) the experimenter continued with instructions to be described shortly, then left the room. In a few minutes a physician entered the room, briefly repeated the experimenter's instructions, took the subject's pulse, and then injected him with Suproxin.

Depending upon condition, the subject received one of two forms of Suproxin—epinephrine or a placebo.

Epinephrine or adrenaline is a sympathomimetic drug whose effects, with minor exceptions, compose an almost perfect mimicry of a discharge of the sympathetic nervous system. Shortly after injection systolic blood pressure increases markedly, heart rate increases somewhat, cutaneous blood flow decreases, while muscle and cerebral blood flow increase, blood sugar and lactic acid concentration increase, and respiration rate increases slightly. As far as the subject is concerned, the major subjective symptoms are palpitation, tremor, and sometimes a feeling of flushing and accelerated breathing. With a subcutaneous injection (in the dosage administered to our subjects), such effects usually begin within 3–5 minutes of injection and last anywhere from 10 minutes to an hour. For most subjects these effects are dissipated within 15–20 minutes after injection.

Subjects receiving epinephrine received a subcutaneous injection of $1/2$ cm^3 of a 1:1000 solution of Winthrop Laboratory's Suprarenin, a saline solution of epinephrine bitartrate.

Subjects in the placebo condition received a subcutaneous injection of $1/2$ cm^3 of saline solution.

Manipulating an Appropriate Explanation

By "appropriate" I refer to the extent to which the subject has an authoritative, unequivocal explanation of his bodily condition. Thus, a subject who had been informed by the physician that as a direct consequence of the injection he would feel palpitations, tremor, etc., would be considered to have a completely appropriate explanation. A subject who had been informed only that the injection would have no side effects would have no explanation of his state. This dimension of appropriateness was manipulated in three experimental conditions called: Epinephrine Informed (Epi Inf), Epinephrine Ignorant (Epi Ign), and Epinephrine Misinformed (Epi Mis).

Immediately after the subject has agreed to the injection and before the physician entered the room, the experimenter's spiel in each of these conditions went as follows:

Epinephrine Informed

> I should tell you that some of our subjects have experienced side effects from the Suproxin. These side effects are transitory and will last only for about 15 or 20 minutes. What will probably happen is that your hand will start to shake, your heart will start to pound, and your face may get warm and flushed. Again, these are side effects lasting about 15 or 20 minutes.

While the physician was giving the injection, she told the subject that the injection was mild and harmless and repeated this description of the symptoms that the subject could expect as a consequence of the shot. In this condition, then, subjects had a completely appropriate explanation of their bodily state. They knew precisely what they would feel and why.

Epinephrine Ignorant

In this condition, when the subject agreed to the injection the experimenter said nothing else relevant to side effects and simply left the room. While the physician was giving the injection, she told the subject that the injection was mild and harmless and would have no side effects. In this condition the subject had no experimentally provided explanation for his bodily state.

Epinephrine Misinformed

> I should tell you that some of our subjects have experienced side effects from the Suproxin. These side effects are transitory and will last only for about 15 or 20 minutes. What will probably happen is that your feet will feel numb, you will have an itching sensation over parts of your body, and you may get a slight headache. Again, these are side effects lasting 15 or 20 minutes.

And, again, the physician repeated these symptoms while injecting the subject. None of these symptoms, of course, are consequences of an injection of epinephrine and, in effect, these instructions provide the subject with a completely inappropriate explanation of his bodily feelings. This condition was introduced as a control condition of sorts. It seemed possible that the description of side effects in the Epi Inf condition might turn the subject introspective, self-examining, possibly slightly troubled. Differences on the dependent variable between the Epi Inf and Epi Ign conditions might, then, be due to such factors rather than to differences in appropriateness. The false symptoms in the Epi Mis condition should similarly turn the subject introspective, etc., but the instructions in this condition do not provide an appropriate explanation of the subject's state.

Subjects in all of the above conditions were injected with epinephrine. Finally, there was a placebo condition in which subjects, who were injected with saline solution, were given precisely the same treatment as subjects in the Epi Ign condition.

Producing an Emotion Inducing Cognition

My initial hypothesis has suggested that given a state of physiological arousal for which the individual has no adequate explanation, cognitive factors can lead the individual to describe his feelings with any of a diversity of emotional labels. In order to test this hypothesis, it was decided to manipulate emotional states which customarily are considered quite different—euphoria and anger.

There are, of course, many ways to induce such states. In my own research I have concentrated on social determinants of emotional states, and my colleagues and I have been able to demonstrate in other studies that people do evaluate their own feelings by comparing themselves with others around them (Schachter, 1959; Wrightsman, 1960). In this experiment we attempted again to manipulate emotional state by social means. In one set of conditions, the subject is placed together with a stooge who has been trained to act euphorically. In a second set of conditions the subject is with a stooge trained to act in an angry fashion.

Euphoria

Immediately[4] after the subject had been injected the physician left the room and the experimenter returned with a stooge whom he introduced as another subject, then said,

[4] It was, of course, imperative that the sequence with the stooge begin before the subject felt his first symptoms, for otherwise the subject would be virtually forced to interpret his feelings in terms of events preceding the stooge's entrance. Pretests had indicated that, for most subjects, epinephrine-caused symptoms began within 3-5 minutes after injection. A deliberate attempt was made then to bring in the stooge within one minute after the subject's injection.

> Both of you have had the Suproxin shot and you'll both be taking the same tests of vision. What I ask you to do now is just wait for 20 minutes. The reason for this is that we must allow 20 minutes for the Suproxin to get from the injection site into the bloodstream. At the end of 20 minutes when we are certain that most of the Suproxin has been absorbed into the bloodstream, we'll begin the tests of vision.

The room in which this was said had been deliberately put into a state of mild disarray. As he was leaving, the experimenter apologetically added,

> The only other thing I should do is to apologize for the condition of the room. I just didn't have time to clean it up. So, if you need any scratch paper or rubber bands or pencils, help yourself. I'll be back in 20 minutes to begin the vision tests.

As soon as the experimenter had left, the stooge introduced himself again, made a series of standard icebreaker comments, and then launched his routine. He reached first for a piece of paper, doodled briefly, crumpled the paper, aimed for a wastebasket, threw, and missed. This led him into a game of "basketball" in which he moved about the room crumpling paper, and trying out fancy basketball shots. Finished with basketball, he said, "This is one of my good days. I feel like a kid again. I think I'll make a plane." He made a paper plane, spent a few minutes flying it around the room, and said, "Even when I was a kid, I was never much good at this." He then tore off the tail of his plane, wadded it up, and making a slingshot of a rubber band, began to shoot the paper. While shooting, he noticed a sloppy pile of manila folders. He built a tower of these folders, then went to the opposite end of the room to shoot at the tower. He knocked down the tower, and while picking up the folders he noticed a pair of hula hoops behind a portable blackboard. He took one of these for himself, put the other within reaching distance of the subject, and began hula hooping. After a few minutes, he replaced the hula hoop and returned to his seat, at which point the experimenter returned to the room.

This routine was completely standard, though its pace, of course, varied depending upon the subject's reaction, the extent to which he entered into this bedlam and the extent to which he initiated activities of his own. The only variations from this standard routine were those forced by the subject. Should the subject originate some nonsense of his own and request the stooge to join in, he would do so. And he would, of course, respond to any comments initiated by the subject.

Subjects in each of the three "appropriateness" conditions and in the placebo condition were submitted to this setup. The stooge, of course, never knew in which condition any particular subject fell.

Anger

Immediately after the injection, the experimenter brought a stooge into the subject's room, introduced the two and, after explaining the necessity for a 20 minute delay for "the Suproxin to get from the injection site into the bloodstream," he continued by saying, "We would like you to use these 20 minutes to answer these questionnaires." Then handing out the questionnaires, he concluded with, "I'll be back in 20 minutes to pick up the questionnaires and begin the tests of vision."

The questionnaires, five pages long, started off innocently by requesting face sheet information and then grew increasingly personal and insulting, asking questions such as, "With how many men (other than your father) has your mother had extra-marital relationships?"

4 and under _____ : 5-9 _____ : 10 and over _____.

The stooge, sitting directly opposite the subject, paced his own answers so that at all times subject and stooge were working on the same question. At regular points in the questionnaire, the stooge made a series of standardized comments about the questions. His comments started off innocently enough, grew increasingly querulous; finally he ended up in a rage, ripping up his questionnaire, slamming it to the floor, saying "I'm not wasting any more time. I'm getting my books and leaving," and stomping out of the room.

In summary, this is a seven-condition experiment which, for two different emotional states, allows us, first, to evaluate the effects of "appropriateness" on emotional inducibility, and, second, to begin to evaluate the effects of sympathetic activation on emotional inducibility. In schematic form the conditions are the following:

EUPHORIA	ANGER
Epi Inf	Epi Inf
Epi Ign	Epi Ign
Epi Mis	Placebo
Placebo	

The Epi Mis condition was not run in the Anger sequence. This was originally conceived as a control condition and it was felt that its inclusion in the Euphoria conditions alone would suffice as a means of evaluating the possible artifactual effect of the Epi Inf instructions.

Measurement

Emotional state was measured in two ways. First, standardized observation, through a one-way mirror, provided a running record of a subject's behavior. To what extent did he act euphoric or angry? Second, on a variety of self-report scales, a subject indicated his moods of the moment.

Observation

Euphoria. Throughout the stooge's standardized routine an observer kept a running chronicle of what the subject did and said. For each unit of the stooge's behavior the observer coded the subject's behavior in one or more of the following categories.

Category 1: Joins in Activity. If the subject entered into the stooge's activities, i.e., if he made or flew airplanes, threw paper basketballs, hula hooped, etc., his behavior was coded in this category.

Category 2: Initiates New Activity. A subject was so coded if he gave indications of creative euphoria; i.e., if, on his own, he initiated behavior outside of the stooge's routine. Instances of such behavior would be the subject who threw open the window and, laughing, hurled paper basketballs at passersby, or the subject who jumped on a table and spun one hula hoop on his leg and the other on his neck.

Categories 3 and 4: Ignores or Watches Stooge. Subjects who paid flatly no attention to the stooge or who, with or without comment, simply watched the stooge without joining in his activity were coded in these categories.

For any particular unit of behavior, the subject's behavior was coded in one or more of these categories. To test reliability of coding, two observers independently coded two experimental sessions. The observers agreed completely on the coding of 88% of the units.

Anger. For each of the units of stooge behavior, an observer recorded the subject's responses and coded them according to the following category scheme:

Category 1: Agrees. In response to the stooge the subject makes a comment indicating that he agrees with the stooge's standardized comment or that he, too, is irked by a particular item on the questionnaire. For example, a subject who responded to the stooge's querulous comment on a question about "father's income" by saying, "I don't like that kind of personal question either," would be coded in this category (scored +2).

Category 2: Disagrees. In response to the stooge's comment, the subject makes a comment which indicates that he disagrees with the stooge's meaning or mood; e.g., in response to the stooge's comment on the "father's income" question, such a subject might say, "Take it easy, they probably have a good reason for wanting the information (scored −2)."

Category 3: Neutral. A noncommittal or irrelevant response to the stooge's remark (scored 0).

Category 4: Initiates Agreement or Disagreement. With no instigation by the stooge, a subject, so coded, would have volunteered a remark indicating that he felt the same way or, alternatively, quite differently than the stooge. Examples would be "Boy I hate this kind of thing," or "I'm enjoying this (scored +2 or −2)."

Category 5: Watches. The subject makes no verbal response to the stooge's comment but simply looks directly at him (scored 0).

Category 6: Ignores. The subject makes no verbal response to the stooge's comment, nor does he look at him; the subject, paying no attention at all to the stooge, simply works at his own questionnaire (scored −1).

A subject was scored in one or more of these categories for each unit of stooge behavior. To test reliability, two observers independently coded three experimental sessions. In order to get a behavioral index of anger, observation protocol was scored according to the values presented in parentheses after each of the above definitions of categories. In a unit-by-unit comparison, the two observers agreed completely on the scoring of 71% of the units jointly observed. The scores of the two observers differed by a value of 1 or less for 88% of the units coded, and in not a single case did the two observers differ in the direction of their scoring of a unit.

Self-Report of Mood and Physical Condition

When the subject's session with the stooge was completed, the experimenter returned to the room, took the pulse of both the subject and the stooge, and said,

> Before we proceed with the vision tests, there is one other kind of information which we must have. We have found that there are many things beside Suproxin that affect how well you see in our tests. How hungry you are, how tired you are, and even the mood you're in at the time—whether you feel happy or irritated at the time of testing—will affect how well you see. To understand the data we collect on you, then, we must be able to figure out which effects are due to causes such as these, and which are caused by Suproxin. The only way we can get such information about your physical and emotional state is to have you tell us. I'll hand out these questionnaires and ask you to answer them as accurately as possible. Obviously, our data on the vision tests will only be as accurate as your description of your mental and physical state.

In keeping with this spiel, the questionnaire that the experimenter passed out contained a number of mock questions about hunger, fatigue, etc., as well as questions of more immediate relevance to the experiment. To measure mood or emotional state the following two were the crucial questions:

1. How irritated, angry or annoyed would you say you feel at present?

I don't feel at all irritated or angry (0)	I feel a little irritated and angry (1)	I feel quite irritated and angry (2)	I feel very irritated and angry (3)	I feel extremely irritated and angry (4)

2. How good or happy would you say that you feel at present?

I don't feel at all happy or good (0)	I feel a little happy and good (1)	I feel quite happy and good (2)	I feel very happy and good (3)	I feel extremely happy and good (4)

To measure the physical effects of epinephrine and determine whether or not the injection had been successful in producing the necessary bodily state, the following questions were asked:

1. Have you experienced any palpitation (consciousness of your own heart beat)?

Not at all (0)	A slight amount (1)	A moderate amount (2)	An intense amount (3)

2. Did you feel any tremor (involuntary shaking of the hands, arms, or legs)?

Not at all (0)	A slight amount (1)	A moderate amount (2)	An intense amount (3)

To measure possible effects of the instructions in the Epi Mis condition, the following questions were asked:

1. Did you feel any numbness in your feet?
2. Did you feel any itching sensation?
3. Did you experience any feeling of headache?

To all three of these questions was attached a four-point scale running from "Not at all" to "An intense amount."

In addition to these scales, the subjects were asked to answer two open-end questions on other physical or emotional sensations they may have experienced during the experimental session. A final measure of bodily state was pulse rate; this was taken by the physician or the experimenter at two times—immediately before the injection and immediately after the session with the stooge.

When the subjects had completed these questionnaires, the experimenter announced that the experiment was over, explained the deception and its necessity in detail, answered any questions, and swore the subjects to secrecy. Finally, the subjects answered a brief questionnaire about their experiences, if any, with adrenaline, and their previous knowledge or suspicion of the experimental setup. There was no indication that any of the subjects had known about the experiment beforehand, but eleven subjects were so extremely suspicious of some crucial feature of the experiment that their data were automatically discarded.

Subjects

The subjects were all male college students taking classes in introductory psychology at the University of Minnesota. Some 90% of the students in these classes volunteer for a subject pool for which they receive two extra points on their final exam for every hour that they serve as experimental subjects. For this study the records of all potential subjects were cleared with the Student Health Service in order to insure that no harmful effects would result from the injections.

Evaluation of the Experimental Design

The ideal test of my propositions would require circumstances which this experiment is far from realizing. First, the proposition that, "A state of physiological arousal for which an individual has no immediate explanation will lead him to label this state in terms of the cognitions available to him" obviously requires conditions under which the subject does not and cannot have a proper explanation of his bodily state. Though Singer and I toyed with such fantasies as ventilating the experimental room with vaporized adrenaline, reality forced us to rely on the disguised injection of Suproxin—a technique which was far from ideal, for no matter what the experimenter told them, some subjects inevitably attributed their feelings to the injection. To the extent that subjects did so, differences between the several appropriateness conditions should be attenuated.

Second, the proposition that, "Given the same cognitive circumstances the individual will react emotionally only to the extent that he experiences a state of physiological arousal" requires for its ideal test the manipulation of states of physiological arousal and of physiological quiescence. Though there is no question that epinephrine effectively produces a state of arousal, there is also no question that a placebo does not prevent physiological arousal. To the extent that the experimental situation effectively produces sympathetic stimulation in placebo subjects, the proposition is difficult to test, for such a factor would attenuate differences between epinephrine and placebo subjects.

Both of these factors, then, can be expected to interfere with the test of my propositions. In presenting the results of this study, I shall first present condition by condition results, and then evaluate the effects of these two factors on experimental differences.

Results

Effects of the Injections on Bodily State

Let us examine first the success of the injections at producing the bodily state required to examine the propositions at test. Does the injection of epinephrine produce symptoms of sympathetic discharge as compared with the placebo injection? Relevant data are presented in Table 1, where it can be immediately seen that, on all items, subjects who were in epinephrine conditions showed considerably more evidence of sympathetic activation than did subjects in placebo conditions. In all epinephrine conditions pulse rate increased significantly when compared with the decrease characteristic of the placebo conditions.[5] On the scales it is clear that epinephrine subjects experience considerably more palpitation and tremor than do placebo subjects. In all possible comparisons on these symptoms, the mean scores of subjects in any of the epinephrine conditions are greater than the corresponding scores in the placebo conditions at better than the .001 level of significance. Examination of the absolute values of these scores makes it quite clear that subjects in epinephrine conditions were, indeed, in a state of physiological arousal, while most subjects in placebo conditions were in a relative state of physiological quiescence.

[5] It can be seen in Table 1 that the rise in the pulse rate of subjects injected with epinephrine is greater in the anger than in the euphoria conditions. This finding, which has been the subject of fairly exotic interpretations in critical discussions of this experiment (Plutchik and Ax, 1967; Stein, 1967), is undoubtedly most simply explained by the fact that the anger manipulation took somewhat less time than the euphoria manipulation, and the second pulse reading was, therefore, taken sooner on the average in the anger than in the euphoria condition. The typical reaction to an injection of adrenaline in the dosage used is a very rapid rise in heart rate, and then a steady and gradual decline.

TABLE 1 THE EFFECTS OF THE INJECTIONS ON BODILY STATE

Condition	N	Pulse		Self-rating of				
		Pre	Post	Palpitation	Tremor	Numbness	Itching	Headache
Euphoria								
Epi Inf	27	85.7	88.6	1.20	1.43	0	0.16	0.32
Epi Ign	26	84.6	85.6	1.83	1.76	0.15	0	0.55
Epi Mis	26	82.9	86.0	1.27	2.00	0.06	0.08	0.23
Placebo	26	80.4	77.1	0.29	0.21	0.09	0	0.27
Anger								
Epi Inf	23	85.9	92.4	1.26	1.41	0.17	0	0.11
Epi Ign	23	85.0	96.8	1.44	1.78	0	0.06	0.21
Placebo	23	84.5	79.6	0.59	0.24	0.14	0.06	0.06

The epinephrine injection, of course, did not work with equal effectiveness for all subjects; indeed for a few subjects it did not work at all. Such subjects reported almost no palpitation or tremor, showed no increase in pulse, and described no other relevant physical symptoms. Since, for such subjects, the necessary experimental conditions were not established, they were automatically excluded from the data and all further tabular presentations will not include them. Table 1, however, does include the data of these subjects. There were four in euphoria conditions, and one in anger conditions.

In order to evaluate further data on Epi Mis subjects it is necessary to note the results of the "numbness," "itching," and "headache" scales also presented in Table 1. Clearly the subjects in the Epi Mis condition do not differ on these scales from subjects in any of the other experimental conditions.

Effects of the Manipulations on Emotional State

Euphoria: Self-Report. The effects of the several manipulations on emotional state in the euphoria conditions are presented in Table 2. The scores recorded in this table are derived for each subject by subtracting the value of the point he checked on the irritation scale from the value of the point he checked on the happiness scale. Thus, if a subject were to check the point "I feel a little irritated and angry" on the irritation scale and the point "I feel very happy and good" on the happiness scale, his score would be +2. The higher the positive value, the happier and better the subject reports himself as feeling. Even though, for expositional simplicity, an index is employed, it should be noted that the two components of the index each yield results completely consistent with those obtained by use of this index.

TABLE 2 SELF-REPORT OF EMOTIONAL STATE IN
THE EUPHORIA CONDITIONS

Condition	N	Self-report scales
Epi Inf	25	0.98
Epi Ign	25	1.78
Epi Mis	25	1.90
Placebo	26	1.61
Comparison		p^a
Epi Inf vs. Epi Mis		<.01
Epi Inf vs. Epi Ign		.02
Placebo vs. Epi Mis, Ign, or Inf		n.s.

^{a}All p values reported throughout this volume are two-tailed.

Let us examine first the effects of the appropriateness instructions. Comparison of the scores for the Epi Mis and Epi Inf conditions makes it immediately clear that the experimental differences are not due to artifacts resulting from the informed instructions. In both conditions the subject was warned to expect a variety of symptoms as a consequence of the injection. In the Epi Mis condition, where the symptoms were inappropriate to the subject's bodily state, the self-report score is almost twice that in the Epi Inf condition, where the symptoms were completely appropriate to the subject's bodily state. It is reasonable, then, to attribute differences between informed subjects and those in other conditions to differences in manipulated appropriateness rather than to artifacts such as introspectiveness or self-examination.

It is clear that, consistent with expectations, subjects were more susceptible to the stooge's mood and, consequently, more euphoric when they had no explanation of their own bodily states than when they did. The means of both the Epi Ign and Epi Mis conditions are considerably greater than the mean of the Epi Inf condition.

Comparing the placebo to the epinephrine conditions, we note a pattern which will repeat itself throughout the data. Placebo subjects are less euphoric than either Epi Mis or Epi Ign subjects, but somewhat more euphoric than Epi Inf subjects. These differences are not, however, statistically significant. We shall consider the epinephrine-placebo comparisons in detail in a later section of this chapter following the presentation of additional relevant data. For the moment, it is clear only that manipulating appropriateness has had a very strong effect on euphoria.

Behavior. Let us next examine the extent to which the subject's behavior was affected by the experimental manipulations. To the extent that his mood

TABLE 3 BEHAVIORAL INDICATIONS OF EMOTIONAL STATE IN THE
EUPHORIA CONDITIONS

Condition	N	Activity index	Mean number of acts initiated
Epi Inf	25	12.72	.20
Epi Ign	25	18.28	.56
Epi Mis	25	22.56	.84
Placebo	26	16.00	.54

	p value	
Comparison	Activity index	Initiates[a]
Epi Inf vs. Epi Mis	.05	.03
Epi Inf vs. Epi Ign	n.s.	.08
Placebo vs. Epi Mis, Ign, or Inf	n.s.	n.s.

[a]Tested by X^2 comparison of the proportion of subjects in each condition initiating new acts.

has been affected, one should expect that the subject will join in the stooge's whirl of manic activity and initiate similar activities of his own. The relevant data are presented in Table 3. The column labeled "Activity index" presents summary figures on the extent to which the subject joined in the stooge's activity. This is a weighted index which reflects both the nature of the activities in which the subject engaged and the amount of time he was active. The index was devised by assigning the following weights to the subject's activities: 5, hula hooping; 4, shooting with slingshot; 3, paper airplanes; 2, paper basketballs; 1, doodling; 0, does nothing. Pretest scaling on 15 college students ordered these activities with respect to the degree of euphoria they represented. Weights were assigned in accordance with this order so that the wilder the activity, the heavier the weight. These weights are multiplied by an estimate of the amount of time the subject spent in each activity and the summed products make up the activity index for each subject. This index may be considered a measure of behavioral euphoria. It should be noted that the same between-condition relationships hold for the two components of this index as for the index itself.

The column labeled "Mean number of acts initiated" presents data on what might be called "creative euphoria"—the extent to which the subject deviates from the stooge's routine and initiates euphoric activities of his own.

On both behavioral indices, we find precisely the same pattern of relationships as those obtained with self-reports. Epi Mis subjects behave somewhat more euphorically than do Epi Ign subjects, who in turn behave more euphorically than do Epi Inf subjects. On all measures, then, there is consistent evidence that a subject will take over the stooge's euphoric mood to the extent that he has no other explanation of his bodily state.

Again, it should be noted that on these behavioral indices, Epi Ign and Epi Mis subjects are somewhat more euphoric than placebo subjects, but, troublingly, not significantly so.

Anger: Self-report. Before presenting data for the anger conditions, one point must be made about the anger manipulation. In the situation devised, anger, if manifested, is most likely to be directed at the experimenter and his annoyingly personal questionnaire. As we subsequently discovered, this was rather unfortunate, for the subjects, who had volunteered for the experiment in order to obtain extra points on their final exam, simply refused to endanger these points by publicly blowing up, admitting their irritation to the experimenter's face, or spoiling the questionnaire. Though, as the reader will see, the subjects were quite willing to manifest anger when they were alone with the stooge, they hesitated to do so on material (self-ratings of mood and questionnaire) that the experimenter might see, and only after the purposes of the experiment had been revealed did these subjects admit to the experimenter that they had been irked or irritated.

This experimentally unfortunate situation pretty much forces us to rely on the behavioral indices derived from observation of the subject's presumably private interaction with the stooge. We do, however, present data on the self-report scales in Table 4. These figures are derived in the same way as the figures presented in Table 2 for the euphoria conditions; i.e., the value checked on the irritation scale is subtracted from the value checked on the happiness scale. Though, for the reasons stated above, the absolute magnitude of these figures (all positive) is relatively meaningless, we can, of course, anticipate precisely the reverse results from those obtained in the euphoria conditions; i.e., the Epi Inf subjects in the anger conditions should again be less susceptible to the stooge's mood and should, therefore, describe themselves as in a somewhat happier frame of mind than subjects in the Epi Ign condition. This is the case;

TABLE 4   SELF-REPORT OF EMOTIONAL STATE IN THE ANGER CONDITIONS

Condition	N	Self-report scales
Epi Inf	22	1.91
Epi Ign	23	1.39
Placebo	23	1.63
Comparison		p
Epi Inf vs. Epi Ign		.08
Placebo vs. Epi Ign or Inf		n.s.

the Epi Inf subjects average 1.91 on the self-report scales, while the Epi Ign subjects average 1.39.

Evaluating the effects of the injections, we note again that, as anticipated, Epi Ign subjects are somewhat less happy than Placebo subjects but, once more, this is not a significant difference.

Behavior. The subject's responses to the stooge, during the period when both were filling out their questionnaires, were systematically coded to provide a behavioral index of anger. The coding scheme and the numerical values attached to each of the categories have been described in the methodology section. To arrive at an "Anger index" the numerical value assigned to a subject's responses to the stooge is summed together for the several units of stooge behavior. With the coding scheme used, a positive value for this index indicates that the subject agrees with the stooge's comment and is growing angry. A negative value indicates that the subject either disagrees with the stooge or ignores him.

It is anticipated, of course, that subjects in the Epi Ign condition will be angrier than subjects in the Epi Inf condition. As can be seen in Table 5, this is indeed the case. The Anger index for the Epi Ign condition is positive and large, indicating that these subjects have become angry, while in the Epi Inf condition the Anger index is slightly negative in value, indicating that these subjects have failed to catch the stooge's mood at all. It seems clear that providing the subject with an appropriate explanation of his bodily state greatly reduces his tendency to interpret his state in terms of the cognitions provided by the stooge's angry behavior.

Finally, on this behavioral index it can be seen that subjects in the Epi Ign condition are significantly angrier than subjects in the Placebo condition. Behaviorally, at least, the injection of epinephrine appears to have led subjects to an angrier state than comparable subjects who received placebo shots.

TABLE 5 BEHAVIORAL INDICATIONS OF EMOTIONAL STATE IN THE ANGER CONDITIONS

Condition	N	Anger index
Epi Inf	22	−0.18
Epi Ign	23	+ 2.28
Placebo	22[a]	+0.79
Comparison		p
Epi Inf vs. Epi Ign		<.01
Epi Ign vs. Placebo		<.05
Placebo vs. Epi Inf		n.s.

[a]For one subject in this condition the sound system went dead and the observer could not code his reactions.

Conformation of Data to Theoretical Expectations

Now that the basic data of this study have been presented, let us examine closely the extent to which they conform to theoretical expectations. If our hypotheses are correct and if this experimental design provided a perfect test for these hypotheses, it should be anticipated that in the euphoria conditions the degree of experimentally produced euphoria should vary in the following fashion:

$$\text{Epi Mis} \geqslant \text{Epi Ign} > \text{Epi Inf} = \text{Placebo}$$

And in the anger conditions, anger should conform to the following pattern:

$$\text{Epi Ign} > \text{Epi Inf} = \text{Placebo}$$

In both sets of conditions, it is the case that emotional level in the Epi Mis and Epi Ign conditions is considerably greater than that achieved in the corresponding Epi Inf conditions. The results for the Placebo condition, however, are ambiguous, for consistently the Placebo subjects fall between the Epi Ign and the Epi Inf subjects. This is a particularly troubling pattern, for it makes it impossible to evaluate unequivocally the effects of the state of physiological arousal, and indeed raises serious questions about our entire theoretical structure. Though the emotional level is consistently greater in the Epi Mis and Epi Ign conditions than in the Placebo condition, this difference is significant at acceptable probability levels only in the anger conditions.

In order to explore the problem further, let us examine the experimental factors identified earlier, which might have acted to restrain the emotional level in the Epi Ign and Epi Mis conditions. As pointed out earlier, the ideal test of the first two hypotheses requires an experimental setup in which the subject flatly has no way of evaluating his state of physiological arousal other than by means of the experimentally provided cognitions. Had it been possible to physiologically produce a state of sympathetic activation by means other than injection, one could have approached this experimental ideal more closely than in the present setup. As it stands, however, there is always a reasonable alternative cognition available to the aroused subject—he feels the way he does because of the injection. To the extent that the subject seizes on such an explanation of his bodily state, we should expect that he will be uninfluenced by the stooge. Evidence presented in Table 6 for the anger condition and in Table 7 for the euphoria conditions indicates that this is, indeed, the case.

As mentioned earlier, some of the Epi Ign and Epi Mis subjects in their answers to the open-end questions clearly attributed their physical state to the injection, e.g., "The shot gave me the shivers." In Tables 6 and 7 such subjects are labeled "Self-informed." In Table 6 it can be seen that the self-informed subjects are considerably less angry than are the remaining subjects; indeed, they

TABLE 6   THE EFFECTS OF ATTRIBUTING BODILY STATE TO THE
INJECTION ON ANGER IN THE ANGER EPI IGN CONDITION

Condition	N	Anger index[a]
Self-informed subjects	3	−1.67
Others	20	+ 2.88

[a]Self-informed vs. Others: $p = .05$.

are not angry at all. With these self-informed subjects eliminated, the difference
between the Epi Ign and the Placebo conditions is significant at the .01 level.

Precisely the same pattern is evident in Table 7 for the euphoria conditions.
In both the Epi Mis and the Epi Ign conditions, the self-informed subjects have
considerably lower activity indices than do the remaining subjects. Eliminating
self-informed subjects, comparison of both of these conditions with the Placebo
condition yields a difference significant at the .03 level. It should be noted, too,
that the self-informed subjects have much the same score on the activity index as
do the experimental Epi Inf subjects (Table 3).

It would appear, then, that the experimental procedure of injecting the
subjects, by providing an alternative cognition, has, to some extent, obscured the
effects of epinephrine. When account is taken of this artifact, the evidence is
good that the state of physiological arousal is a necessary component of an
emotional experience, for when self-informed subjects are removed, epinephrine
subjects give consistent indications of greater emotionality than do placebo
subjects.

TABLE 7 THE EFFECTS OF ATTRIBUTING BODILY STATE TO THE INJECTION ON
EUPHORIA IN THE EUPHORIA EPI IGN AND EPI MIS CONDITIONS

Epi Ign		
	N	Activity index[a]
Self-informed subjects	8	11.63
Others	17	21.14
Epi Mis		
	N	Activity index[b]
Self-informed subjects	5	12.40
Others	20	25.10

[a]Self-informed vs. Others, $p = .05$.
[b]Self-informed vs. Others, $p = .10$.

Let us examine next the fact that consistently the emotional level, both reported and behavioral, in Placebo conditions is greater than that in the Epi Inf conditions. Theoretically, of course, it should be expected that the two conditions will be equally low, for by assuming that emotional state is a joint function of a state of physiological arousal and of the appropriateness of a cognition we are, in effect, assuming a multiplicative function, so that if either component is at zero, emotional level is at zero. As noted earlier, this expectation should hold if we can be sure that there is no sympathetic activation in the Placebo conditions. Such an assumption, of course, is completely unrealistic, for the injection of placebo does not prevent sympathetic activation. The experimental situations were fairly dramatic, and certainly some of the placebo subjects gave indications of physiological arousal. If our general line of reasoning is correct, it should be anticipated that the emotional level of subjects who give indications of sympathetic activity will be greater than that of subjects who do not. The relevant evidence is presented in Tables 8 and 9.

As an index of sympathetic activation, Singer and I used the most direct and unequivocal measure available—change in pulse rate. It can be seen in Table 1 that the predominant pattern in the Placebo condition is a decrease in pulse rate. We assumed, therefore, that those subjects whose pulse increased or remained the same gave indications of sympathetic activity, while those subjects whose pulse decreased did not. In Table 8, for the euphoria condition, it is immediately clear that subjects who gave indications of sympathetic activity are considerably more euphoric than are subjects who show no sympathetic activity. This relationship is, of course, confounded by the fact that euphoric subjects are considerably more active than noneuphoric subjects—a factor which, independent of mood, could elevate pulse rate. However, no such factor operates in the anger condition where angry subjects are neither more active nor talkative than calm subjects. It can be seen in Table 9 that Placebo subjects who show signs of sympathetic activation give indications of considerably more anger than do subjects who show no such signs. Conforming to expectations, sympathetic activation accompanies an increase in emotional level.

It should be noted, too, that the emotional levels of subjects showing no signs of sympathetic activity are quite comparable to the emotional levels of

TABLE 8 SYMPATHETIC ACTIVATION AND EUPHORIA IN THE EUPHORIA PLACEBO CONDITION

Subjects whose:	N	Activity index[a]
Pulse decreased	14	10.67
Pulse increased or remained same	12	23.17

[a]Pulse decrease vs. pulse increase or same, $p = .02$.

TABLE 9 SYMPATHETIC ACTIVATION AND ANGER IN ANGER
PLACEBO CONDITION

Subjects whose :	N^a	Anger index^b
Pulse decreased	13	+0.15
Pulse increased or remained same	8	+1.69

$^a N$ reduced by two cases owing to failure of sound system in one
case and experimenter's failure to take pulse in another.

^{b}Pulse decrease vs. pulse increase or same, $p = .01$.

subjects in the parallel Epi Inf conditions (see Tables 3 and 5). The similarity of
these sets of scores and their uniformly low level of indicated emotionality
would certainly make it appear that both factors are essential to an emotional
state. When either the level of sympathetic arousal is low, or a completely
appropriate cognition is available, the level of emotionality is low.

Discussion

Let us summarize the major findings of this experiment and examine the
extent to which they support the propositions offered in the introduction of this
chapter. It has been suggested, first, that given a state of physiological arousal
for which an individual has no explanation, he will label this state in terms of the
cognitions available to him. This implies, of course, that by manipulating the
cognitions of an individual in such a state we can manipulate his feelings in
diverse directions. Experimental results support this proposition for, following
the injection of epinephrine, those subjects who had no explanation for the
bodily state thus produced gave behavioral and self-report indications that they
had been readily manipulable into the disparate feeling states of euphoria and
anger.

From this first proposition, it must follow that given a state of physiological
arousal for which the individual has a completely satisfactory explanation, he
will not label this state in terms of the alternative cognitions available.
Experimental evidence strongly supports this expectation. In those conditions in
which subjects were injected with epinephrine and told precisely what they
would feel and why, they proved relatively immune to any effects of the
manipulated cognitions. In the anger condition, such subjects did not report or
show anger; in the euphoria condition such subjects reported themselves as far
less happy than subjects with an identical bodily state but no adequate
knowledge of why they felt the way they did.

Finally, it has been suggested that given constant cognitive circumstances, an individual will react emotionally only to the extent that he experiences a state of physiological arousal. Without taking account of experimental artifacts, the evidence in support of this proposition is consistent but tentative. When the effects of "self-informing" tendencies in epinephrine subjects and of "self-arousing" tendencies in placebo subjects are partialed out, the evidence strongly supports the proposition.

The pattern of data, then, falls neatly in line with theoretical expectations. However, the fact that we were forced, to some extent, to rely on internal analyses in order to partial out the effects of experimental artifacts inevitably makes our conclusions somewhat tentative. In order to further test these propositions on the interaction of cognitive and physiological determinants of emotional state, several additional experiments were conducted.

Chapter II

Sympathetic Arousal
and Emotionality

I. Epinephrine, Chlorpromazine, and Amusement

Though the euphoria-anger experiment demonstrated the contribution of cognitive factors to emotional experiences, the effects of the physiological manipulations were somewhat obscured by experimental artifacts which I have called "self-informing" tendencies in epinephrine subjects and "self-arousing" tendencies in placebo subjects. Assuming, for the moment, that physiological arousal is a necessary component of emotional states, one of the factors that might account for this failure to find larger differences between epinephrine and placebo subjects seems reasonably apparent. The experimental situations employed to manipulate emotional state were fairly effective. The injection of placebo does not, of course, prevent the subject from self-arousal of the sympathetic system, and indeed there is considerable evidence (Woodworth and Schlosberg, 1954) that the arousal of an emotional state is accompanied by general excitation of the sympathetic nervous system.

A test of the proposition at stake, then, would require comparison of subjects who have received injections of epinephrine with subjects who, to some extent, are rendered incapable of self-activation of the sympathetic nervous system. Thanks to a class of drugs known generally as autonomic blocking agents, such blockade is, to some degree, possible. If the proposition is correct that a state of sympathetic discharge is a necessary component of an emotional experience, it would be anticipated that whichever emotional state is experimentally manipulated, it should be most intensely experienced by subjects who have received epinephrine, next by placebo subjects, and least of all by subjects who have received injections of an autonomic blocking agent.

To test these expectations, Schachter and Wheeler (1962) cast an experiment in the framework of a study of the effects of vitamins on vision. As soon as a subject arrived, he was taken to a private room and told by the experimenter:

> I've asked you to come today to take part in an experiment concerning the effects of vitamins on the visual processes. We know a great deal about vision, but only night vision has been studied in relation to nutrition. Our experiment is concerned with the effects of Suproxin on vision. Suproxin is a high-concentrate vitamin C derivative. If you agree to take part in the experiment, we will give you an injection of Suproxin and then subject your retina to about 15 minutes of continuous black and white stimulation. This is simpler than it sounds; we'll just have you watch a black and white movie. After the movie, we'll give you a series of visual tests.
>
> The injection itself is harmless and will be administered by our staff doctor. It may sting a little at first, as most injections do, but after this you will feel nothing and will have no side effects. We know that some people dislike injections, and if you take part in the experiment, we want it to be your own decision. Would you like to? (All subjects agreed to take part.)

This much said, the experimenter gave the subject a test of visual acuity and of color vision, took the subject's pulse, and left the room. Shortly thereafter, the doctor arrived, gave the subject a quick ophthalmoscopic examination, then gave him an injection and informed him that the experimenter would be back for him shortly "in order to take you and some other subjects who have also received shots of Suproxin into the projection room."

Injections

There were three forms of Suproxin administered—epinephrine, placebo, and chlorpromazine.

1. Epinephrine: subjects in this condition received a subcutaneous injection of ½ cc of a 1 : 1000 solution of Winthrop Laboratory's Suprarenin.

2. Placebo: subjects in this condition received a subcutaneous injection of ½ cc of saline solution.

3. Chlorpromazine: subjects in this condition received an intramuscular injection of a solution consisting of 1 cc (25 milligrams) of Smith, Kline, and French Thorazine, and 1 cc of saline solution.

The choice of chlorpromazine as a blocking agent was dictated by considerations of safety, ease of administration, and known duration of effect. Ideally, one would have wished for a blocking agent whose mechanism and effect was precisely and solely the reverse of that of epinephine—a peripherally acting agent which would prevent the excitation of sympathetically innervated structures. Though it is certainly possible to approach this ideal more closely with agents other than chlorpromazine, such drugs tend to be dangerous, or difficult to administer, or of short duration.

Chlorpromazine is known to act as a sympathetic depressant. It has a moderate hypotensive effect, with a slight compensatory increase in heart rate. It has mild adrenergic blocking activity, for it reverses the pressor effects of small doses of epinephrine and depresses responses of the nictitating membrane to preganglionic stimulation. Killam (1959) summarizes what is known and supposed about the mechanism of action of chlorpromazine as follows: "Autonomic effects in general may be attributed to a mild peripheral adrenergic blocking activity and probably to central depression of sympathetic centers, possibly in the hypothalamus (p. 27)." Popularly, of course, the compound is known as a "tranquilizer."

It is known that chlorpromazine has effects other than the sympatholytic effect of interest to us. For purposes of experimental purity this is unfortunate but inevitable in this sort of research. It is clear, however, that the three conditions do differ in the degree of manipulated sympathetic activation.

Subjects

Subjects were again male college students from a subject pool made up from introductory psychology classes at the University of Minnesota. The records of all potential subjects were cleared with the Student Health Service to insure that no harmful effects would result from injections of either epinephrine or chlorpromazine.

Each experimental group was made up of three subjects—one from each of the injection conditions. Their appointments were staggered slightly so as to insure sufficient time for the particular drug to be absorbed. Thus, the chlorpromazine subject received his injection about 15 minutes before the movie began. Pretests had revealed that, with this dosage and mode of administration, about this time interval was required for the onset of sympathetic effects. Placebo subjects were injected 5–10 minutes before onset of the movie. Epinephrine subjects were injected immediately before the movie so that at most 3–4 minutes went by between the time they were injected and the beginning of the film. Pretests had shown that the effects of epinephrine began within 3–5 minutes of injection. It was, of course, basic to the experimental design that these effects begin only after the movie had started.

Film

Rather than the more complicated devices employed in the previous experiment, an emotion inducing film was used as a means of manipulating the cognitive component of emotional states. In deciding on the type of film, two extremes seemed possible—a horror film or a comedy. Since it is a common stereotype that adrenaline makes one nervous and that the tranquilizer, chlorpromazine, makes one tranquil and mildly euphoric, the predicted pattern of results with a horror film would be subject to alternative interpretation. It was deliberately decided, then, to use a comedy. If our hypothesis is correct, it should be anticipated that epinephrine subjects would find the film somewhat funnier than placebo subjects who, in turn, would be more amused than chlorpromazine subjects.

The film chosen was a 14-minute 40-second excerpt from a Jack Carson movie called *The Good Humor Man*. This excerpt is a self-contained, comprehensible episode involving a slapstick chase scene.

The projection room was deliberately arranged so that the subjects could neither see nor hear one another. Facing the screen were three theater-type seats separated from one another by large, heavy partitions. In a further attempt to maintain the independence of the subjects, the sound volume of the projector was turned up so as to mask any sounds made by the subjects.

Measurement

Observation

During the showing of the movie an observer, introduced as an assistant who would help administer the visual tests, systematically scanned the subjects and recorded their reactions to the film. He observed each subject once every 10 seconds, so that over the course of the film 88 units of each subject's behavior were categorized. The observer simply recorded each subject's reaction to the film according to the following scheme:

1. Neutral: straight-faced watching of film with no indication of amusement.
2. Smile.
3. Grin: a smile with teeth showing.
4. Laugh: a smile or grin accompanied by bodily movements usually associated with laughter, e.g., shaking shoulders, moving head, etc.

5. Big laugh: belly laugh—a laugh accompanied by violent body movement such as doubling up, throwing up hands, etc.

In a minute-by-minute comparison, two independent observers agreed in their categorization of 90% of the 528 units recorded in six different reliability trials.

The observer, of course, never knew which subject had received which injection.

Evaluation of the Film

The moment the movie ended the lights were turned on and the experimenter proceeded:

> Before beginning the visual tests, we want your eyes to recover somewhat from the constant stimulation they've just received. The rate of neurolimnal recovery under conditions of perfectly normal lighting and coloring is of major interest to us. The recovery will have begun in about 12 minutes and after that time you will receive a visual examination.
>
> In the meantime, I'd like to ask your help. As I told you, we need about 15 minutes of retinal stimulation, for which purpose we use a movie. Obviously, it doesn't matter at all to us which movie we use, so long as it is black and white. We can use one movie just as easily as another, but we do want to use a film that you like. I'm sure that you can see the necessity of using a film which our subjects will like. Of course, the only way to find out if you like it is to ask you. We're just beginning the experiment and will have many more subjects like you. Since you are one of the first groups, it will be a big help if you will give us your personal reactions to the film. If you like it, we'll keep it, and if you don't like it, we can just as easily get another. If you'll use these mimeographed questionnaires, it will make it easier for us.

The experimenter then handed out a questionnaire whose chief items, for present purposes, were the following:

1. How funny did you find this film?

Extremely dull (1)	Very dull (2)	Somewhat dull (3)	Mildly funny (4)	Very funny (5)	Extremely funny (6)

2. All in all, how much did you enjoy this film?

Disliked it intensely (1)	Disliked it very much (2)	Disliked it a little (3)	Enjoyed it a little (4)	Enjoyed it very much (5)	Enjoyed it ·enormously (6)

The figures in brackets represent the values used in computing the means presented in later tables.

> 3. Would you recommend that we should show this particular film to our future subjects?
>   (3) strongly recommend keeping this film
>   (2) moderately recommend keeping this film
>   (1) recommend you get another film

Physical Condition

In order to check on whether or not the drugs were having the desired effect on the subject's internal state, after the subjects had evaluated the film, the experimenter continued with the following spiel:

> Before we begin the eye tests, we need a bit more information about you. Earlier studies have shown that a person's physical and emotional states influence the visual processes. Because of this it is necessary to know how you feel physically and emotionally at this time. We know, for example, that certain states such as hunger, or fatigue, or boredom, do have a noticeable effect on these processes. Naturally, we have to know these things about you in order to interpret your results and the only way we can find out such things is to ask you.

A bit more on this line and the experimenter then handed round a questionnaire whose chief items were the two questions on palpitations and tremor used in the previous study of epinephrine and two questions designed to evaluate the effects of chlorpromazine. Any direct measure (such as blood pressure) of the effects of the chlorpromazine injection on each subject was pretty much out of the question owing to limitations of time and personnel. It is known, however, that chlorpromazine does have something of a dehydrating effect. As some indication that within the experimental time interval the chlorpromazine had been absorbed, the following questions were asked:

Does your mouth feel dry?

| Not at all dry (0) | A little dry (1) | Somewhat dry (2) | Very dry (3) | Extremely dry (4) |

Does your nose feel stuffy?

| Not at all stuffy (0) | A little stuffy (1) | Somewhat stuffy (2) | Very stuffy (3) | Extremely stuffy (4) |

Film Detail Questionnaire

Since it is known that chlorpromazine produces drowsiness, it seemed possible that experimental differences might be due to the fact that subjects had simply not watched the film. In order to check on this, a 10-item, multiple-choice test concerned with small details of the film was administered. This test was rationalized to the subjects as a means of measuring the amount of time they had watched the movie, and, therefore, the amount of retinal stimulation received. Presumably the more they had watched the screen the more details they would remember. Subjects in the three conditions made virtually identical scores on this test—epinephrine subjects scoring an average of 9.29 items correct, placebo subjects scoring 9.15, and chlorpromazine subjects, 9.38. It seems unlikely, then, that any differences in reaction to the film are due to differences in attention.

Following the Film Detail Questionnaire the purpose of the experiment was disclosed, the deception was explained in detail, and the subjects were sworn to secrecy. Finally, the subjects filled out a brief questionnaire concerned with their past experiences with adrenaline and tranquilizers and with their suspicion, if any, of the experiment.

Results

Physical Effects of the Injections

Evaluating first the effects of the injections, it can be seen in Table 10 that epinephrine has produced the required pattern of sympathetic activation. On self-reports of palpitation and tremor, subjects in the epinephrine condition report considerably more disturbance than subjects in either the placebo or chlorpromazine condition. On pulse measures, epinephrine subjects increase significantly when compared with placebo subjects. A subject's pulse was measured immediately before the injection and shortly after the movie. Pulse increased for some 63% of the epinephrine subjects and for 28% of the placebo subjects.

As to the effects of chlorpromazine, it can be seen in Table 10 that subjects in this condition report considerably stuffier noses and drier mouths than subjects in the placebo or epinephrine conditions. This may be taken as indirect evidence that within the time limits of the experiment, chlorpromazine was taking effect. The increase in pulse rate (61% of chlorpromazine subjects increase) is a standard reaction to chlorpromazine and appears to be compensa-

TABLE 10   PHYSICAL EFFECTS OF THE INJECTION

		Pulse				Mouth	Nose
Condition	N	Pre-injection	Post-injection	Palpitation	Tremor	dry	stuffy
Epinephrine	44	81.4	87.3	2.00	1.86	0.72	0.39
Placebo	42	78.7	75.5	0.30	0.12	0.30	0.68
Chlorpromazine	46	81.4	86.0	0.52	0.26	1.12	2.16
			p value				
Epinephrine vs. placebo				< .001	< .001	< .01	n.s.
Epinephrine vs. chlorpromazine				< .001	< .001	< .07	< .001
Placebo vs. chlorpromazine				n.s.	n.s.	< .001	< .001

tory for the decreased blood pressure caused by this agent. It should be noted, however, that unlike epinephrine subjects the chlorpromazine subjects were unaware of this increased heart rate, for on the palpitation scale they are quite similar to subjects in the placebo condition.

Six subjects (included in Table 10) in the epinephrine condition were unaffected by the injection. They reported virtually no palpitation or tremor and their pulse rates were not affected. Since for these subjects the necessary experimental state was not produced, they are not included in any further presentation of data.

Overt Reactions to the Film

The observation record provides a continuous record of each subject's reaction to the film. As an overall index of amusement, the number of units in which a subject's behavior was recorded in the categories of Smile, Grin, Laugh, and Big laugh are summed together. The means of this amusement index are presented in Table 11. The larger the figure, the more amusement manifested. Differences are in the anticipated direction. Epinephrine subjects gave indications of greater amusement than did placebo subjects who, in turn, were more amused than chlorpromazine subjects. The U Test was used to test for significance of differences, since the variance in the epinephrine condition was significantly greater than that in either the placebo or chlorpromazine condition. The means of both the epinephrine and the placebo conditions are significantly greater than the mean of the chlorpromazine condition.

TABLE 11   THE EFFECTS OF EPINEPHRINE,
PLACEBO, AND CHLORPROMAZINE
ON AMUSEMENT

Condition	N	Mean amusement index
Epinephrine	38	17.79
Placebo	42	14.31
Chlorpromazine	46	10.41

p value

Epinephrine vs. placebo	n.s.
Epinephrine vs. chlorpromazine	.01
Placebo vs. chlorpromazine	.05

Though the trend is clearly in the predicted direction, epinephrine and placebo subjects do not differ significantly in this overall index. The difference between these two groups, however, becomes apparent when we examine strong reactions to the film. Considering just the categories Laugh and Big laugh, as indicating strong reactions to the film, we find an average of 4.84 such units among the epinephrine subjects and of only 1.83 such units among placebo subjects. This difference is significant at better than the .05 level of significance. Epinephrine subjects tend to be openly amused at the film, and placebo subjects to be quietly amused. Some 16% of epinephrine subjects reacted at some point with belly laughs, while not a single placebo subject did so. It should be noted that this is much the state of affairs one would expect from the disguised injection of epinephrine—a manipulation which, I have suggested, creates a bodily state "in search of" an appropriate cognition. Certainly laughter may be considered a more appropriate accompaniment to the state of sympathetic arousal than quietly smiling.

It would appear, then, that degree of overt amusement is directly related to the degree of manipulated sympathetic activation.

Evaluation of the Film

Responses to the post-movie questionnaire in which the subjects evaluated the film are presented in Table 12. The column headed Funny includes answers to the question "How funny did you find this film?"; the heading Enjoy includes answers to the question "All in all, how much did you enjoy the film?";

TABLE 12   EVALUATION OF THE FILM

Condition	N	Funny	Enjoy	Recommend
Epinephrine	38	4.09	3.99	2.04
Placebo	42	4.01	3.95	1.93
Chlorpromazine	46	3.85	3.85	1.85

and the heading Recommend presents answers to the question, "Would you recommend that we show this particular film to our future subjects?"

For all three questions, the trend is in precisely the same direction; epinephrine subjects like the film slightly more than do placebo subjects, who like it more than do chlorpromazine subjects. On all questions, however, the differences between conditions are small, and, at best, significant at only borderline probability levels.

The fact that between-condition differences are large on the behavioral measure and quite small on the attitude scales administered after the film is an intriguing one. The most reasonable explanation comes from the subjects themselves. For example, after the experiment an epinephrine subject said, "I just couldn't understand why I was laughing during the movie. Usually I hate Jack Carson and this kind of nonsense, and that's the way I checked the scales."

For this subject, then, his long-time preferences determined his answers to the questions, whereas his immediate bodily state seems to have determined his reaction while watching the movie. If this is widespread, it should be anticipated that there will be relatively little relationship between past preferences and overt behavior in the epinephrine condition, and a considerably stronger relationship in the placebo condition. For chlorpromazine, too, one should anticipate slight relationship between past preferences and behavior. No matter what the long-time feeling about such films, the immediate reaction to the movie should be restrained owing to a lack of sympathetic activity. However, as pointed out earlier, chlorpromazine is a weak blocker and, most reasonably, one should expect a somewhat weaker relationship with this drug than with the placebo.

To measure general attitude toward the sort of film shown, at the time they were evaluating the film the subjects also answered the question, "In general, how well do you like this kind of slapstick film?" by checking one of the five points along a scale ranging from "Slapstick is the kind of film I like least" to "Slapstick is my favorite kind of film." General attitudes to this sort of film are related to reactions to this particular film in Table 13. The subjects are divided into two groups—those who dislike slapstick and those who like it as much or more than they do other kinds of film. The entries in the table are the mean laugh indices for each of the breakdowns.

Attitude to slapstick	Epinephrine		Placebo		Chlorpromazine	
	N^a	Laugh index	N^a	Laugh index	N^a	Laugh index
Dislike	25	15.12	29	10.52	29	7.34
Like	12	21.75	12	23.25	16	14.69
t		1.18		3.40		2.04
p		n.s.		< .01		.05

^{a}One subject in each condition did not answer the question concerned with general attitude to such films.

It is evident that there is a very strong relationship between general attitude toward such films and laughter in the placebo condition, a considerably weaker relationship in the chlorpromazine condition, and the weakest relationship of all in the epinephrine condition.

Summarizing the simple facts of this study, we know that subjects injected with adrenaline are more openly amused at a slapstick movie than are subjects injected with placebo, who in turn are more amused than are subjects injected with chlorpromazine. In addition, we know that these joint cognitive-physiological manipulations can affect amount of laughter at a movie as well as the intensity of situationally determined states that we have labeled euphoria and anger. Turning to theoretical considerations, this study does provide additional support for the proposition that the degree of emotionality is directly related to the degree of physiological arousal. Extending the range of manipulated sympathetic activity extends the range of emotional responsivity. This conclusion, however, must be sharply tempered by two facts. First, the use of chlorpromazine as an agent for extending the manipulated range of arousal can hardly be considered an experimentally "pure" manipulation. Like it or not, chlorpromazine does have effects other than the sympatholytic property of interest to us. Though it may seem far fetched to attribute the nonresponsivity of chlorpromazine subjects to some effect of the drug such as its demonstrated antipyritic property, there is obviously no possibility of ruling out such an alternative within this experimental context. Second, as in the earlier experiment, though epinephrine subjects are more responsive than placebo, this difference, except for extreme reactions, is not statistically significant. In the euphoria-anger experiment, this pattern of results was explained in terms of a "self-informing" tendency; that is, epinephrine subjects who attributed their arousal state to the injection were considerably less emotional than were subjects who did not make this attribution. There is little question that such a tendency also operated in this study and I suggest, of course, that this is one of the chief factors attenuating differences between epinephrine and placebo conditions. Such a self-informing tendency will probably operate in any experiment on humans which employs an injection technique. In order, once and for all, to make the epinephrine-placebo comparison under conditions which would rule out the operation of this artifact, two additional experiments were conducted.

Chapter III

Sympathetic Arousal
and Emotionality

II. Two Experiments on Adrenaline and Fear

Since, at this point, the chief block to a conclusive test of the adrenaline-placebo relationship is the simple fact that a certain proportion of human subjects seem inevitably to attribute their physiological symptoms to the injection, a proper test requires either a totally covert means of administering a sympathomimetic substance or the use of a subject species incapable of making such an attribution. Though it is possible to administer a sympathomimetic agent in a more subtle fashion than injection, the technical problems involved are so formidable as to make alternative techniques virtually useless for present purposes. It seemed simplest, then, to make the adrenaline-placebo comparison on rats—a species unlikely to attribute a state of sympathetic arousal to an injection. Two experiments were conducted.

In one study, Singer (1963) examined the effects of epinephrine, placebo, and chlorpromazine on fear. His technique was straightforward and simple. One hour after injection, his animals were individually placed in a small box so constructed that when a switch was flicked all hell broke loose—a jarring door buzzer exploded, a door bell clanged, and a 150-watt bulb vigorously flickered off and on. There were two basic conditions. In the fear condition, 10 seconds after the rat was put in the box the switch was turned on and for 90 seconds the animal was exposed to this small chaos. In the nonfear condition, the animal was in the box for the same length of time, but the switch was never flicked.

To measure fear, Singer had an observer systematically code the rat's behavior in the box along five dimensions—defecation, urination, activity, trembling, and face washing—all responses which had previously been demonstrated to indicate fear or emotionality (Hall, 1934; Singer, 1961). Scores on these dimensions were combined to yield a single number called a fright index. There were three drug conditions.

Adrenaline: Twenty-four rats were given a .5 ml intraperitoneal injection containing .100 mg/kg body weight of epinephrine suspended in oil. Twelve rats were given a .25 ml intraperitoneal injection containing .050 mg/kg body weight of epinephrine hydrochloride suspended in oil. As there were no differences attributable to dosage levels, results for the two epinephrine groups are reported together.

Placebo: Twelve rats in each of two dosage groups received .5 ml and .25 ml intraperitoneal injections of sterile peanut oil; as there were no differences between the groups, their results are combined.

Chlorpromazine: Twelve rats were given a .5 ml intraperitoneal injection containing 2.0 mg/kg body weight of chlorpromazine hydrochloride solution in physiological saline. The chlorpromazine was administered in saline to make its time of onset approximate that of epinephrine.

The results of this experiment are presented in Table 14 and the statistical analysis of these data in Table 15. It is clear that in the fear condition, the drugs have an effect, for adrenaline injected rats are more frightened than placebo rats ($p < .05$), who in turn are more frightened than chlorpromazine rats ($p < .05$). In the nonfear condition, on the other hand, the drugs have no effect at all, for the three scores are virtually identical. Though the point may be obvious, it is worth noting that the similarity of scores in the three drug nonfear conditions is an indication that this "interactional" view of emotion is as appropriate for rats as it appears to be for humans. The degree of drug-induced sympathetic arousal has no effect on the measured behavior in the nonstressful situation. Only in the fear producing situation is the measured display of fright directly related to the degree of drug manipulated arousal.

In a second experiment comparing the effects of adrenaline and placebo injections, Latané and Schachter (1962) examined the effects of adrenaline on

TABLE 14 MEAN FRIGHT INDICES FOR EACH
EXPERIMENTAL CONDITION

Drug treatment	Experimental condition			
	Fear		Nonfear	
	⇀N	M	N	M
Adrenaline	18	13.20	18	7.33
Placebo	12	11.38	12	7.16
Chlorpromazine	6	9.72	6	7.94

TABLE 15 ANALYSIS OF VARIANCE OF FRIGHT
INDEX SCORES

Source of variation	df	MS	F	p
Drug condition	2	12.41	3.32	< .05
Fear condition	1	411.30	109.97	< .001
Drugs × Fear	2	19.61	5.24	< .01
Error	66	3.74		
	71			

avoidance learning. If, as is commonly assumed, avoidance learning depends upon the arousal of an emotional response to the conditioned stimulus, then it should be anticipated from our general line of reasoning that manipulated autonomic arousal will facilitate avoidance learning. To test this expectation, rats were run in a modified Miller-Mowrer shuttle box. This is simply a box which is divided into two chambers by a metal guillotine door, and which has as a floor in both chambers an electrifiable grid. In use, the animal is placed in one of the compartments. At the beginning of a trial, a light in the rat's compartment goes on and simultaneously the door is lifted. If the rat crosses into the other compartment within 5 seconds, the light is turned off, the door lowered, and the trial is scored as an avoidance. If the rat does not cross within 5 seconds, it receives a 1½ mA shock through the grid until it crosses, at which point the shock is terminated, the door lowered, and, shortly, a new trial begun. In this study each rat was given 200 trials at the rate of two trials per minute. With this apparatus, one can easily ascertain the rate at which an animal learns to avoid shock.

The experimental animals received either a subcutaneous injection of placebo—½ ml of peanut oil—or ½ ml of a .0001 solution of adrenaline in peanut oil, or, since the average rat weighed about 400 gm, a dose of about .0125 mg adrenaline per 100 gm of body weight. Forty-five minutes after injection, the animal was transferred from a detention cage to the shuttle box where for 10 minutes it was allowed to explore with the door between compartments open. During this time a count was kept of spontaneous crossings between compartments in order to obtain a rough measure of the effects of the injections on general activity level. Following this exploration period, the experiment proper began.

The results of this study are presented in Fig. 1 which plots the frequency of avoidance as a function of block of training trials for each group. It is immediately clear that adrenaline has had a powerful effect on avoidance learning. Over the total experimental period adrenaline rats average 101.2 avoidances and placebo rats only 37.3 avoidances ($p < .001$). Employing a learning criterion of five consecutive avoidances, all adrenaline rats reach criterion and only 33% of placebo rats do so ($p < .001$).

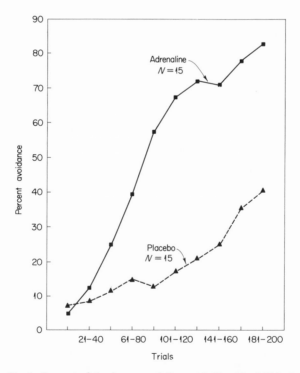

Fig. 1. Percent of shocks successfully avoided by 20-trial block.

TABLE 16 SUMMARY OF STUDIES TESTING THE RELATIONSHIP OF ADRENALINE
TO "EMOTIONAL" BEHAVIOR

Investigator	Situation	Dosage mg/100 gm	Mode of administration	Adrenaline-placebo difference
Kosman and Gerard (1955)	Bar-press	.60	Subcutaneous in oil	Adrenaline avoid less
Sieling and Benson (1959)	CER	.06–.25	Subcutaneous in oil	No difference
Moyer and Bunnell (1958)	Shuttlebox	.03–.09	Intraperitoneal in saline solution	No difference
Singer (1963)	Frightbox	.005–.01	Intraperitoneal in oil	Adrenaline more frightened
Latané and Schachter (1962)	Shuttlebox	.0125	Subcutaneous in oil	Adrenaline avoid more

There is little question, from the results of these two studies, that fear and fear-related behavior are directly related to drug manipulated sympathetic arousal. There is also little question that other studies of this relationship have revealed no differences between adrenaline and placebo-injected rats. Table 16 summarizes the salient features of the several relevant studies. It is evident that the Singer (1963) and the Latané and Schachter (1962) studies differ from previous experiments in dosage concentration. Our dose is approximately one-fiftieth of that used by Kosman and Gerard, one-fifth of the minimum Sieling and Benson dosage, and less than one-half of the Moyer and Bunnell minimum dosage. The Moyer and Bunnell dose, moreover, is not comparable to any of the other studies for they alone use adrenaline in a saline solution and use intraperitoneal injections. Both of these factors would strongly increase the potency of the injection and decrease the duration of its effects.

Only when the concentration of adrenaline is low is there a positive relationship between adrenaline and fear-motivated behavior.[1]

These differences in dosage, of course, suggest that the relationship between adrenaline concentration and avoidance learning is a nonmonotonic, inverted U

[1] Too late for consideration in this volume, I learned of Moran, Ahmed, and Meagher's (1970) series of studies on adrenaline, emotionality, and avoidance behavior. Their experiments replicate Singer's findings, but fail to replicate Latané's and my findings on avoidance learning. They conclude, "Schachter's theory of emotion is supported but the reliability of avoidance learning as an indicant of emotionality is seriously questioned." Perhaps so, and perhaps they are being overly generous. In either case, their failure to reproduce our findings on avoidance learning is troubling, for their experiments appear to have been almost identical to ours.

relationship. In order to test for this possibility, two additional groups of rats were run in the avoidance learning set-up: one group with an adrenaline dosage equivalent to .25 mg per 100 gm of body weight, and a second group with an adrenaline dosage equivalent to .50 mg per 100 gm of body weight. The effects of these heavier concentrations on avoidance learning are presented in Table 17. Since the results of the .25 mg and the .50 mg groups are virtually identical, data for the two groups are pooled in the table. The strong dosage group clearly does not learn to avoid as well as the weaker dosage group. Though the strong dosage group learns somewhat more effectively than does the placebo group, differences between these two groups are not significant. The indications are good, then, that the discrepant results of these several studies can be reconciled by the assumption of a nonmonotonic relationship between adrenaline concentration and avoidance learning.

Probably the simplest explanation of the poor performance of the heavy dosage rats is the pathological effects of large doses of adrenaline. Indeed, Kosman and Gerard report that their adrenaline-injected rats showed signs of physiological debilitation. Moyer and Bunnell observed diarrhea and sluggishness in rats given an intraperitoneal adrenaline injection of .09 mg/100 gm. Fifteen out of twenty-five animals in this injection condition died before reaching the learning criterion, as compared with one out of twenty animals given smaller doses. Though none of the rats in the present study gave any clear-cut indications of debilitation, there is evidence presented in Table 17 that strong dosage rats made significantly fewer crossings during the preexperimental observation period than did either of the other experimental groups.

TABLE 17   THE EFFECTS OF ADRENALINE CONCENTRATION
ON AVOIDANCE LEARNING

Condition	Dosage mg/100 gm	N	Precrossings	Percent of rats reaching avoidance criterion	Total no. avoidances
Placebo	–	15	19.9	33	37.3
Weak adrenaline	.0125	15	21.1	100	101.2
Strong adrenaline	.25–.50	20	14.7	65	62.5
				p value	
Strong vs. weak adrenaline			.05	.05	.01
Strong adrenaline vs. placebo			.05	n.s.	n.s.

Given this array of facts, it seems reasonable to conclude that evidence contradictory to our proposition can be explained by dosage considerations. When, in appropriate circumstances, nondebilitating concentrations of adrenaline are used as a means for manipulating sympathetic arousal, the degree of fear is directly related to the degree of arousal.

Chapter IV

Peripheral and Central Theories of Emotion and Motivation

Let us summarize the facts of the four studies that have been presented. We know that:

1. Given a state of epinephrine-induced sympathetic arousal, subjects may be manipulated into states of euphoria and anger if they have not been provided with an appropriate explanation of their bodily state.

2. Given the same state of arousal, subjects are virtually nonmanipulable into such emotion or mood states if they have a proper explanation of their bodily feelings (e.g., "My heart is pounding because of the injection)."

3. Making allowance for experimental artifacts, subjects injected with placebo are less manipulable into euphoric and angry states than are subjects injected with epinephrine and given no explanation of their feelings.

4. Amusement at a movie is directly related to the degree of arousal as manipulated by injections of epinephrine, placebo, and chlorpromazine.

5. In fear-inducing situations, the intensity of fear and fear-related behavior in rats is, within nondebilitating dose limits, directly related to manipulated sympathetic arousal. In nonfear-inducing situations, manifestations of fear are few and are unrelated to sympathetic arousal.

Given this assortment of facts the evidence in support of the propositions that generated these studies seems strong and convincing. It does appear experimentally useful to conceive of emotional states as a function of both cognitive or situational factors, and of physiological arousal.

Other than their relevance to my own line of thought these facts do, it seems to me, have critical implications for some of the central controversies that over the years have dominated research and debate in the fields of emotion and motivation. Since William James' day the study of emotion has tended to polarize around two sets of facts:

1. Emotional states are accompanied by various marked peripheral or visceral physiological changes such as modification of blood pressure, heart rate, endocrine levels, and the like.

2. Directly manipulating various lower brain structures, by lesion or electric stimulation techniques, may directly manipulate emotional states such as rage and fear.

This pair of complementary facts has been the focus of the famous James-Cannon debate over the peripheral versus the central nature of emotion. James, Lange, and their followers, even of today, have maintained that the feeling state accompanying the various peripheral bodily "changes as they occur *is* the emotion." Cannon, Bard, and probably most contemporary brain physiologists maintain that peripheral activity is irrelevant, and that emotional states are controlled by the activation of particular structures in the central nervous system.

It is of interest to note that this peripheral-central dimension of controversy has also been the focus of much of the scientific activity in the study of bodily states such as hunger or thirst, which, like emotion, are accompanied by "feelable," measurable, peripheral activity. The gist of the vast body of research on the physiological correlates of hunger, for example, can be summarized in a fashion that perfectly parallels my summary of the study of the physiological correlates of emotion:

1. Food deprivation leads to peripheral physiological changes such as modification of various blood constituents, increase in gastric motility, changes in body temperature, and the like.

2. Directly manipulating hypothalamic structures, by lesion or electric stimulation techniques, can directly manipulate the amount eaten.

And, again, this pair of facts has provided the basis for a long-term, active controversy on peripheral versus central mechanisms of hunger regulation. (See Rosenzweig, M. R., 1962, for an absorbing scientific history of this controversy.)

Whether for emotion, or hunger, or thirst, this peripheralist-centralist controversy has been marked, then, by the opposition between those who choose to identify a particular state with some visceral process, processes, or structure, and those who choose to identify the same state with some brain process or structure. Note, in both cases, the state is identified with a particular physiological process, or structure, or change. Though no one has bothered to make the assumption explicit, both peripheralists and centralists accept what, in other contexts, I have called the assumption of "identity" (Schachter, 1970); that is, the assumption that there is a one-to-one relationship between a set or pattern of physiological processes or biochemical changes and a specific behavior or psychological state. It is this assumption of identity which is, I believe, most seriously called into question by my series of experiments on emotion and adrenaline which demonstrate that precisely the same physiological state, a state of epinephrine-induced arousal, can, depending on cognitive circumstances, be interpreted as euphoria, anger, amusement at a movie, fear, or, as in the Epi Inf conditions, no emotion or mood state at all. It is this assumption of identity which is at the heart of the peripheralist-centralist difficulties and which, as I will try to demonstrate, is responsible for the fact that neither a purely central nor a purely peripheral point of view can possibly cope with the existing facts.

Let us first review the recognized inadequacies of a purely visceral formulation of emotion and examine the extent to which the addition of cognitive factors allows us to cope with these shortcomings. Since Cannon's critique (1927, 1929) has been the most lucid and influential attack on a visceral view of emotion, I shall focus discussion around Cannon's five criticisms of the James-Lange theory. Each of these critical points, it will be noted, is essentially an attack on the "identity" implications of James' view of matters.

A Reexamination of Cannon's Critique of a Visceral Formulation of Emotion

Criticisms Overcome by Cognitive Considerations

1. Cannon's criticism that "artificial induction of the visceral changes typical of strong emotions does not produce them" is based on the results of Marañon's (1924) study and its several replications. The fact that the injection of adrenaline produces apparently genuine emotional states in only a tiny minority of subjects is, of course, completely damning for a theory that equates visceral activity with affect. This is, on the other hand, precisely the fact that inspired the series of studies described in the previous chapters. Rather than being a criticism, the fact that the injection of adrenaline, in and of itself, does not lead to an emotional state is one of the strong points of the cognitive-physiological formulation, since, with the addition of cognitive propositions, we are able to specify and manipulate the conditions under which such an injection will or will not lead to an emotional state.

2. Cannon's point that "the same visceral changes occur in very different emotional states" is again damning for a purely visceral viewpoint. Since we are aware of a great variety of feeling and emotional states, it must follow from a purely visceral formulation that the variety of emotions will be accompanied by an equal variety of differentiable bodily states. Though the evidence as of today

is by no means as one-sided as it appeared in Cannon's day, it does seem that the gist of Cannon's criticism is still correct. Following James' pronouncement, a formidable number of studies were undertaken in search of the physiological differentiators of the emotions. The results, in those early days, were usually failure to find any discriminable patterns. All of the emotional states experimentally manipulated were characterized by a general pattern of activation of the sympathetic nervous system, but there appeared to be no clear-cut physiological discriminators of the various emotions.

More recent work, has given some indication that there may be differentiators. Ax (1953) and Schachter (1957) studied fear and anger. On a large number of indices both of these states were characterized by a similar level of sympathetic activation, but on several indices they did differ in the degree of activation. Wolf and Wolff (1943) studied a subject with a gastric fistula and were able to distinguish two patterns in the physiological responses of the stomach wall. It should be noted, though, that for many months they studied their subject during and following a great variety of moods and emotions, but were able to distinguish only two patterns.

Whether there are physiological distinctions among the various emotional states must still be considered an open question. Recent work might be taken to indicate that such differences are at best rather subtle, and that the variety of emotion, mood, and feeling states is by no means matched by an equal variety of visceral patterns—a state of affairs hardly compatible with the Jamesian formulation. On the other hand, the question of the physiological differentiability of the various emotions is essentially irrelevant to the present formulation, which maintains simply that cognitive and situational factors determine the labels applied to any of a variety of states of physiological arousal.

The experimental search for the physiological differentiators of emotional states has involved such a substantial, long-term effort that I would like to comment further on the problem. Taken together, these experiments have yielded inconclusive results. Most, though not all, of these studies have indicated no differences among the various emotional states. Since, as human beings, rather than as scientists, we have no difficulty identifying, labeling, and distinguishing among our feelings, the results of these studies have long seemed rather puzzling and paradoxical. Perhaps, because of this, there has been a persistent tendency to discount such results as being due to ignorance or to methodological inadequacy, and to pay far more attention to the very few studies that demonstrate some sort of physiological differences among emotional states than to the very many studies that indicate no differences at all. It is conceivable, however, that these results should be taken at face value and that emotional states may, indeed, be generally characterized by a high level of sympathetic activation with few, if any, physiological distinguishers among the many emotional states. If this is so, the cognitive-physiological formulation I have outlined and the findings of the studies I have described may help to resolve the problem. Obviously these studies do not rule out the possibility of differences among the emotional states. However, given precisely the same state of epinephrine-induced sympathetic activation, we have, by means of cognitive manipulations, been able to produce in our subjects the very disparate states of euphoria, anger, and amusement at a movie. It may, indeed, be the case that cognitive factors are major determiners of the emotional "labels" we apply to a common state of sympathetic arousal.

A novelist's view of this position is Ambler's (1958) description of a fugitive who introspects:

> Rather to his surprise, he found that being wanted for murder produced in him an effect almost identical to that of a dentist's waiting-room—a sense of discomfort in the intestinal region, a certain constriction in the chest. He supposed that the same glands discharged the same secretions into the blood stream in both cases. Nature could be absurdly parsimonious.

If these speculations are correct, nature may indeed be far more parsimonious than Ambler suggests.

3. Cannon's point that "the viscera are relatively insensitive structures" is again damaging to a formulation which virtually requires a richness of visceral sensation in order to be able to match the presumed richness of emotional experience. For the present formulation, of course, the criticism is irrelevant. Just so long as there is some visceral or cardiovascular sensation, the cognitive-physiological hypotheses are applicable.

The introduction of cognitive factors does allow us, then, to cope with three of Cannon's criticisms of a purely visceral formulation. Let us turn next to Cannon's remaining two points, which are quite as troublesome for a cognitive-physiological view of emotion as for the Jamesian view.

Visceral Separation and Emotion

Cannon's remaining criticisms are these: "visceral changes are too slow to be a source of emotional feeling" (i.e., the latency period of arousal of many visceral structures is longer than the latency of onset of emotional feelings reported in introspective studies), and "total separation of the viscera from the central nervous system does not alter emotional behavior." Both criticisms make essentially the same point, since they identify conditions in which there are apparently emotions unaccompanied by visceral activity. The data with which Cannon buttresses his latter criticism are based on his studies (Cannon, Lewis, and Britton, 1927) of sympathectomized cats, and Sherrington's (1900) study of sympathectomized dogs. For both sets of experimental animals "the absence of reverberation from the viscera did not alter in any respect the appropriate emotional display; its only abbreviation was surgical." (Cannon, 1929, p. 349.) In the presence of a barking dog, for example, the sympathectomized cats manifested almost all of the signs of feline rage. Finally, Cannon notes the report of Dana (1921) that a patient with a spinal-cord lesion and almost totally without visceral sensation still manifested normal emotionality.[1]

For either the Jamesian or the present formulation, such data are crucial, since both views demand visceral arousal as a necessary condition for emotional arousal. When faced with this evidence, James' defenders (e.g., Wenger, 1950; Mandler, 1962) have consistently made the point that the apparently emotional behavior manifested by sympathectomized animals and men is well-learned behavior, acquired long before sympathectomy. There is a dual implication in this position: first, that sympathetic arousal facilitates the acquisition of emotional behavior, and, second, that sympathectomized subjects act but do not feel emotional. There is a small but growing body of evidence supporting these contentions. Wynne and Solomon (1955) have demonstrated that sympathecto-mized dogs acquire an avoidance response considerably more slowly than control dogs. Furthermore, on extinction trials most of their 13 sympathectomized animals extinguished quickly, whereas not a single one of 30 control dogs gave any indications of extinction over 200 trials. Of particular interest are two dogs who were sympathectomized after they had acquired the avoidance response. On extinction trials these two animals behaved precisely like the control dogs—giv-ing no indication of extinction. Thus, when deprived of visceral innervation, animals are quite slow in acquiring emotionally-linked avoidance responses and, in general, quick to extinguish such responses. When deprived of visceral innervation only after acquisition, the animals behave exactly like normal dogs—they fail to extinguish. A true Jamesian would undoubtedly note that these latter animals have learned to act as if they were emotional, but would ask if they feel emotional.

This apparently unanswerable question seems on its way to being answered in a thoroughly fascinating study of the emotional life of paraplegics and quadriplegics conducted by Hohmann (1962, 1966). Hohmann studied a sample of 25 patients of the Spinal Cord Injury Service of the Veterans Administration Hospital at Long Beach, California. The subjects were divided into five groups according to the height of the clinically complete lesions as follows:

---

[1] More recent work supporting Cannon's position is that of Moyer and Bunnell (Moyer, 1958; Moyer and Bunnell, 1959, 1960a, 1960b), who have in an extensive series of studies of bilaterally adrenalectomized rats, consistently failed to find any indication of differences between experimental and control animals on a variety of emotionally linked behaviors such as avoidance learning. The effects of adrenalectomy are by no means clear-cut, however, for other investigators (Levine and Soliday, 1962) have found distinct differences between operated and control animals.

Group I, with lesions between the second and seventh cervical segmental level, have only the cranial branch of the parasympathetic nervous system remaining intact.

Group II, with lesions between the first and fourth thoracic segmental level, have, in addition to the above, at least partial innervation of the sympathetically innervated cardiac plexus remaining intact.

Group III, with lesions between the seventh and twelfth thoracic segmental level, have, additionally, at least partial innervation of the splanchnic outflow of the sympathetics remaining intact.

Group IV, with lesions between the first and fifth lumbar segmental level, have, in addition, at least partial sympathetic innervation of the mesenteric ganglia.

Group V, with lesions between the first and third sacral segments, have, in addition, at least partial innervation of the sacral branch of the parasympathetic nervous system.

These groups, then, fall along a continuum of visceral innervation and sensation. The higher the lesion, the less the visceral sensation. If the present conception of emotion is correct, one should expect to find decreasing manifestation of emotion as the height of the lesion increases.

With each of his subjects Hohmann conducted an extensive, structured interview, which was "directed toward his feelings rather than toward the concomitant ideation." Hohmann asked his subjects to recall an emotion-arousing incident prior to their injury and a comparable incident following the injury. They were then asked to compare the intensity of their emotional experiences before and after injury. Changes in reported affect comprise the body of data. I have adapted Hohmann's data for presentation in Fig. 2. Following Hohmann's coding schema, a report of no change is scored as 0; a report of mild change (e.g., "I feel it less, I guess") is scored −1 for a decrease and +1 for an increase; a report of strong change (e.g., "I feel it a helluva lot less") is scored as −2 or +2.

Hohmann's data for the states of fear and anger are plotted in Fig. 2. It can be immediately seen that the higher the lesion and the less the visceral sensation, the greater the decrease in emotionality. Precisely the same relationship holds for the states of sexual excitement and grief. The sole exception to this consistent trend is "sentimentality," which, I suspect, should be considered a cognitive rather than a "feeling" state. It is clear that for these cases, deprivation of visceral sensation has resulted in a marked decrease in emotionality.

If, in an attempt to assess the absolute level of emotionality of these cases one examines their verbalized introspections, one notes again and again that subjects with cervical lesions describe themselves as acting emotionally but not feeling emotional. A few typical quotes follow:

> It's sort of cold anger. Sometimes I act angry when I see some injustice. I yell and cuss and raise hell, because if you don't do it sometimes, I've learned people

will take advantage of you, but it just doesn't have the heat to it that it used to. It's a mental kind of anger.

Seems like I get thinking mad, not shaking mad, and that's a lot different.

I say I am afraid, like when I'm going into a real stiff exam at school, but I don't really feel afraid, not all tense and shaky, with that hollow feeling in my stomach, like I used to.

In effect, these subjects seem to be saying that when the situation demands it, they make the proper emotional-appearing responses but they do not feel emotional. Parenthetically, it should be noted that these quotations bear an almost contrapuntal resemblance to the introspections of Marañon's subjects who, after receiving an injection of adrenaline, described their feelings in a way that led Marañon to label them "cold" or "as if" emotions. Many of these

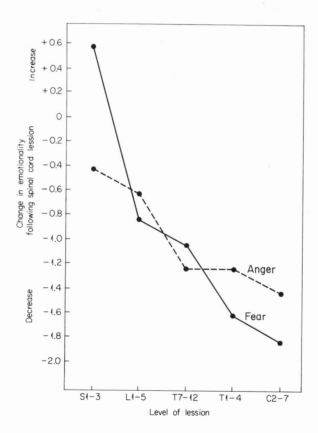

Fig. 2. Changes in emotionality as related to height of spinal cord lesion. (Adapted from Hohmann, 1962).

subjects described their physical symptoms and added statements such as "I feel as if I were very frightened; however, I am calm."

The two sets of introspections are like opposite sides of the same coin. Marañon's subjects report the visceral correlates of emotion, but in the absence of veridical cognitions do not describe themselves as feeling emotion. Hohmann's subjects describe the appropriate reaction to an emotion-inducing situation, but in the absence of visceral arousal do not seem to describe themselves as emotional. It is as if they were labeling a situation, not describing a feeling. Obviously, this contrasting set of introspections is precisely what should be anticipated from a formulation of emotion as a joint function of cognitive and physiological factors.

The line of thought stimulated by the Wynne and Solomon (1955) and the Hohmann (1962) studies may indeed be the answer to Cannon's observation that there can be emotional behavior without visceral activity. From the evidence of these studies, it would appear, first, that autonomic arousal greatly facilitates the acquisition of emotional behavior but is not necessary for its maintenance if the behavior is acquired prior to sympathectomy and, second, that in the absence of autonomic arousal, behavior that appears emotional will not be experienced as emotional.

On the whole, it does appear that the explicit recognition of cognitive variables does allow us to cope with the generally recognized shortcomings of a purely peripheral or visceral formulation of emotion. More importantly, though, this cognitive-physiological, interactionist formulation does permit us to predict and cope with phenomena (e.g., the results of the euphoria-anger experiment) which are well beyond the scope of any purely visceral or purely central theory.

Though I realize that this presentation smacks of neo-Jamesianism, I rather hope not to become embroiled in any revival of the peripheralist-centralist battles, for I believe neither view of matters is, of itself, adequate to cope with present day experimental data and that cognitive or situational factors are of equal importance for either point of view. In the past (Schachter, 1964) I have, in fact, been inclined to interpret the results of my experiments within a modified peripheralist framework. I have, however, become increasingly convinced that this interpretation was almost an accident of the experimental techniques my students and I employed. The injection of adrenaline is a means of directly activating peripheral structures—an experimental fact which makes likely a peripheralist interpretation of these particular results.

Central Theories and the Assumption of Identity

Let us turn next to the central theories—that variety of theory that from Cannon's day on has involved one or another of the lower brain stem structures as crucial to emotion or motivation. In essence, such theories have rested upon the numerous demonstrations that brain lesions or brain stimulation can induce intense emotional and drive states. From the present point of view, the crucial question, of course, is this—does such brain manipulation inevitably lead to modification of specified emotion or drive states, or are the consequences of such manipulation contingent upon stimulus, environmental, or cognitive circumstances? The effects of peripheral manipulation of bodily state are demonstrably dependent on external circumstances and the implications of this fact constitute the substance of the chief criticisms leveled at purely visceral formulations. Are the central theories any less vulnerable to precisely the same order of criticisms?

Though I claim flatly no expertise, my talks with researchers in this area and my reading of the publications to which they have directed me have convinced me that a purely central theory of emotion or motivation is as inadequate at coping with all of the facts as a purely peripheral theory. The external circumstances surrounding the experimental animal appear to play an extraordinary role in determining whether or not brain manipulation has motivational or emotional effects. In the field of hunger, for example, we know that there is a feeding control center in the ventromedial area of the hypothalamus. Experimentally produced lesions in this area lead to hyperphagia and immensely obese animals. This is one of a large number of related findings which has led many scholars (e.g., Rosenzweig, 1962) to the conclusion that feeding behavior is entirely under central control. However, as both Miller, Bailey and Stevenson (1950) and Teitelbaum (1955) have demonstrated, such lesions lead to overeating and obesity only when the available food is palatable. When the food is unpleasant (coarse in texture or adulterated with quinine) the experimental animals eat considerably less and grow thinner than control animals presented with the same diet. It would appear that this feeding control center operates in intimate interaction with environmental stimuli.

In the area of emotion, experiments explicitly dealing with this point seem rare, but what I have found so far certainly supports the suspicion that external circumstances play a major part in determining whether or not electrical brain stimulation leads to emotional display. Von Holst's and von Saint Paul's (1962) studies of aggression in the rooster neatly illustrate the point. When presented with a stuffed weasel (a natural enemy) an unstimulated rooster ignores the stuffed animal. When electrically stimulated, the rooster attacks it. If the stuffed animal is absent, the rooster will, after sustained stimulation, attack its keeper's face. However, in von Holst's words (p.61),

> If all substitutes for an enemy are lacking—when there is, so to speak, no hook on which to hang an illusion—the rooster exhibits only motor restlessness. Moreover, the same motor restlessness is observed if one stimulated brain areas

associated with hunger, thirst, courtship, or fighting[2] under conditions in which the environment does not permit the unreeling of the entire behavior sequence. For this reason it is often necessary to vary the external conditions to be sure which particular behavior sequence—which complex drive—has in fact been activated.

Even more convincing are the studies of Hutchinson and Renfrew (1966) which demonstrate that stimulation of a single area in the lateral hypothalamus can lead to either predatory attack or to eating behavior, depending entirely on the nature of the situational cues. If a cat is stimulated in the presence of a rat, it will attack; if stimulated in the presence of food, it will eat; if stimulated in the presence of both food and a rat, it will either eat or attack, depending entirely on which of the cues is physically closest.

It would appear, then, that the central theorists of emotion are faced with many of the same problems as are the peripheralists. Direct stimulation of brain stem structures does produce emotional behavior, but only in the presence of appropriate external stimuli. The experimental production of the peripheral correlates of emotion also produces emotional behavior but, again, only in the presence of appropriate external stimuli. Neither a purely central nor a purely peripheral view of emotion is adequate at coping with the facts. Nor is any sort of compromise formulation—one suggesting that both peripheral and central processes are important—likely to be any more successful. Any physiologically based formulation of emotion must specify the fashion in which physiological processes interact with stimulus, cognitive, or situational factors.

If we are eventually to make sense of these areas, I believe we will be forced to adopt a set of concepts with which most physiologically inclined scientists feel somewhat uncomfortable and ill-at-ease, for they are concepts which are difficult to reify, and about which it is, at present, difficult to physiologize. We will be forced to deal with concepts about perception, about cognition, about learning, and about the social situation. We will be forced to examine a subject's perception of his bodily state and his interpretation of it in terms of his immediate situation and his past experience.

In order to avoid any misunderstanding, let me make it completely explicit that I am most certainly not suggesting that such notions as perception and cognition do not have physiological correlates. I am suggesting that at present we know little about these physiological correlates, but that we can and must use such nonphysiologically anchored concepts if we are to make headway in

---

[2] The one exception noted by von Holst is escape behavior which "can be evoked in the absence of the appropriate external object (or its substitute) if the brain stimulation is sufficiently intense." Von Holst seems so convinced of the importance of external circumstances that he suggests for this exception: "it is probable that the absent object of fear is being hallucinated."

understanding the relations of complex behavioral patterns to physiological and biochemical processes. If we don't, my guess is that we will be just about as successful at deriving predictions about emotion or any other complex behavior from a knowledge of biochemical and physiological conditions as we would be at predicting the destination of a moving automobile from an exquisite knowledge of the workings of the internal combustion engine and of petroleum chemistry.

Part II

Cognitive and Physiological
Determinants of Pain and Hunger

Chapter V

Cognitive Manipulation of Pain

Though the experiments described in the first two chapters have been couched within the broad framework of emotion, the specifics of the experiments proper raise issues which go far beyond this conventional context. Free of a theoretical load, these studies have simply demonstrated that the exogenous injection of adrenaline can, under specifiable circumstances, lead a human subject to label his bodily state with any of a diversity of situationally derived labels. These demonstrations of the plasticity of interpretation of bodily state have depended upon the experimental trick of simultaneously and independently manipulating physiological and cognitive factors. In nature, of course, matters are quite otherwise, for cognitive or situational factors trigger physiological processes, and the triggering stimulus usually imposes the label we attach to our feelings. We see the threatening object; this perception-cognition initiates a state of sympathetic arousal, and this joint cognitive-physiological experience is labeled "fear."

Several considerations suggest that the line of reasoning guiding these experimental studies of emotion may be extended to these naturally occurring states, and that the intensity of such states may be as modifiable, as are experimentally induced states of arousal.[1] As an example of this possibility,

[1] Though this "modifiability" has been demonstrated in my own work only for the exogenous administration of adrenaline, the numerous demonstrations of the impact of set and context on the effects of a variety of psychogenic drugs provide ample evidence that these results generalize to virtually any other drug-induced bodily state. (See Wikler, 1957, and Schachter, 1964, for further consideration of this work.) Probably the most intriguing of these studies is Becker's (1953) fascinating study of marijuana, in which he demonstrates that marijuana users must be taught to notice and identify what they feel, must be taught to label the state as "high," and must be taught that the state is to be called "pleasant" rather than "sick."

consider pain. Broadly, we can conceive of the intensity of experienced pain and of one's willingness to tolerate pain as a function of the intensity of stimulation of the pain receptors, of the autonomic correlates of such stimulation, and of a host of cognitive and situational factors. To the extent that we can convince a subject undergoing electric shock that his shock-produced symptoms and arousal state aren't due to shock but, rather, to some outside agent such as a drug, he should, following the above considerations, experience less pain and be willing to tolerate more shock. Such an individual would, of course, regard his arousal as a drug-produced state rather than an indicator of pain or fear.

Since we would not expect that an individual undergoing extreme pain, fear, or rage could easily be persuaded to attribute the accompanying physiological arousal to an artificial source, there should be limits placed on the generality of these notions. We should be able to alter the labeling of a bodily state only within a range bounded at the lower end by the existence of at least some arousal, and at the upper end by experiences so extreme that no manipulation of cognitions will persuade the individual to attribute his bodily state to an artificial source. Common sense would indicate that no amount of argument would persuade a man dodging machine-gun bullets that his physiological arousal was due to anything but the exigencies of his situation. The present experiment examines the extent to which relabeling processes affect pain thresholds under conditions of high and low fear.

The experimental test of these ideas requires (1) administration of a placebo, (2) the "natural" production of an aroused bodily state by a painful stimulus, (3) manipulation of the extent to which this arousal can be attributed to the placebo, and (4) measurement of the extent to which the pain stimulus is tolerated and labeled as painful. To satisfy these requirements Nisbett and Schachter (1966) designed an experiment which was described to subjects as one on skin sensitivity where the test of sensitivity would be electric shock. They were given a brief lecture on the importance of shock sensitivity research for the prevention of accidents and the control of shock dosage for patients undergoing electro-shock therapy. This was followed by a description of the shock stimulus which the subject was to take. The shock was described to one group as being extremely painful, and to the other as being mild and easily tolerable.

Subjects were then told that the experimenters were interested in the effects on skin sensitivity of a drug called Suproxin. The drug was described as being a mild one that could do no harm, but which had certain transitory side effects which would last for 15 or 20 minutes. The description of the "side effects" of the placebo differed across conditions. In one set of conditions, the "side effects" were actually symptoms produced by the shock. In the other pair of conditions, the symptoms were irrelevant to shock. After taking the placebo tablet, subjects were told that they could expect the side effects to start within two to four minutes. They were then left to wait alone for a 10-minute period.

After the waiting period, subjects were taken into a room containing the shock apparatus. Electrodes were attached and subjects were given a series of shocks of gradually increasing intensity. Subjects reported when they could first feel the shock, when the shock first became painful, and when the shock was too painful to endure.

Manipulating Fear

High Fear

After describing the nature of the research, the experimenter concluded his patter with,

> So what we'll ask you to do is very simple. We'd like to give you a series of electric shocks. Now I should be very honest with you and tell you what you're in for. These shocks will hurt, they will be painful. If we're going to learn anything at all in this kind of research, it's necessary that the shocks be intense. What we'll do is put electrodes on your hand and give you a series of electric shocks. Again, I want to be honest with you and tell you that these shocks will be quite painful, but of course they won't do any permanent damage.

The experimenter then continued with instructions about Suproxin; the subjects took the pill and then waited alone for 10 minutes. At this point they were taken to the experimental room, the instructions about the painfulness of the shock were repeated, and the subjects were given a sample "standardizing" shock which, to reinforce the manipulation, was a rather jarring and unpleasant 55 μA.

Low Fear

In introducing the experiment, the experimenter reassured the subject by saying, "Before you get worried, let me tell you not to let the word 'shock' bother you. There's not going to be any discomfort and I'm sure you'll enjoy the experiment." He then continued his description of the research, concluding with, "So what we will ask you to do will be very simple. We would like to give you a series of very mild electric shocks. What you will feel will be more like a tickle or a tingle than anything unpleasant. So we will put some electrodes on your hand and give you a series of very mild shocks." The subject then took the pill, waited 10 minutes, and was given a sample shock of a barely perceptible 22 μA.

Manipulating Attribution of Bodily State

The extent to which bodily state could be attributed to an external source was manipulated by instructing the subjects in one condition to expect, as "side effects" of the placebo, symptoms which would actually be caused by the shock (Pill Attrib condition), and in another condition by making subjects anticipate symptoms which were irrelevant to the shock (Shock Attrib condition).

Pill Attrib subjects were told the following about the side effects of the placebo: "What will happen is that you may have some tremor, that is, your hand will start to shake; you will have some palpitation, that is, your heart will start to pound; your rate of breathing may increase. Also, you will probably get a sinking feeling in the pit of your stomach, like butterflies." All of these are symptoms which were widely reported by pretest subjects who introspected about their physiological reactions to shock. To the extent that the manipulation is effective, subjects in this condition should attribute these shock-produced symptoms to the pill.

Shock Attrib subjects were told: "What will probably happen is that your feet will feel numb, you may have an itching sensation over parts of your body, and you may get a slight headache." None of these symptoms, of course, is produced either by the shock or the placebo. As in the Schachter and Singer (Chapter I) study, it seemed a distinct possibility that reeling off a list of symptoms, any symptoms, might make a subject more introspective and concerned with his bodily state. Therefore we again employed this technique of "false" symptoms rather than telling a subject that the pill would have no effects at all as a means of making the two attribution conditions somewhat more comparable. Subjects in this condition, then, will experience the physiological symptoms produced by shock and anticipation of shock and, since no plausible alternative exists, will perforce attribute these symptoms to the shock experience.

After the 10-minute waiting period, subjects were reminded of the symptoms appropriate to their condition, and told that they were probably just starting. A second reminder immediately preceded the administration of the shock series.

In summary, there were four conditions: Hi Fear Pill Attrib, Hi Fear Shock Attrib, Lo Fear Pill Attrib, and Lo Fear Shock Attrib. There were 16 subjects in each of the Hi Fear groups and 12 in each of the Lo Fear groups. All were male volunteers from introductory psychology courses at Long Island University.

Measurement

Pain Thresholds. After the 10-minute waiting period, the subject was ushered into the experimental room and introduced to a second experimenter who proceeded to apply the electrodes to the fingers of the subject's left hand, to administer the sample "standardizing" shock, and to explain the procedure to the subject. It was explained that a series of shocks would be administered and that they would progressively increase in intensity. Shocks were administered every 15 seconds and the shock proper had a duration of .10 second. Starting with a subthreshold 20 μA, each successive shock in the early part of the series was roughly 5–10 μA more intense than the preceding shock. This gap widened during the series to an average of about 100 μA. These intervals were determined on the basis of pretests to be subjectively equal increments. There were a total of 37 steps in the shock series, with the final step delivering 3000 μA of current.

Subjects were requested to report (1) when they first felt the shock (sensitivity threshold), (2) when the shock first became painful (pain threshold), and (3) when the shock was too painful to endure and they wanted it stopped (tolerance threshold).

The subjects were told that when they reached a point too painful to endure, the shocks would be terminated. If a subject endured the entire 37 steps of the series without so complaining, the experiment automatically ended after the thirty-seventh trial.

The shocks were administered by the experimenter's assistant. He was aware of the fear condition of the subject, but ignorant of his attribution condition.

Questionnaires. In order to get measures of the effectiveness of the fear manipulation, subjects answered a questionnaire about "general physical and mental" state at the very end of the 10-minute waiting period. Embedded among a series of dummy items were two relevant scales dealing with how frightened they were about taking shock, and how worried they were about the effects of the shock.

At the end of the shock series, the subjects answered a questionnaire concerned with the painfulness of the shocks, the extent to which the subject experienced the symptoms which had been described, when they occurred, and the extent to which they were attributed to the placebo.

A Note on the Noncomparability of Fear Conditions

As must be evident, the primary interests of this study are the examination of (1) the effects of the symptom-attribution manipulation on pain, and (2) the interaction of the attribution and fear manipulations. In no sense were we directly concerned in this experiment with the effects of manipulated fear on pain. Because of these interests we deliberately sacrificed the elegance of a completely symmetrical experimental design in order to maximize the effects of the fear manipulation. For example, in the Hi Fear condition the sample shock was jolting and painful, while in the Lo Fear condition it was simply a tickly sensation. The language used in describing the various thresholds was slightly different in high and low fear conditions, e.g., for the sensitivity threshold, Lo Fear subjects were asked to note when they "first felt a tingle," while Hi Fear subjects noted when they first felt a "shock." Without question, experimental touches such as these made Hi Fear subjects more fearful and Lo Fear subjects less fearful than they might otherwise have been. It is the case, however, that such variations in procedure make direct comparison of Hi and Lo Fear subjects dubious. Among other things, for example, the sample shock may have provided a different point of reference for the two groups of subjects in making judgments of pain. Similarly, describing thresholds somewhat differently to Hi and Lo Fear subjects obviously will affect threshold values. For reasons such as these, direct comparison of Hi and Lo Fear conditions is meaningless, and we shall not discuss the effects of the fear manipulation on the dependent variable.

Within fear conditions, of course, the pairs of experimental conditions are identical in every respect other than the attribution manipulation.

Results

The experimental test of the hypotheses requires first, the successful manipulation of fear, second, the actual production of symptoms described in the Pill Attrib condition, and third, the successful manipulation of attribution.

Effectiveness of Fear Manipulation

Evaluating first the effect of the fear manipulation, it can be seen in Table 18 that Ss in the Hi Fear conditions report significantly more fear and worry after the waiting period than do Ss in the Lo Fear conditions. Means in Table 18

TABLE 18 MEAN REPORTED FEAR AND
WORRY SCORES AFTER WAITING PERIOD

Condition	N	Fear	Worry
Lo Fear Pill Attrib.	12	.46	.42
Lo Fear Shock Attrib.	12	.58	.31
Hi Fear Pill Attrib.	16	1.00	.70
Hi Fear Shock Attrib.	16	.92	.91
t Hi vs. Lo		2.50	2.78
p		$< .02$	$< .01$

are for responses on four-point rating scales (0 = not at all, 3 = extremely) to the questions "How frightened are you about taking shock?" and "How worried are you about the effects of the shock?" The fear manipulation was clearly successful.

The Level of Physiological Arousal.

Table 19 presents the proportion of subjects in each condition who reported actually experiencing one or more of the symptoms (palpitation, tremor, breathing rate change, butterflies in the stomach) that we associate with receiving or anticipating shock. These data are simply tabulations of answers to the questions about each of these symptoms on the questionnaire administered at the end of the shock portion of the experimental session. There are no significant differences between conditions, and obviously the large majority of subjects in each of the conditions report experiencing one or more of the physiological symptoms associated with shock.

That subjects actually did experience these symptoms and are not simply being suggestible or accommodating is indicated by a comparison of these figures with the proportion of subjects reporting the irrelevant symptoms. While 78.6% of all subjects reported experiencing the true symptoms described in the Pill Attrib manipulation, only 21.2% of all subjects reported one or more of the "false" symptoms (itching skin, numb feet, headache) described in the Shock Attrib conditions.

Effectiveness of Attribution Manipulation

From their answers to the postexperimental questionnaire, most of the subjects who reported any arousal at all could be categorized as either

TABLE 19 PROPORTION OF SUBJECTS
WHO REPORTED AROUSAL SYMPTOMS

Condition	N	Percent of subjects reporting "true" shock-produced symptoms
Lo Fear Pill Attrib.	12	75.0
Lo Fear Shock Attrib.	12	83.3
Hi Fear Pill Attrib.	16	75.0
Hi Fear Shock Attrib.	16	81.3
	56	78.6

TABLE 20 ATTRIBUTION OF SYMPTOMS[a]

Condition	Exclusive attribution to placebo	Some attribution to shock or fear
Lo Fear Pill Attrib.	6	4
Lo Fear Shock Attrib.	1	7
Hi Fear Pill Attrib.	2	10
Hi Fear Shock Attrib.	1	9
Comparison		p^b
Lo PA vs. Hi PA		.05
Lo PA vs. Hi SA		.03
Lo PA vs. Lo SA		.05
Lo PA vs. all others		.01

[a]Entries are the number of subjects with the designated attribution. The total for each condition is less than the number of subjects in the condition because some subjects reported no symptoms or could not be categorized as to attribution.

[b]p values are Fisher's exact p.

attributing all of their symptoms to the pill or as attributing some or all of their symptoms to shock or fear. The frequencies in these categories are reported in Table 20. It can be seen that in Lo Fear conditions the manipulation has worked. Some 60% of the Pill Attrib subjects attributed their symptoms to the pill, while only one of eight Shock Attrib subjects did so. Where the shock is presumed to be mild and harmless, the subjects accept the immediately provided explanation and attribute the shock-induced symptoms to the pill rather than the shock. In marked contrast, most of the Hi Fear subjects, regardless of attribution condition, attribute their symptoms to the shock. This, of course, is precisely what was anticipated, for the Hi Fear conditions were deliberately made as frightening as possible in order to provide subjects with a plausible alternative explanation for their bodily state. Obviously, the intensity of the Hi Fear manipulation has made it more plausible for subjects in these conditions to attribute their arousal to shock or fear than to the pill.

Clearly, the experimental conditions necessary to test the hypotheses have been established. The subjects actually experienced symptoms of physiological arousal, the manipulation of fear was successful, and the attribution of symptoms conforms to the manipulations in the Lo Fear and not in the Hi Fear conditions.

Effect of the Manipulation on Tolerance of Shock

Our formulation of the pain experience as, in part, a function of the intensity of arousal symptoms, and of the attribution of these symptoms leads us to expect first, that the attribution manipulation will have effects only in the Lo Fear conditions and, second, that these effects will be manifested only when arousal symptoms are prominent. In Lo Fear conditions, then, one should anticipate marked differences in Tolerance Threshold, for at this point of "unbearableness" the arousal symptoms produced by shock and anticipation of shock are undoubtedly at a maximum. In contrast, the attribution manipulation should have no effect on Sensitivity Threshold, for this is the point at which subjects first report that they are aware of some (nonpainful) sensation, and shock-produced arousal symptoms are nil. The effects on Pain Threshold should depend on the extent to which this "first sign of pain" is arousing. A low intensity pain is considerably less autonomically arousing (Valins, 1967) than is an intense pain. We should, then, expect the attribution manipulation to have relatively small effects on Pain Threshold. In Hi Fear, on the other hand, there should be no difference between the attribution conditions on any of the thresholds.

The extent to which the data support these expectations can be evaluated in Table 21, which presents the means for each of these thresholds. The figures in this table represent the average step in the series of 37 increasingly intense shocks at which subjects reported that they had reached a particular threshold. It can be seen that in the Lo Fear conditions, as anticipated, there is no difference in Sensitivity Threshold, a small difference in Pain Threshold, and a marked and extremely large difference in Tolerance Threshold. Translating these steps into amperage, Pill Attribution subjects on the average were able to

TABLE 21 MEAN SHOCK THRESHOLDS

Condition	Sensitivity threshold	Pain threshold	Tolerance threshold
Lo Fear Pill Attrib.	4.58	11.58	25.75
Lo Fear Shock Attrib.	4.58	8.00	15.75
t	0	1.55	2.90
p	n.s.	n.s.	$<.01$
Hi Fear Pill Attrib.	5.44	15.06	26.31
Hi Fear Shock Attrib.	5.13	19.31	28.19
t	.63	1.47	0.59
p	n.s.	n.s.	n.s.

tolerate 1450 μA while the Shock Attribution subjects found an average of 350 μA intolerable. Obviously, the attribution of shock-produced symptoms to the pill has had a profound effect on the subject's ability or willingness to withstand pain.

In Hi Fear conditions, pill and shock attribution subjects are similar on all three thresholds. As shown previously, the Hi Fear manipulation was successful enough to compel almost all of these subjects to attribute their symptoms to being shocked, and they behaved accordingly.

Testing the Fear X Attribution interaction, on the Pain Threshold, an interaction t test yields $t = 2.01$ with $p = .05$. For the Tolerance Threshold, the interaction $t = 2.52$ with $p < .02$. The attribution manipulation affects the willingness to withstand pain only in the Lo Fear conditions.

In addition to these differences in tolerance of pain, there is evidence that the Lo Fear Pill Attrib subjects consciously experienced less pain than subjects in other conditions. On the post-experiment questionnaire, subjects were asked how painful they found the last shock they were willing to endure. The means for these responses are presented in Table 22. It can be seen that the Lo Fear Pill Attrib subjects reported less pain than any of the other groups, despite the fact that they actually tolerated as much shock as subjects in any other group. A comparison of the mean for the Lo Fear Pill Attrib group with the mean of all other groups yields a t of 2.34 that is significant beyond the .05 level.

Finally, the categorization of subjects, in Table 20, into those who attributed their symptoms to the shock or fear versus those who attributed their symptoms exclusively to the drug, suggests another means of analyzing the data. To the extent that subjects in any condition attributed their symptoms to the drug, they should have behaved like subjects in the Lo Fear Pill Attrib condition. If the tolerance threshold scores of the ten subjects in Table 20 who attributed their symptoms to the pill are contrasted with those of the thirty subjects who attributed their symptoms mainly to fear or to the shock, it is found that four of the ten subjects in the former category were willing to take more shock than the

TABLE 22 MEAN REPORTED PAIN
OF LAST SHOCK

Condition		Pain
Lo Fear Pill Attrib.		1.37
Lo Fear Shock Attrib.		1.79
Hi Fear Pill Attrib.		2.16
Hi Fear Shock Attrib.		1.86
	t	p
Lo PA vs. all others	2.34	$< .05$

shock apparatus could deliver, while this was true of none of the thirty subjects in the latter category. This difference is significant at the .003 level by Fisher's exact test. Further, the mean reported pain of the last shock for the pill-attributers is 1.53, and that for the shock-or-fear attributers is 2.16. This difference yields a t of 2.83, which is significant beyond the .01 level.

The gist of the data is clear. Where subjects attribute shock-produced autonomic symptoms to the pill, they tolerate far more shock and report considerably less pain than when they attribute these symptoms to the shock proper. Earlier studies have demonstrated the cognitive manipulability of bodily states produced by the injection of epinephrine. This study demonstrates that, within the limits of plausibility, the labeling of naturally occurring bodily states is similarly manipulable.

A Replication

In an entirely different experimental context, Ross, Rodin, and Zimbardo (1969) have replicated this finding that the misattribution technique can have major effects on fear and anxiety. In their experiment, attribution was manipulated by exposing subjects to blasts of noise while they anticipated electric shock. In one condition, the subjects were led to believe that this noise bombardment produced palpitations, tremor, etc.—the usual battery of physiological symptoms accompanying fear. In a second condition, the noise was presumed to produce ringing in the ears, dull headache, and so on—symptoms having nothing to do with fear. From the misattribution hypothesis, it should follow that subjects will experience less fear when they attribute the fear-produced symptoms to the noise.

The test of the hypothesis involved simply allowing a subject to work, as she wished, on either of two puzzles during a three-minute period of noise bombardment. If she solved puzzle A, she would win money. If she solved puzzle B, she would avoid being shocked. Both puzzles were insoluble; the subject was free to work on either or both puzzles as she chose, and the amount of time the subject spent working on the shock avoidance puzzle is, of course, considered an index of fear.

The results are marked and dramatic. When subjects attribute palpitations and tremor to the noise, they work on the shock avoidance puzzle for an average of 88 of a possible 180 seconds. In the comparison condition, where the subjects, of course, are very likely to attribute their symptoms to fear of shock, they work on the shock avoidance puzzle for 140 seconds ($p < .001$). Obviously, attribution of fear-related physiological symptoms to noise has a major effect.

Discussion

Since both pain and fear are notoriously manipulable, these experimental effects may not be completely surprising. More revealing, perhaps, is some of the Russian work which has demonstrated that even such presumably nonmalleable states as the feelings associated with micturition are astonishingly manipulable. Razran (1961) and Gwynne-Jones (1956) describe a series of studies conducted by Ayrapetyants *et al.* (1952) and Bykov (1953) of patients with urinary bladder fistulas. In these experiments warm water or air was introduced into the bladder and bladder pressure was recorded on a manometer with conspicuous dials which were always watched by the subjects. During the course of a session, subjects reported on the intensity of the urge to urinate, thus establishing a connection between the manometer reading and intensity of this urge. Apparently, a series of such training sessions were conducted. At one point in this series, unknown to the subject, the manometer was disconnected from the bladder and its dial placed under the experimenter's control so that dial readings could be varied independently of the actual bladder pressure. In these circumstances, the fake dial reading rather than the actual volume of fluid in the bladder appeared to control the reported intensity of the urge to urinate. When the manipulated manometer reading was high, subjects reported an urgent need to urinate even when the bladder was virtually empty. Conversely, when the meter reading was quite low or at zero, subjects failed to report any particular desire to urinate even when the volume of fluid in the bladder was far greater than that normally associated with such a report. These results appear to be consistent from subject to subject and this technique has been used with remarkable therapeutic success by Gwynne-Jones (1956) in the treatment of a patient with long-standing neurotic micturition problems.[2]

[2] In analogous sorts of studies, Valins (1966) has used the technique of phony cardiac feedback as a means of manipulating sexual interest. His procedure involved simply giving subjects the impression that they were listening to their own heartbeat. While doing so, they are exposed to a series of pin-up, girlie pictures. For some of these pictures, the experimenter creates the impression that the subject's heartrate is accelerating, while for other pictures his heartrate remains constant or decelerates. In post-experimental judgments, subjects rate those pictures for which their heartrate had presumably increased as markedly more attractive than those pictures for which their heartrate had remained unchanged. Valins and Ray (1967) have also used this phony cardiac feedback procedure on snake phobic subjects as a means of desensitizing them to snake stimuli.

Such studies essentially involve giving the subject pseudo information about the state of one of his organs and are probably successful because they pit the experimenter's scientific prestige and know-how against a subject's vague and amorphous knowledge of his internal state. Though these studies are impressive, they should not be considered as clinical analogs of the relabeling or misattribution processes which, I believe, are exemplified in the studies

The point seems well-established. The labels ascribed to bodily states produced by the exogenous administration of adrenaline prove manipulable by cognitive techniques. The intensity of the pain experience is, within the limits of plausibility, similarly manipulable. Even the feeling states associated with purely internal conditions such as the volume of liquid in the bladder prove readily manipulable by essentially cognitive procedures. There seems little question that cognitive factors are indeed major determinants of the labels we attach to bodily states and of the affective tone we attribute to these states. There is little need to belabor the point further, and let us proceed to examine some of the implications of these facts and of this way of thinking about bodily states.

---

of pain and fear described in this chapter. There are studies, however, that have been designed as direct tests of the usefulness of these misattribution techniques in clinically oriented settings. In a remarkable study, Storms and Nisbett (1970) have demonstrated that the sleeping behavior of chronic insomniacs can be successfully manipulated by reattribution techniques. Their subjects, all insomniacs, are given a placebo pill to take one hour before bedtime. In one condition, the placebo is described as producing flight of ideas, feelings of warmth, and a general feeling of arousal—all symptoms classically accompanying an inability to fall asleep. In another condition, the placebo is described as having no side effects. Subjects told to anticipate "flight of ideas," etc. (and, therefore, able to attribute these symptoms to the pill rather than to their own "condition") report falling asleep significantly sooner than subjects told that the pill would have no effects.

Chapter VI

*The Physiological
Correlates of
Hunger*

These simple demonstrations that the interpretation and labeling of even naturally occurring bodily states are so readily manipulable open up questions with almost metaphysical overtones. Obviously attaching a particular label to any particular internal or visceral syndrome is a learned, cognitively, and socially determined act. Though we are inclined to assume that such labels are invariant and universal, it is evident that there is no compelling reason for this to be so. As an example, consider the state of hunger. About hunger we know that food deprivation leads to various peripheral physiological changes such as modification of blood constituents, increase in gastric motility, changes in body temperature, and the like. By means of some still debated mechanism, these changes are detected by a hypothalamic feeding center. Presumably some or all facets of this activated machinery lead the organism to search out and consume food. There appears to be no doubt that peripheral changes and activation of the hypothalamic feeding center are inevitable consequences of food deprivation. On the basis of current knowledge, however, one may ask, when this biological machinery is activated, do we necessarily describe ourselves as hungry, and eat? For most of us raised on the notion that hunger is the most primitive of motives, wired into the animal and unmistakable in its cues, the question may seem farfetched, but there is increasing reason to suspect that there are major individual differences in the extent to which these physiological changes are associated with the desire to eat.

On the clinical level, the analyst Hilde Bruch (1961) has observed that her obese patients literally do not know when they are physiologically hungry. To account for this observation she suggests that, during childhood, these patients were not taught to discriminate between hunger and such states as fear, anger, and anxiety. If this is so, these people may be labeling almost any state of arousal as hunger, or, alternatively, labeling no internal state as hunger.

If Bruch's observations are correct, it should be anticipated that the set of physiological symptoms which are considered characteristic of food deprivation are not labeled hunger by the obese. In other words the obese literally may not know when they are physiologically hungry. For at least one of the presumed physiological correlates of food deprivation, this does appear to be the case. In an absorbing study, Stunkard (1959; 1964) has related gastric motility to self-reports of hunger in 37 obese and 37 normally sized subjects. Stunkard's experiment was simple and clear-cut. Subjects who had eaten no breakfast came to the laboratory at 9:00 A.M. and swallowed a gastric balloon, and for the next four hours Stunkard continuously recorded gastric motility. Every fifteen minutes the subject was asked whether or not he was hungry. He answered "yes" or "no" and that is all there was to the study. We have, then, a record of the extent to which a subject's self-report of hunger corresponds to his gastric motility. Stunkard found that when the stomach was not contracting, obese and normal subjects were quite similar, both groups reporting hunger roughly 38% of the time. When the stomach did contract, however, the two groups differed markedly. For normals, self-report of hunger coincided with motility 71.0% of the time. For the obese the coincidence was only 47.6%. This difference is significant at considerably better than the .01 level of confidence.

Two additional facts are helpful in interpreting these findings. First, during the four-hour experimental period in this study, gastric contractions were equally frequent for obese and normal subjects. Second, Griggs and Stunkard (1964) and Stunkard (in press) have demonstrated that obese subjects can be readily trained to recognize gastric contractions—a fact which they interpret as indicating that the obese do not suffer from a defective visceral sensorium. It would appear, then, that the obese do have gastric contractions, that they are, at least, capable of perceiving them, and that, unlike normals, they do not describe themselves as feeling hungry when their stomachs are contracting. Hunger, then, appears to be a label which is not universally applied to an identical set of physiological symptoms.

If all of this is correct, it seems reasonable to assume that the actual eating behavior of obese and normal subjects will correspond to this same pattern; that is, the amount of food eaten should, for normal subjects, relate directly to the state of the viscera, while, for obese subjects, there should be no relation. The test of this expectation is certainly simple enough, requiring only the experimental manipulation of visceral states and the measurement of food consumption.

In an experiment conducted by Schachter, Goldman, and Gordon (1968) the physiological correlates of food deprivation were manipulated by two means:

first, by the obvious method of directly manipulating food deprivation so that some subjects entered an experimental eating situation with empty stomachs and others with full stomachs; second, by manipulating fear so that some subjects entered the eating situation frightened and others calm. Carlson (1916) has presented evidence indicating that fear inhibits gastric motility; Cannon (1929) has demonstrated that the state of fear leads to the suppression of gastric movement and the liberation from the liver of sugar into the blood. Hypoglycemia and gastric contractions are generally considered among the chief peripheral physiological correlates of food deprivation. If it is correct that the obese do not label these symptoms as hunger, it should follow that the eating behavior of obese subjects will be unaffected by these manipulations. They should eat just as much when their stomachs are full as when they are empty, and just as much when they are frightened as when they are calm. Normal subjects, on the other hand, should be directly affected by the manipulations. They should eat less with full stomachs than with empty ones, and should eat more when they are calm than when frightened.

Procedure

The experiment was conducted within the framework of a study of taste. Subjects, all male students at Columbia, came to the laboratory in midafternoon (2:00 or 3:00) or evening (7:00 or 8:00). Two subjects were always scheduled to run at the same time. If one of the subjects didn't show up, a stooge was run in his place. All subjects had been contacted the previous evening and asked not to eat the meal (lunch or dinner) preceding their experimental appointment. The experimenter's introductory patter was an expanded version of the following:

> A subject of considerable importance in psychology today is the interdependence of the basic human senses, that is, the way the stimulation of one sense affects another. To take a recent example, research has discovered that certain sounds act as very effective pain killers. Some dentists are, in fact, using these sounds, instead of Novocain, to block out pain when they work on your teeth. Some psychologists believe that similar relationships exist for all the senses—the experiment we are working on now concerns the effect of tactile stimulation on the way things taste.

> The reason we asked you not to eat before coming here is that in any scientific experiment it is necessary that the subjects be as similar as possible in all relevant ways. As you probably know from your own experience, an important factor in determining how things taste is what you have recently eaten. For example, after eating any richly spiced food such as pizza, almost everything else tastes pretty bland.

Manipulating Preloading

Following this introduction, the experimenter manipulated preloading in the following manner. In the Full Stomach condition he said,

> In order to guarantee that your recent taste experiences are entirely similar, we should now like you each to eat exactly the same thing. Just help yourself to the roast beef sandwiches on the table. Eat as much as you want—till you're full.

The subjects spent about 15 minutes eating and, while they ate, filled out a long food preference questionnaire.

In the Empty Stomach[1] condition, the subjects, of course, were not fed. They simply spent the 15-minute period filling out the questionnaire about food.

Subjects who were fed were presented with two large roast beef sandwiches and a glass of water. Obese subjects consumed an average of 1.88 sandwiches before stopping eating, while normal subjects averaged 1.74 sandwiches.

Setting up the Experimental Eating Situation

Following the 15-minute eating period, the subject was seated in front of five bowls of crackers and told,

> Now that we are through with the preliminaries we can get to the main part of the experiment. What we are going to have each of you do is to taste five different kinds of crackers and tell us how they taste to you. These are very low-calorie crackers designed to resemble commercial products.

The experimenter then presented the subject with a long set of rating scales and said,

> We would like you to judge each cracker on each of the dimensions (salty, cheesy, garlicky, etc.) listed on this sheet. Taste as many or as few crackers of each type as you want in making your judgments; the important thing is that your ratings be as accurate as possible.

Manipulating Fear

Before permitting the subjects to eat crackers, the experimenter continued with the final stage of the experiment—the manipulation of fear: "As I mentioned before, our primary interest in this experiment is the effect of tactile stimulation on taste. Electric stimulation is the means we have chosen to excite

---

[1] The gaucheness of these condition labels is unfortunate but inevitable. I assume it is self-evident that given the line of reasoning underlying this study I cannot speak of high or low "hunger" conditions.

your skin receptors. We use this method so that we can carefully control the amount of stimulation you receive."

In Low Fear conditions, the subject was told, "In order to create the effect in which we are interested we need to use only the lowest level possible. At most you will feel a slight tingle in your skin. Probably you will feel nothing at all. We are only interested in the effect of very weak stimulation."

In High Fear conditions, the experimenter pointed to an eight-foot high, jet black console loaded with electrical junk and said, "That machine is the one we will be using. I am afraid that these shocks will be painful. In order for them to have any effect on your taste sensations, they must be of a rather high voltage. There will, of course, be no permanent damage."

The subject was then connected to the console by attaching a very large electrode to each ankle. While doing this, the experimenter looked up at the subject and asked, "You don't have a heart condition, do you?"

Following the manipulation of high or low fear, the experimenter concluded with, "The best way for us to test the effect of the tactile stimulation is to have you rate the crackers now, before the electric shock, to see how the crackers taste under normal circumstances, and then rate them again, after the shock, to see what changes in your ratings the shock has made."

Before the subjects ate they filled out a very brief questionnaire designed to evaluate the effectiveness of the manipulations. This was explained to the subject as a means of evaluating the effects of his mood and bodily states on his taste discriminations. That this manipulation of fear was effective is demonstrated by responses to two rating scales headed:

How anxious do you feel at present?

How nervous or uneasy do you feel about taking part in this experiment and being shocked?

On the first of these scales, High Fear subjects averaged 1.70 and Low Fear subjects averaged .96 ($t = 3.81; p < .001$). On the second question, High Fear subjects scored 2.02 and Low Fear subjects 1.34 ($t = 3.04, p < .01$). Obviously the manipulation succeeded in creating differential fear in the two groups of subjects.

Measuring Eating

The questionnaire answered, the experimenter provided each subject with water, pulled a sliding partition in order to completely separate the two subjects, and then left the subjects alone for 15 minutes, during which time the subject tasted and rated crackers. The subject was under the impression that he was tasting while, through one-way mirrors, observers simply counted the number of crackers he ate. This experimental disguise was designed to cope with the possiblility that some subjects, particularly obese ones, might be self-conscious and restrained about eating in an experiment. Subjects in this study do not eat, they taste.

The taste rating scales were deliberately designed so that most of the subjects were able to complete them within ten minutes. When the subject had completed these ratings, he was left with nothing to do for exactly two minutes, free to nibble or not at the crackers as he chose.[2] At the end of this interval the observer signaled the experimenter who promptly entered the room with a new set of taste rating scales which kept almost all subjects fully occupied for the remainder of the eating period.[3] This period over, the experimenter returned and announced that shocking was about to begin, but first asked the subjects to fill out the same questionnaire on mood and bodily state that they had answered immediately before tasting the crackers. This much done, the experiment was over, the deceptions and their rationale were explained in detail, and the subjects were impressed with the necessity for not talking about the experiment to their fellow students. Subjects in the Empty Stomach condition were fed roast beef sandwiches, all subjects filled out a weight history questionnaire, and, finally, each subject was weighed and measured.

We have then a measure of the eating behavior of subjects who were empty or full, and who were frightened or calm. Finally, of course, there were two groups of subjects—obese and normals. We are then covarying three variables—preloading, fear, and obesity—in an eight-condition factorial experiment.

Subjects

To provide a pool of subjects, data on the weight, height, and age of Columbia students were obtained from university records and classroom surveys. From these data, the percent of weight deviation was computed using norms published by the Metropolitan Life Insurance Company (1959).

Potential subjects were contacted by telephone and asked to take part in an experiment on taste. Roughly 70% of all those contacted agreed to do so. The decision was made to consider all students who were 15% overweight or more as

[2] This two-minute period was introduced in order to determine if the anticipated relationships would be affected by a "free" eating situation in contrast with the experimentally required eating of the "tasting" situation. The patterns of results obtained in the two eating situations were precisely the same. For purposes of expositional simplicity, these two sets of data are combined in presenting the results of the experiment.

[3] A few subjects finished this second set of rating scales before the 15-minute eating period was over. When this happened the observer signaled the experimenter to bring the subject a third set of rating scales. Since the number of crackers eaten is to some extent affected by the number of rating scales filled out, possible effects of this artifact were examined. The experimental effects cannot be accounted for by this artifact.

obese, and those who were 10% overweight or less as normal; subjects were assigned to conditions on the basis of these calculations. Inevitably anomalies of classification occurred, for either some of the students were not particularly accurate in reporting their own measurements or their weight or height had changed. In some cases, subjects who were originally classified as obese proved, when weighed after the experiment, to be lighter than subjects originally classfied as normal. Even with such subjects eliminated, there still remained such absurdities as a subject originally classified as obese proving to be 12.3% overweight on weighing, and a subject originally classified as normal proving to be 12.1% overweight. In order to cope with such classification problems, the final distribution of subject weight deviations was examined for, those cut-off points which permitted roughly a 5% weight differential between the lightest obese and the heaviest normal subject, and at the same time involved the absolute minimal loss of subjects. These cut-off points proved to be 9.0% overweight for the normal group and 13.6% overweight for the obese group. Eight subjects whose weight deviations fell between these points were automatically eliminated from the data analysis. In addition, all athletes (six subjects), members of the varsity squad in some body contact sport, were automatically eliminated as subjects. Welham and Behnke (1942) have demonstrated that football players, though overweight by standard weight charts, are not obese for their excessive weight is due to disproportionately large muscle and bone content, not to high body fat—a fact which is small surprise to experimenters who, anticipating a nice, plump boy as a subject, found themselves with a Greek god.[4] Finally, nine students were eliminated for though they had done without the requested meal they had eaten a snack at a nonmeal time.

The experimentally relevant characteristics of the final group of subjects are presented in Table 23. On all characteristics except, of course, weight and percent of weight deviation, the various experimental groups are all quite similar.

TABLE 23 PHYSICAL CHARACTERISTICS OF THE SUBJECTS

Subjects	N	Age	Height in inches	Weight in pounds	Mean percent weight dev.	Range percent weight dev.
Obese	43	20.5	68.9	184.1	+25.1	+13.6 to +74.5
Normal	48	19.9	69.4	152.6	+ 2.3	− 8.1 to + 9.0

[4] These problems of classification are, in large part, responsible for the clumsily unequal condition N's revealed in Table 24. In later experiments (Nisbett, 1968, Schachter and Gross, 1968) we were able to cope with these problems by obtaining more reliable and recent records of height and weight, by establishing initially more extreme cutoff points, and by learning beforehand whether or not a potential subject was an athlete.

Obese subjects outweigh normals by an average of 31.5 pounds and are on the average 25.1% overweight as compared with the normal group average of 2.3% overweight.

Results

To review expectations briefly: if it is correct that gastric contractions, hypoglycemia, and the like, signal hunger for normal subjects and not for obese subjects, if these experimental manipulations have succeeded in altering these physiological states, it should follow that the amount eaten in the several conditions will vary, as follows, for normal subjects:

Low Fear, Empty > Low Fear, Full = High Fear, Empty > High Fear, Full

When the subject is neither fearful nor full of roast beef sandwiches, the physiological correlates of food deprivation should be at a maximum and normal subjects in the Low Fear, Empty condition should be expected to eat more than subjects in any of the other conditions. Conversely, for subjects who are both frightened and full, these physiological states should be at a minimum and subjects in the High Fear, Full condition should eat less than those in the other conditions. The relationship of the remaining two conditions depends on the relative impact of the Fear versus the Preloading manipulations. Since there is no a priori reason for differentially weighting these variables, we arbitrarily assume that Low Fear, Full = High Fear, Empty.

For obese subjects, the amount eaten in the several conditions should vary as follows:

Low Fear, Empty = Low Fear, Full = High Fear, Empty = High Fear, Full

Unless it is assumed that fear has some special effect on obese subjects (a matter to which I shall return), there should be no difference in the amounts eaten in any of the conditions; for no matter how successful the manipulations, they are affecting physiological states which are unrelated to hunger in obese subjects.

Reducing these multiple predictions to essentials: two interaction effects must follow from this general line of reasoning.

1. Fear should reduce the amounts eaten by normal subjects and should not do so for obese subjects.

2. Preloading should reduce the amounts eaten by normal subjects and should not do so for obese subjects.

No predictions are made about the relative amounts eaten by obese and normal subjects in the several conditions for, of course, we know nothing of base rate eating by these two groups of subjects in this experimental setup.

The data necessary to test these predictions are presented in Table 24, and the analysis of variance of these data in Table 25. It will be noted immediately

TABLE 24 THE EFFECTS OF FEAR AND PRELOADING ON THE EATING BEHAVIOR
OF NORMAL AND OBESE SUBJECTS

Condition	N	Normal Subjects Average number of crackers eaten	N	Obese Subjects Average number of crackers eaten
Hi Fear, Full	14	13.78	11	19.64
Hi Fear, Empty	11	15.89	10	19.60
Lo Fear, Full	13	16.98	11	17.66
Lo Fear, Empty	10	28.28	11	16.34

TABLE 25 ANALYSIS OF VARIANCE OF THE EFFECTS
OF FEAR, PRELOADING, AND WEIGHT DEVIATION
ON EATING

Source	SS	df	F	p
Preloading (P)	18.21	1	3.09	$< .10$
Fear (F)	13.44	1	2.28	n.s.
Weight Deviation (W)	.34	1	.06	n.s.
P × W	27.34	1	4.63	$< .05$
F × W	54.34	1	9.21	$< .01$
P × F	7.74	1	1.31	n.s.
P × F × W	13.60	1	2.30	n.s.
Error	488.89	83		

that the predictions are supported for the two basic interactions are significant. For normals, subjects in the Low Fear, Empty condition eat by far the greatest number of crackers (eating more than twice as many as subjects in the High Fear, Full condition) with the two remaining conditions falling between these extremes. For the obese, the four condition means are all quite similar; none of the differences are statistically significant, and what trends there are in the data are exactly opposite to those manifested by normal subjects. Obviously, preloading and fear have had a major effect on the eating behavior of normal subjects, and no effect at all on obese subjects.

These interactions are represented in Fig. 3 and 4. From Fig. 3, it will be a surprise to no one to learn that normal subjects eat considerably fewer crackers when their stomachs are full of roast beef sandwiches than when they are empty. The obese stand in fascinating contrast. They eat as much, in fact slightly more, when their stomachs are full as when they are empty. Obviously, within this

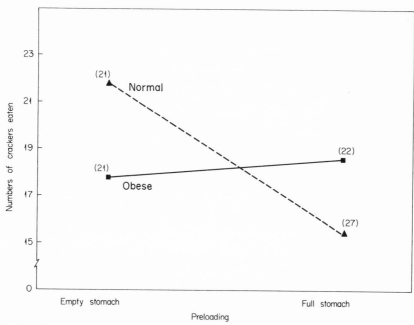

Fig. 3. Effects of preliminary eating on the amounts eaten during the experiment by normal and obese subjects. Numbers in parentheses are numbers of subjects.

context, the actual state of the stomach has nothing to do with how much the obese eat.

Turning to fear in Fig. 4, we note much the same picture. High fear markedly decreases the number of crackers normal subjects eat and has no effect on the amount eaten by the obese. Again there is a small, though nonsignificant reversal, with the fearful obese eating slightly more than the calm obese.

It is rather interesting to note that the overall amounts eaten by obese and normal subjects are virtually identical. Combining conditions, obese subjects ate an average of 18.3 crackers and normal subjects, 18.1 crackers. As will be seen in the following chapter, the Schachter and Gross (1968) experiment also found no difference in the overall amounts eaten by obese and normal subjects. Crackers were the test food in both of these studies and we believe that this fact accounts for the findings. Crackers are, after, a neutral sort of food, neither liked nor disliked by most people. Nisbett's (1968) experiment (described in Chapter VIII) has demonstrated that only when the food is good do obese out-eat normal subjects.

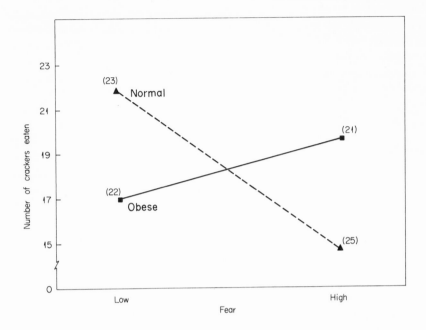

Fig. 4.   Effects of fear on the amounts eaten by normal and obese subject. Numbers in parentheses are numbers of subjects.

Discussion

There appears to be little question that eating by the obese is not related to the same set of bodily symptoms as is the eating of normal subjects. Whether one measures gastric motility, as in Stunkard's studies, or manipulates it, as I assume we have done in this study, there is a high degree of correspondence between the state of the viscera and the eating of normal subjects, and virtually no correspondence for fat subjects.

Clear-cut as these facts appear to be, they do pose a major dilemma. The obese are fat; obviously they eat. The feelings associated with gastric motility and hypoglycemia appear to trigger eating in normal subjects. What triggers eating for the obese? Given the fact that the bodily circumstances that prompt a self-report of hunger and subsequent eating seem to have nothing in common for obese and normal subjects, one may conjecture that:

1. The obese label an entirely different set of physiological symptoms and feeling states as hunger, or that,

2. The obese label no bodily states as hunger and their eating is unrelated to any physiological condition, in which case, since the obese do eat, we must

assume that their eating is triggered either by (a) psychic states such as anxiety, fear, loneliness, feelings of unworthiness, and so on, or, by (b) external food related stimuli such as the smell of food, the sight of other people eating, discussions of food, and so on.

Considering these alternatives, let us turn first to the hypothesis that psychic states precipitate eating in the obese, a hypothesis which unquestionably is the single most pervasive theme in psychosomatic theorizing about obesity (see Kaplan and Kaplan, 1957, for a review of the literature). In essence, such treatments assume that overeating by the obese represents an attempt to cope with anxiety, or fear, or emotional disturbance of some kind. This assumption is so accepted as a working hypothesis by experienced psychotherapists that I am reluctant to question it without a wealth of relevant data, but the simple fact is that to date we have found no evidence to support it. Certainly the results of the present experiment offer little support, for as Fig. 4 shows, in the High Fear conditions, obese subjects eat only trivially and nonsignificantly more ($t = 1.28$, $p > .20$) than they do in Low Fear conditions. In an internal analysis of the High Fear data, as one would expect, there is, for normal subjects, a correlation of $-.42$ ($p < .05$) between self ratings of fear and the number of crackers eaten. For the obese the correlation is $+.13$, in the direction required by the psychosomatic hypothesis, but again a nonsignificant relationship.

The effect of eating on anxiety level is another datum from this study relevant to any psychosomatic formulation which rests on the assumption that, for the obese, eating is anxiety reducing. Table 26 presents indices derived by subtracting subjects' self ratings of fear before they had eaten crackers from their ratings after eating. For both groups of subjects there is a slight decline in fear and there are no differences of consequence between obese and normal subjects. If anything, the trends are in a direction opposite to that required by the psychosomatic hypothesis, for on both scales fear is reduced more for normal than for obese subjects.

In a longitudinal study of the weight of graduate students during the Stürm und Drang of graduate study, Schachter and Nesbitt found little indication that

TABLE 26 REDUCTION IN FEAR PRODUCED BY EATING

| | N | Mean ratings after eating minus mean ratings before eating | |
		How anxious are you?	How nervous about shock?
Obese	43	$-.23$	$-.02$
Normals	48	$-.30$	$-.27$

the fatter students gain weight during examination periods or at other times of personal stress. Finally, in an unpublished study of the effects of job stress on weight change, John Maher has found absolutely no evidence that fat executives in stressful jobs gain any more weight than fat executives in nonstressful jobs. Relevant to later concerns of this book, he does find a marked tendency for skinny executives in stressful jobs to lose weight as compared with their skinny colleagues in nonstressful jobs. Given the weight of clinical experience, I do not feel free to reject the psychosomatic hypothesis, but obviously the data my colleagues and I have collected compel us to turn to more serious consideration of other alternatives.

Let us turn next to the possibility that the obese label an entirely different set of physiological symptoms as hunger—a logical possibility, certainly. But which symptoms? Some years ago, I suggested (Schachter, 1964) that the obese label as hunger the state of arousal of the sympathetic nervous system—an elegant hypothesis, for if correct it not only provides a physiological underpinning for the psychosomatic thesis, but allows integration of the psychosomatic and the "labeling" view of matters. Elegant or not, I have been able to muster no particular support for this notion. Certainly the effects of the fear manipulation in this experiment argue as strongly against this hypothesis as they do against the psychosomatic thesis. Furthermore, in case studies in which we attempted experimentally to separate the "psychic" from the physiological components of the arousal state by use of a disguised injection of adrenaline, there was no evidence that the obese ate more when injected with adrenaline than when injected with placebo.

If not the state of sympathetic activation, then what? I confess a certain feeling of helplessness for, short of utter absurdities, it is difficult to conceive of any set of alternative physiological symptoms that one can, with any justification, suggest. Nor are the obese themselves of much assistance, for they seem as inept at describing their visceral states as are any of the rest of us when, not sick, we are suddenly asked to describe what's going on beneath the skin. Casual interviews with the obese centered on the theme, "What do you feel when you say, 'I'm hungry'?" more often than not terminated with an exasperated "I don't know, I just feel like I want to eat."

All of which has led to serious consideration of the possibility that internal state is irrelevant to eating by the obese, and that external, food-relevant cues trigger eating for such people.

Chapter VII

External Control
of Eating Behavior

In the work described so far, there is nothing that we have been able to do—from feeding, to frightening, to injecting with adrenaline—that has any effect at all on the eating behavior of the obese subject, or that fails to have an effect on the eating behavior of the normal subject. Keeping these facts in mind, let us turn to the work of the members of the Nutrition Clinic in St. Luke's Hospital in New York, chiefly Drs. Hashim and Van Itallie (1965). Summarizing their findings, virtually everything they do seems to have a major effect on the eating behavior of the obese, and almost no effect on the eating behavior of the normal subject.

These researchers have prepared a bland and homogenized liquid diet similar in taste and composition to the vanilla flavors of such commercial preparations as Nutrament or Metrecal. The subjects are restricted to this diet. They can eat as much or as little as they want of this tasteless and uninteresting pap, but this and this alone is all they can eat for periods ranging from a week to several months. Some of their subjects get a large pitcher full of the stuff and can pour themselves a meal anytime they are so inclined. Other subjects are fed by a machine which delivers a mouthful of this food every time the subject presses a button. Whichever feeding technique is used, the eating situation is characterized by the following properties: first, the food itself is dull and unappealing and, second, eating is entirely self-determined; whether or not the subject eats, how much and when he eats, is up to the subject and no one else. It should be specifically noted that absolutely no pressure is put on the subject to limit his consumption. Finally, the eating situation is totally devoid of any social or domestic trappings. It is basic eating; it will keep the subject alive, but it's not much fun.

To date (1970) ten grossly obese and eight normally sized adult subjects have been run in this setup. In Fig. 5 the eating curves for a typical pair of subjects over a 21-day period are plotted. Both subjects were healthy, normal people who lived in and did not leave the hospital the entire period of the study. The obese subject was a 52-year-old woman, 5 feet 3 inches tall and weighing 307 pounds on admission. The normal subject was a 30-year-old male, 5 feet 7 inches tall and weighing 132 pounds.

On the left of the figure is shown, for each subject, estimated daily caloric intake before entering the hospital—estimates based on very detailed interviews with each subject. While in the hospital, but before entering the experimental regime, each subject was placed on a general hospital tray diet. The obese subject was placed on a 2400-calorie diet for seven days, and a 1200-calorie diet for the

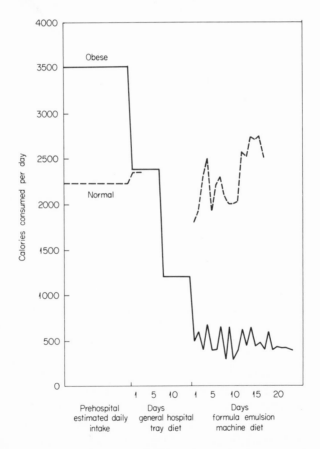

Fig. 5. The effects of a formula emulsion diet on the eating behavior of an obese and a normal subject.

next eight days. As can be seen in the figure, she consumed everything on her tray during this 15-day period. The normal subject was placed on a 2400-calorie general hospital diet for two days and he too ate everything on his tray.

With the beginning of the experiment proper, the difference in the amounts eaten by the two subjects becomes dramatic and startling. You will note immediately that the food consumed by the obese subject dropped precipitously the moment she entered on this regime and remained at this incredibly low level for the duration of the experiment. This effect is so dramatic that one of the obese subjects who remained in the experiment for eight months dropped from 410 pounds to 190 pounds. The normal subject on the other hand dropped slightly on the first two days, then returned to a fairly steady 2300 calories or so of food a day. These are typical curves. Every one of the fat adult subjects has been characterized by this marked and persistent decrease in food consumption.[1] Every one of the normal subjects has fairly steadily consumed about his normal amount of food.

Before worrying through possible interpretations of this data, I must note that there are certain marked differences between these two groups of subjects. Most important, the obese subjects have come to the clinic for help in their weight problems and are, of course, motivated to lose weight. The normal subjects are simply volunteers for an experiment. With no question, this difference could account for these effects, and until a group of obese volunteers who are unconcerned with their weight are run through this procedure we cannot be completely sure of this phenomenon. However, I would like to be sure that we do not dismiss these findings only on the grounds of methodological fastidiousness. At the very least, let us note that it was concern with weight that brought each of the obese subjects to the Nutrition Clinic. Obviously every obese subject was highly motivated to lose weight before entering the hospital, and certainly while in the hospital and before going on the formula emulsion diet. Yet despite this motivation no one of these subjects was capable of successfully restricting his at-home diet. When placed on the general hospital

---

[1] Though this pattern is characteristic of every obese adult who has been a subject in the Hashim and Van Itallie study, Hashim, Van Itallie and Campbell (personal communication) have recently run two brain-damaged, juvenile, obese subjects in their setup with strikingly different results. One of these was a 13-year-old girl who had an excised cranial pharyngioma (hypothalamic tumor). Another was a 14-year-old boy who had grown obese following an accident that produced severe skull fractures and brain injury of a nonlocalized nature. Both of these subjects consumed sufficient formula (3000–4000 calories/day) to maintain their excessive weight. Whether to attribute these deviant results to brain damage or to the youth of the subjects is, at the moment, equivocal. These investigators are in the process of running four additional, obese, otherwise healthy boys whose ages range from 11–14 years. Three of these four have decreased their daily caloric intake as abruptly and dramatically as any of the adult subjects. The fourth is consuming a relatively large quantity of formula and maintaining his weight.

tray diet, motivated or not, every one of these obese subjects polished off his tray. Only when the food is dull and the act of eating self-initiated and devoid of any ritual trappings does the obese subject, motivated or not, severely limit his consumption.

On the one hand, then, we have a series of experiments which indicate virtually no relationship between internal state and the eating behavior of the obese subjects; on the other hand, these case studies seem to indicate a very close tie-up between the eating behavior of the obese and what might be called the circumstances of eating. When the food is uninspired and the eating situation uninteresting, the fat subject eats virtually nothing. For the normal subject, the relationships are quite the reverse—his eating behavior seems directly linked to internal state but relatively unaffected by the external circumstances surrounding the eating routine and ritual.

Given this set of facts it seems eminently clear that the eating behavior of obese and normal subjects is not triggered by the same set of bodily symptoms. Indeed, there is growing reason to suspect that the eating behavior of the obese is relatively unrelated to any internal gut state but is, in large part, under external control; that is, eating behavior is initiated and terminated by stimuli external to the organism. A few examples should convey what is meant by external control. A person whose eating behavior is under external control will stroll by a pastry shop, find the window irresistible, and, whether or not he has recently eaten, buy something. He will wander by a hamburger stand, smell and see the broiling meat, and though he may have recently eaten, he will buy a hamburger. Obviously such external factors—smell, sight, taste, what other people are doing, etc.—to some extent affect anyone's eating behavior. However, for normals, such external factors clearly interact with internal state. They may affect what, where, and how much the normal eats, but chiefly when he is in a state of physiological hunger. For the obese, I suggest, internal state is irrelevant and eating is determined very largely by external factors.

This hypothesis obviously fits the various data presented beautifully, as well it should since it is an ad hoc construction designed specifically to fit these data. Let us, then, see what independent support there is for the hypothesis, and where it leads.

Now the essence of this notion of the external control of eating behavior is this—stimuli outside of the organism trigger eating behavior. In effect, since internal states such as gastric motility and hypoglycemia are not labeled as hunger, some cue outside of the organism must tell it when it is hungry and when to eat. Such cues are, of course, multiple, but one of the most intriguing of cues is simply the passage of time. Everyone "knows" that four to six hours after eating his last meal he should eat his next one. Everyone "knows" that within narrow limits there are set times to eat regular meals. In the absence of alternative cues, in the absence of competing alternatives to eating, the eating behavior of the externally controlled person should be time bound. We should, then, expect that if we manipulate time we should be able to manipulate the eating behavior of the obese subject.

The experimental test of this expectation requires measuring the eating behavior of normal and obese subjects under conditions where they believe the time to be later than it actually is, and under conditions where they believe the time to be earlier than it actually is—a state of affairs managed simply by the use of doctored clocks, one gimmicked to run at twice the normal speed, the other at half normal speed.

The context within which Schachter and Gross (1968) satisfied these experimental requirements was the following. The experimental session always began at 5:00 p.m. When a subject arrived, he was ushered into a small experimental room and told,

> This is an experiment on the relation between physiological reactions and psychological characteristics. As you know there are a number of physiological reactions that continually vary in rate. For example your heart rate is always varying to some extent; your breathing rate fluctuates, as does the sweat gland activity in your skin. As you also undoubtedly know, these variations are affected by situational factors in your environment.

The experimenter gave a series of examples and continued,

> It also looks as though these variations are related to various personality characteristics and physical traits. In other words, some people seem to be highly volatile and excitable and react strongly even in relatively neutral situations; others, more tranquil, hardly react even in extreme situations. This is the sort of thing we are trying to get at. The way we do it is quite simple. I'm going to attach these electrodes to you and get simple base-line reaction levels on two of these physiological processes—heartrate and GSR or sweat gland activity—in a completely neutral situation, namely this room and with nothing for you to do but sit here alone. After we have enough base-line data, I will come back and get some simple psychological and background information, and that will be all.

The experimenter then began attaching electrodes to the subject's wrists, picked up a tube of electrode jelly, and said, "This stuff is necessary to get a good contact but unfortunately it gums up everything in the world—it also corrodes metal so you had better take off your watch. Here, let me put it away so this goo won't get on it."

This much done, the experimenter left the subject who, other than thinking his private thoughts, had only two things to do—watch the presumed record of heartrate and GSR roll off the polygraph, and stare at a large faced clock mounted on the wall directly facing him.

After a true thirty minutes the experimenter returned, shut off the machine, removed the electrodes, and handed paper towels to the subject to wipe off the electrode jelly. He left the room for a moment and returned with a sheaf of paper in one hand and a box of crackers called Wheat Thins under his arm. Munching at a cracker, he seated himself opposite the subject, put down his papers and the box of crackers, and said, "I like to mix a little pleasure with business; help yourself if you want any."

The experimenter then administered a truncated version of the Embedded Figures Test—an operation consuming roughly four to five minutes. Twice during this period he took two crackers and told the subject to help himself. He then handed the subject a long questionnaire saying, "I'll leave you to fill this out." While leaving the room, he pointed to the box of crackers and said, "I'll leave this here, you might want some." In exactly ten minutes, the experimenter returned, left additional questionnaire material with the subject, casually picked up the box, ate a cracker, and left the room with the box under his arm.

Allowing for the crackers eaten by the experimenter, the measure of the dependent variable—amount eaten—is simply the weight of the box when it was first brought into the room minus the weight of the box when it was finally removed.

This experiment, then, covaried weight deviation and apparent time flow, and examined the impact of these variations on eating. There were four experimental conditions:

> Obese—Fast Time
> Obese—Slow Time
> Normal—Fast Time
> Normal—Slow Time

The Manipulation of Time

In designing this study a crucial consideration was the exact time for running the experiment. Should the study be conducted between regular meal times so as to simply create the impression that more or less time had passed or, should the study be run around lunch or dinner time thus not only manipulating the passage of time but also creating the impression that it was before or after regular eating times? Though, certainly, the experiment could have been run at both times, thus doubling the number of conditions, our resources (i.e., the number of fat subjects) were limited, and it was necessary to choose between the two times. For a variety of semi-intuitive reasons, it seemed to us that the strategic choice was to run the experiment at a regular meal time. From our line of reasoning about the obese, there seemed no good reason to expect that creating the impression that it was 2:30 p.m. versus 3:15 p.m. would have any effect on the eating behavior of obese subjects, whereas the difference between 5:30 p.m. and 6:15 p.m. could be critical. Assuming that dinner time for most of our subjects was roughly at 6:00 p.m., we designed the experiment so that the cracker-eating period fell either before or after this critical time.

The exact sequence of events and its relation to both true time and the clock readings in the fast and slow time conditions is presented in the following outline:

| | | Clock reading in: | |
True time	Event	Slow condition	Fast condition
5:00–5:05	S arrives, receives experimental instructions, watch removed, electrodes attached	5:00–5:05	5:00–5:05
5:05–5:35	Period for getting "baseline" readings of EKG and GSR. S alone in room	5:05–5:20	5:05–6:05
5:35–5:40	E brings in box of crackers, administers Embedded Figures Test	5:20–5:25	6:05–6:10
5:40–5:50	S alone with crackers, fills out questionnaire	5:25–5:35	6:10–6:20
5:50–	E removes crackers, S fills out questionnaires	5:35–	6:20–

All told there were a total of 15 minutes during which the subject could nibble at crackers. While doing so, in the Slow condition he believed the time to be 5:20–5:35; in the Fast condition, he believed the time to be 6:05–6:20. The exact times noted above varied slightly, of course, depending upon the exact moment a subject arrived. In all cases, however, the variations are trivial and a matter of only a few minutes.

It will be noticed that clock rate was varied only during the true thirty minute base line period when the subject was alone. This was done in order to avoid arousing unnecessary suspicion. During the first five minutes, of course, the subject still had his watch. During the cracker-eating period, it seemed a reasonable guess that the subject would have at least a rude notion of the rate at which he could fill out questionnaires. On the whole, the manipulation worked astonishingly well. Only two subjects volunteered that there was something wrong with the clock and disbelieved the time, one subject simply asked if the clock was a little fast, and no other subject raised any question.

Subjects

All subjects were male students registered in Columbia College. From records in various campus offices it was possible to get data on the height, weight, and age of most of the student body. The Metropolitan Life Insurance Company (1959) norms were used to calculate weight deviations, and a pool of obese and normally sized subjects was assembled. Subjects were solicited by phone and, if agreeable (as most were), an experimental appointment was made.

The experimentally relevant characteristics of the subjects are presented in Table 27 where it can be seen that normal and obese subjects are similar in age and height but, of course, differ markedly in weight. Before beginning the experiment the decision was made to classify all potential subjects as obese if they were 15% overweight or more, and as normal if they were 10% overweight or less. Students whose weight deviations fell between these cut-off points were not considered as subjects.

Besides the 46 subjects tabulated in Table 27, eight subjects were run but eliminated from the experiment—two because they flatly refused to believe the clock, and six because they had either eaten dinner or a substantial snack within an hour of the beginning of the experiment—states of affairs which obviously violated the experimental requirements.

Results

Given the design of the study, let us now spell out the specific predictions generated by the line of thought presented in the introduction to this experiment. We have assumed that external cues are the major determiners of eating behavior for the obese, while both external and internal cues determine the eating behavior of normals. Ignoring, for the moment, all other stimulants or inhibitors of eating, if one grants that the passage of time is a potent external cue, it should follow that Obese Fast (6:05) subjects will eat more than Obese Slow (5:20) subjects. For the Fast subjects it is past dinner time. For Slow subjects it is before dinner time. For normals, one should also anticipate that Fast (6:05) subjects will eat somewhat more than Slow (5:20) subjects. However, since we assume that external cues have less of an impact on normal

TABLE 27 CHARACTERISTICS OF THE SUBJECTS

	N	Age	Height in inches	Weight in pounds	Percent weight deviation from norm	Range of weight deviation
Obese	22	19.2	70.3	202.0	+31.5	+15.0% to +85.0%
Normal	24	18.6	69.2	153.9	+2.6	−10.8% to +9.8%

than on obese subjects, this difference should be smaller for normal than for obese subjects, and the crucial prediction is that of a significant interaction between degree of obesity and time.

The basic data are presented in Table 28 and the statistical analysis of these data is presented in Table 29. It is immediately evident that there are profound differences in the effects of the manipulations of time on the eating behavior of the two groups of subjects. Obese Fast subjects eat almost twice as much as Obese Slow subjects. The impression that it is roughly dinner time is a spur to the eating behavior of the obese. For normal subjects, the effect of the time manipulation is the reverse of its effect on obese subjects, for they eat much more in the slow than in the fast time condition. The expected Time X Obesity interaction is strongly supported, though not quite in the form anticipated. Where the Fast time manipulation appears to stimulate eating among obese subjects, it inhibits the eating of normal subjects.

TABLE 28 AMOUNT EATEN
(IN GM) BY SUBJECTS·
IN THE FOUR CONDITIONS

Weight	Time	
	Slow	Fast
Obese	19.9	37.6
Normal	41.5	16.0

TABLE 29 STATISTICAL ANALYSIS OF THE EFFECTS
OF OBESITY AND TIME MANIPULATION
ON EATING BEHAVIOR

Analysis of variance

Source	df	MS	F	p
Weight (W)	1	.17	.01	n.s.
Time (T)	1	19.28	.51	n.s.
W X T	1	447.74	11.94	.002
Error	42	37.49		

The explanation of this turnabout seems to us embarrassingly simple and is documented by the several Normal Fast subjects who politely declined the experimenter's offer of crackers saying, "No thanks, I don't want to spoil my dinner." If, as seems likely, some factor of this sort was widespread among Normal Fast subjects it does, of course, suggest that the fast time manipulation has acted as a major inhibitor of eating among normal subjects. Obviously, cognitive factors have affected the eating behavior of both normal and obese subjects with, however, a vast difference. While this cognitive manipulation serves to trigger or stimulate eating among the obese, it has the opposite effect on normals, most of whom are at this hour physiologically hungry, aware in the Fast condition that they will eat dinner very shortly, and unwilling to wreck dinner by filling up on crackers.

If this is correct, it does raise the following question: Why has this purely cognitive manipulation which served to inhibit the eating of normal subjects failed to inhibit the eating of obese subjects? The answer, I suspect, is simple. Eating crackers (or anything else) does not "spoil" dinner for the fat subject. It has probably occurred to the reader that this experiment and our several related studies have in good part been concerned with the "start" mechanisms of eating, i.e., the relative role of internal and external cues in triggering eating behavior. It seems a reasonable guess that this general line of reasoning applies equally well to the "stop" mechanism. If the state of the stomach is unrelated to the hunger experience in fat subjects, it is probably also unrelated to the satiety experience. Evidence from several sources inferentially supports this guess. The food deprivation-fear experiment demonstrated that fat subjects eat just as much in an experimental eating situation conducted immediately after they have eaten a meal as they do when they have been deprived of food for some ten hours, whereas normal subjects, of course, eat considerably more after food deprivation than after they have eaten a meal. Similarly the notorious binge eating (Stunkard, 1961) of the obese can be considered as indicative of some failure of the stop or satiety mechanism.

If this general line of interpretation is correct, it does suggest that the effects of the time manipulation on normal subjects are a result of the decision to make experimental eating a casual, predinner affair. Should such an experiment be conducted in a dinner or full meal context, we would certainly anticipate that the original expectations for normal subjects would be supported.[2]

It should be specifically noted that the difference between Obese Fast and Slow subjects is significant ($p = .07$) at a somewhat uncomfortable level of

---

[2] Precisely what to anticipate for obese subjects in such an experiment is somewhat more obscure. As the reader will shortly see (Chapters IX and X) the obese, under the proper circumstances, can be considerably more flexible about eating or not eating than normal subjects—a condition which could lead one to expect no effects of a time manipulation on the obese in the experimental context of a delicious, full meal.

confidence, and that the substantial interaction effect is as much due to the unexpected reversal of the two normal groups as to the predicted difference between the obese conditions. Since the point is crucial, the following section is devoted to a more refined analysis of the effects of the time manipulation on these two groups of subjects.

The Effects of "Usual" Eating Time

In the course of this experiment, a subject is faced with two possibly dissonant sets of cues relevant to eating; first, the actual state of his viscera and, second, the clock which leads him to believe that it is either earlier or later than true time. The experiment, as designed, manipulates clock time and makes the deliberately naive working assumption that physiological hunger is constant for all subjects, or, at least, effectively randomized among conditions. To the extent, however, that we can make reasonable guesses about the actual physiological state of the subject, we should be able to examine the relative effects of these two sets of cues.

Though, of course, we have no physiological measures, we can make a guess as to a subject's state from his answer to the question, "What is your usual dinner time?" We shall simply assume that people organize and routinize their lives in such a way that those who normally eat before the experimental eating period are physiologically hungrier during the experimental hour than those who normally eat a late dinner. Making this assumption, we can to some extent examine the differential operation of these two sets of cues by comparing the effects of the true discrepancy between the subjects' normal eating times and the cracker eating period with the effects of the clock manipulated discrepancy.

For both "true" time and "clock" time, subjects are divided into two groups—those who normally eat dinner coincidentally with or before the start of the cracker eating period, and those who usually eat dinner after the start of the cracker eating period. Obviously, a subject's classification as experimentally eating before or after his usual dinner time may be different for the true and clock time distributions. Thus, in the Fast Time condition, a subject who normally eats at 6:00 p.m. would be classified as eating crackers after his usual dinner hour according to clock time (the clock reads 6:05–6:20 during the cracker eating period), and classified as eating before his usual mealtime according to true time (5:35–5:50).

Given these distinctions, it should be anticipated that the amount eaten by externally controlled, obese subjects will be directly related to clock time and bear little relationship to true time.

For normal subjects, the relationship to anticipate is unclear, for two opposing tendencies are involved. If our general framework is correct, certainly the actual time should have a relatively greater impact on the eating behavior of normals than of the obese. On the other hand, the "spoil dinner" artifact should attenuate the effects of true time, for those who are actually closest to dinner seem most likely to inhibit cracker eating. Knowing absolutely nothing of the relative impacts of these two tendencies, only one guess seems reasonable—clock time should have relatively less effect on the eating behavior of normals than of obese subjects.

The relevant data for obese subjects are presented in Table 30. Fast and Slow conditions are combined and the subjects are divided into categories according to the relationship of their usual dinner time to both clock and actual time. Given this additional breakdown, the number of cases in some of these cells is quite small, and in some respects this must be treated as case study material. However, it should be noted that on crucial comparisons, the magnitude of the differences are so large and the data so consistent in the distributions compared, that even with the small number of cases involved statistical tests yield respectable levels of significance.

It can be seen in Table 30 that in every possible comparison, clock time determines the amount eaten and actual time has virtually no effect. Those obese subjects who in actuality are eating crackers before their usual dinner time, eat more than twice the amount of crackers if the clock indicates that it is after usual dinner time than do those for whom the clock indicates that it is before dinner time ($p = .05$). Similarly, for those who actually eat crackers after their usual dinner hour, clock time is all-determining. Those to whom the clock indicates that it is before dinner time eat less than one-third the amount eaten by those who, by the clock, believe it to be after dinner time ($p = .07$).

**TABLE 30 THE EFFECTS OF ACTUAL AND CLOCK TIME
ON THE AMOUNTS EATEN BY OBESE SUBJECTS**

		Clock time	
		Grams eaten when S thinks it is:	
		Before usual dinner time	After usual dinner time
		A	B
	Before usual dinner time	23.9 (12)[a]	52.3 (3)
Actual time		C	D
	After usual dinner time	13.3 (4)	45.7 (3)

[a]Number of subjects.

The most dramatic and revealing comparison is that between cells B and C in Table 30, for here the two sets of cues are in direct opposition. If one accepts the assumption that physiological hunger is greater for those subjects for whom it is actually after usual dinner time than for those for whom it is before usual dinner time, we should expect that cell C subjects are physiologically hungrier than cell B subjects. In the face of this presumed internal difference, it is evident that the external cue, clock time, is all powerful, for cell B subjects eat almost four times as much as do cell C subjects ($p = .02$).

Reversing this analytic approach by holding clock time constant in order to compare the effects of actual time, the differences are small, nonsignificant, and, if anything, in a direction opposite to what one would expect from the assumption that eating behavior is related to actual time. Obviously, within this experimental context, for obese subjects, eating behavior has nothing to do with actual time and is wholly determined by the external, manipulated cue of clock time.

For normal subjects, in comparison, there are absolutely no indications that clock time has acted as a spur to eating behavior. In Table 31 it can be seen that there are no differences of consequence between categories, and any trends that exist are in a direction opposite to those evident for the obese. By this analysis, manipulation of the external cue, time, has major effects in triggering eating behavior in obese subjects and no such effects on normals. By the same token, there are no indications within the short time limits of this experiment that actual time has had an effect on normal eating behavior—a fact which we have attributed to the "spoil dinner" artifact. Though we cannot, in this experiment, support the assertion that the eating behavior of normal subjects is directly

TABLE 31 THE EFFECTS OF ACTUAL AND CLOCK TIME
ON THE AMOUNTS EATEN BY NORMAL SUBJECTS

		Clock time	
		Grams eaten when S thinks it is:	
		Before usual dinner time	After usual dinner time
		A	B
Actual time	Before usual dinner time	$29.1 (13)^a$	28.9 (3)
		C	D
	After usual dinner time	36.0 (1)	26.9 (7)

[a]Number of subjects.

related to internal state, other studies which have directly manipulated internal state indicate that this is the case. Limiting ourselves, however, to the present study, the most conservative summary and conclusion that can be drawn is this—manipulation of the external cue, time, has strong stimulating effects on the eating behavior of the obese and no such effect on normals.

Chapter VIII

The Effects of Taste and Quantity of Food on Eating

The Schachter and Gross (1968) experiment has demonstrated that one external cue—the manipulated passage of time—has marked stimulating effects on the amounts eaten by obese subjects and no such effects on normal subjects. Though this finding does support our general proposition, the effect has been demonstrated for only one cue, and an exotic one at that. Before this suggestion that the obese are generally more sensitive to external, food-related cues can be taken seriously, this effect must be demonstrated with a variety of other sorts of external cues. To do this Nisbett (1968a, 1968b) conducted two experiments. In one he manipulated the quality or taste of food; in a second, he manipulated the quantity of food available to the subject.

In addition to testing the effects of taste and the quantity of food, both of these experiments extended the range of weight deviation by including groups of very skinny subjects, as well as obese and normally sized subjects. Nisbett's purpose in doing this was to examine the hypothesis that the relative potency of external versus internal controls is a dimension directly related to the degree of overweight. If this is correct, it should be anticipated that external cues will have the greatest impact on the amounts eaten by obese subjects, and the least effect on skinny subjects. Conversely, internal cues should have a greater effect on the skinny subjects than on either normal or obese subjects.

The Effects of Taste

Of the battery of external cues which trigger eating and, in part, determine how much is eaten, certainly food quality or taste is among the most consequential. Following our general schema, it should be anticipated that the taste of food should have the greatest impact on the amounts eaten by obese subjects, and the least effect on skinny subjects. When the food tastes good, obese subjects should eat more; when it tastes bad, they should eat less than skinny subjects.

To test these expectations, Nisbett examined the effects of taste (good and bad) on the amounts eaten by overweight, normal, and underweight subjects. In addition, he covaried deprivation (full and empty) so as to yield a 12-condition experiment.

The experiment was introduced as concerned with the effects of hunger on the ability to concentrate. All subjects had been asked to skip the meal (lunch or dinner) preceding their experimental appointment. When they arrived they were told that they would be fed and then would take a variety of ability tests. Half of the subjects filled up on sandwiches and then, as dessert, ate the experimental test ice cream. The other half of the subjects ate only ice cream. For half of the subjects, the ice cream was delicious; for the other half, vile.

Manipulating Taste

The good ice cream was an expensive, creamy, and delicious French vanilla. The bad ice cream was an acrid brew of cheap vanilla and 2.5 gm of quinine sulphate per quart of ice cream. Since this lent a bitter flavor, both good and bad ice creams were, for plausibility's sake, introduced to the subject as a new commercial flavor called "Vanilla Bitters."

Manipulating Deprivation

Subjects were recruited by phone and asked to skip the meal before their experimental appointment. If scheduled for the afternoon (1:00, 2:15, or 3:30 p.m.), they were asked to eat nothing after 9:00 a.m. If scheduled for an evening hour (6:00, 7:15, or 8:30 p.m.), they were asked to eat nothing after 1:00 p.m.

In the Full condition, subjects, on arrival, were seated at a table loaded with three roast beef sandwiches, three Swiss cheese sandwiches, and a 12-ounce Coke. The presumed purpose of the experiment was explained and the subject was told that he had been assigned to the condition which required that he be fed before taking the "concentration tests." He was asked to rate how hungry he felt on a 6-point scale and given a food preference questionnaire to fill out while he ate. This much done, the experimenter told the subject to eat as much or as little as he liked, and left the room announcing that he would be back in about 15 minutes.

When it became clear, through a one-way mirror, that the subject had finished eating, the experimenter returned with a plastic carton containing exactly a quart of ice cream and said expansively,

> O.K. To finish off, we have ice cream. I'll leave this container here and you can just spoon ice cream into the bowl (the experimenter dips one spoonful from the container into a bowl) as you want it. The flavor is vanilla bitters, and since we're just starting this study we'd like to find out whether we should use this flavor. So please eat at least one spoonful so you can tell us later how you like it. Beyond that, eat as much or as little as you like. I'll be back in 10 minutes.

On his way out, the experimenter removed the unfinished food. He returned in 10 minutes when, before beginning concentration testing, he asked the subject to evaluate the ice cream on the following form:

How good was the ice cream which you ate?

Excellent	Very good	Fairly good	Not very good	Bad	Terrible
(6)	(5)	(4)	(3)	(2)	(1)

In the Empty condition, the subjects, of course, were not fed sandwiches. They were simply asked to rate their hunger and fill out the food preference questionnaire during the 15 minutes in which the experimenter would be gone. When he returned, carrying the same container of ice cream, the experimenter said,

> O.K. The food we'd like you to eat is ice cream, since it has known effects on the digestive system and on gastric motility. There'll be a control group, of course, who won't eat anything before they take the tests. I'll leave this container here. . .

From this point on, the treatment of full and empty subjects was identical.

After completing the concentration tests—a battery of ability tests and disguised persuasion attempts irrelevant to present concerns—all subjects filled out questionnaires concerned with their weight history, general eating behavior, and eating behavior during the experiment. They were then weighed, measured, thanked, and, if in the Empty condition, fed sandwiches and Coke.

Subjects

Subjects were Columbia University undergraduates selected in precisely the fashion described for the two previous experiments. Table 32 summarizes the pertinent physical characteristics of the three groups of subjects.

TABLE 32 SUMMARY STATISTICS FOR WEIGHT GROUP

Weight group	N	Average height	Average weight	Average percent weight deviation	Range of percent weight deviation
Underweight	56	69.8	137.8	−8.8	−25 to −2
Normal	56	69.6	157.6	4.7	0 to +11
Overweight	56	69.8	196.3	30.1	+15 to +70

Results

The condition-by-condition results of Nisbett's experiment are presented in Table 33. These results and their complexities are, of course, treated in detail in Nisbett's (1966, 1968) account of this experiment. For present purposes, I shall be concerned only with the major effects of the manipulated variables and shall consider first the effects of taste and second the effects of the deprivation manipulation.

The Effects of Taste

From the hypothesis of differential sensitivity to external cues, it should follow that the taste manipulations will have the strongest effects on obese subjects and the weakest on underweight subjects. The obese, then, should eat more good ice cream than normal subjects, who, in turn, should eat more than skinny subjects. For bad ice cream, the reverse relationship should obtain. The results, combining deprivation conditions, are presented in Fig. 6. For the good ice cream, results conform exactly to expectations. A trend analysis of the three weight groups reveals a significant $(F = 10.77, p < .01)$ relation between weight deviation and amount eaten—the heavier the subject, the more of the good ice cream he eats. For the bad ice cream the prediction is not supported. Though skinny subjects do eat more $(p < .05)$ than do normal subjects, so do obese subjects. In fact, the three groups all eat relatively similar and quite small amounts of bad ice cream. I suspect that this may be due to the fact that Nisbett's bad ice cream really was pretty bad, and that many of the subjects simply ate the token spoonful or two requested by the experimenter's instruction (40% of the subjects ate less than 20 grams), while most others ate only enough more to satisfy themselves that the taste was quite as weird as they had first thought. If correct, differences between the obese and normals should be anticipated if the experimental food, though still bad, was slightly more palatable and less strange, much as in the Hashim and Van Itallie (1965) study using a Metrecal-like food.

TABLE 33   GRAMS OF ICE CREAM EATEN AS A FUNCTION OF WEIGHT, DEPRIVATION CONDITION, AND TASTE CONDITION[a]

| | | Weight Condition | | | | | |
| | | Underweight | | Normal | | Overweight[b] | |
	Taste condition:	Good	Bad	Good	Bad	Good	Bad
Deprivation Condition:	Empty	182.4	77.1	159.3	48.4	264.3 (246.8)	75.1 (78.8)
	Full	102.7	46.0	167.1	15.6	196.4 (238.1)	44.5 (47.0)
	Empty and full	142.6	61.6	163.2	32.0	230.4 (242.7)	59.8 (62.5)

[a]$N = 14$ in each cell.

[b]Figures in parentheses are for nondieters, i.e., those who were not on a diet at the time of the experiment and who reported that their eating of the ice cream had not been affected by a desire to watch their weight. There were 11 such subjects in the Good Empty condition, 10 in the Good Full condition, and 13 in both Bad conditions.

A Replication

In another study of the effects of taste on eating, Elisabeth Decke (unpublished) collected data which indicate that this guess is probably correct. In her experiment, Decke used milkshakes. Being aware of Nisbett's results, she deliberately concocted a bad milkshake which, though unappealing, was hardly appalling. It consisted of condensed milk, water, vanilla ice cream, and a touch of quinine. Her good milkshake (regular milk and vanilla ice cream) was a decent shake, not a great shake. Her subjects were a small sample of the prisoners at the Vermont State Prison, all volunteers for a program of research on metabolism. The experiment was conducted as a taste test in which the subject was asked to judge each milkshake on a variety of dimensions such as sweetness, creaminess, etc. He was supplied with a cardboard container holding 40 ounces of milkshake and was told to drink as much or as little as he wanted in order to make the judgments of taste. Each subject was run twice; on one day judging the good, and on another day the bad milkshake. Subjects were fed a standard breakfast of a cup of coffee and two slices of toast. Approximately two and a half hours after breakfast, the taste test began.

The number of ounces each subject drank is presented in Table 34. Though the number of cases is unfortunately small, the trends in the data clearly support initial expectations. The obese subjects drank more than five times as much of the good as of the bad milkshake, whereas normal subjects drank roughly one

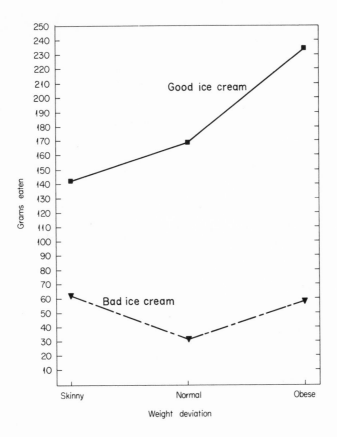

Fig. 6. The effects of taste on eating behavior. (Adapted from Nisbett, 1968.)

and a half times as much good as bad milkshake. Obese subjects drank somewhat more of the good and considerably less of the bad milkshake than did normal subjects.

Given these findings, it seems at least reasonable to suggest that Nisbett's failure to find evidence of differential taste sensitivity in his bad ice cream condition was indeed due to the fact that his ice cream was so very bad. Where Decke's bad milkshakes contained .04 grams of quinine per quart, Nisbett's ice cream contained 2.5 grams of quinine per quart.

Unquestionably additional work is needed to cement down the relationship. All things considered, however, it does seem to me that the hypothesis that the obese and normals are differentially responsive to taste does have reasonable support.

TABLE 34 THE EFFECT OF TASTE ON THE AMOUNT OF MILK SHAKE
CONSUMED BY OBESE AND NORMAL PERSONS

Subjects	N	Ounces of milkshake consumed		
		Good	Bad	p value
Obese	5	13.90	2.60	< .01
Normal	9	10.55	6.44	n.s.
	p value	n.s.	< .05	
			Interaction p = .07	

Gourmet or Glutton

The hypothesis of differential taste sensitivity does convey implications of discrimination and refinement. Certainly the notion that the obese are maximally sensitive to taste suggests a feinschmecher—a gourmet of exquisite palate and discrimination whose consumption is carefully tuned to the quality of the food.

Neither the Nisbett nor the Decke experiment is adequate to test for such a picture, for both experiments manipulate only two points on the taste dimension. However, Nisbett performed an internal analysis of his data, the results of which suggest that the hypothesis and its implications are in sharp need of refinement. He simply related the amount of ice cream each subject had eaten to his liking for the ice cream as measured by answers to a six point rating scale asking, "How good was the ice cream which you ate?" A simple-minded interpretation of the hypothesis of differential taste sensitivity would lead one to expect that the relationship between liking and the amount eaten would, for the obese, be best represented by a straight line of steep slope—the better the food, the more would be eaten, and relatively sharp discriminations would be made from point to point along the rating scale. In contrast, the relationship for the nondiscriminating, skinny subject should be relatively flat.

The results of this internal analysis are presented in Fig. 7. For each of the weight groups, these curves collapse the data across both taste and deprivation conditions.[1] It is evident that the simple-minded version of the hypothesis is wrong, for the obtained curve for obese subjects suggests that glutton might be a more appropriate image than gourmet. When the ice cream is rated as bad they do indeed eat very little; when the ice cream is good, however, they eat huge amounts, and it seems to make no difference at all just how good the ice cream

[1] The relationship indicated in Fig. 7 in no way depends upon combining the data across conditions, for the individual condition curves reveal precisely the same relationships among the three experimental groups.

is. Obese subjects who rate the ice cream as "fairly good" eat as much, in fact slightly more, than fat subjects who rate it as "very good" or "excellent." It is as if once the decision is made that the food is good, the fat person will eat large amounts, and it doesn't much matter just how good the food is. Further evidence for this step-like function comes from an analysis of the Schachter, Goldman and Gordon (Chapter 6) experiment on the effects of fear and deprivation on eating. It will be remembered that as part of the experimental format the subjects in that study were asked to rate how much they liked the various crackers they tasted. Since almost no one either detests or adores crackers, most subjects rated the various crackers as either fairly good or not very good. If one can generalize about the relationships indicated in Fig. 7, it should be anticipated that the difference between the number of positively and negatively rated crackers eaten should be far greater for obese than for normal subjects. This is the case. Obese subjects ate an average of 2.03 of the positively rated crackers and 1.47 of the negatively evaluated crackers ($t = 3.80, p < .001$). For normals, this difference was considerably smaller, for they ate 1.86 of the positively rated and 1.64 of the negatively rated crackers ($t = 1.10, p = $ n.s.).

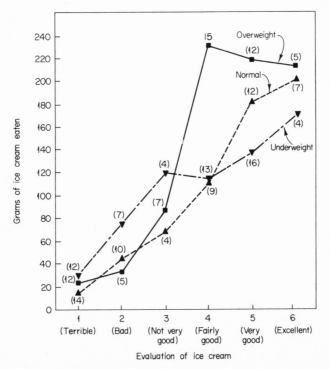

Fig. 7. The effects of food quality on the amount eaten by obese, normal, and underweight subjects. Numbers in parentheses are numbers of subjects.

If, on the basis of the ice cream and cracker eating data, one is willing to concede that glutton is a more appropriate term for the obese than gourmet, it should be noted that if anyone is the gourmet it's the normal. The curve for normals in Fig. 7 is almost a straight line with each increment in judged quality yielding large and virtually identical increments in the amounts eaten.

Though it is a digression, the engaging implications of these data for the basic question of who makes a good cook are well worth considering. If it is agreed that a good palate is the sine qua non of a good cook, if one is willing to accept the assumptions necessary to translate these relationships in Nisbett's study into statements about quality of palate, and most tenuous assumption of all, if the subjective scale of food quality is identical for the three groups of subjects, it should follow that skinny people will make appalling cooks, normals good, occasionally great cooks, and that the fat are the most likely of all to prepare a good meal (for of all the groups they discriminate most sharply between the unacceptable point 3 and the acceptable point 4 in Fig. 7), and the least likely to prepare a great one.

The Effects of Deprivation

Given our earlier findings on the effects of manipulated deprivation and the hypothesis that underweight subjects are particularly sensitive to internal cues, it should follow in this study that the difference in the amounts eaten in Full and Empty conditions will be greatest for skinny subjects and least for obese subjects. Table 35, which, for expositional simplicity, combines the data for good and bad conditions, presents the relevant data. It can be immediately seen that the deprivation manipulation has had very strong effects on the amounts eaten by skinny subjects, for when empty they eat roughly 75% more than when full. In contrast, deprivation has had virtually no effects on the amounts of ice cream eaten by normal and overweight subjects.[2] Though the relative absence of a deprivation effect among obese subjects is the anticipated relationship, the failure to find any indications of such an effect among normal subjects is, of course, contrary to expectations and to our earlier results. It seems very likely, however, that this failure is due to the particular sensitivity of normals to the fact that the experimental food was a dessert rather than "food." Some evidence that this is the case comes from answers to the postexperimental question, "Did you deliberately eat a small amount of ice cream in order to avoid filling up on ice cream?" Six of the 14 empty normal subjects given good ice cream answered

[2] Table 35 omits the data for the 9 dieting obese subjects. In this comparison I believe it makes sense to compare only nondieters, for obviously fat dieters who have filled up on sandwiches will selfconsciously limit the amounts of dessert they eat. If one includes dieters in this comparison, the difference is somewhat larger but still nonsignificant.

TABLE 35   GRAMS OF ICE CREAM EATEN AS A FUNCTION OF WEIGHT AND
DEPRIVATION CONDITION

		Weight Condition		
		Underweight	Normal	Overweight[a]
Deprivation	Empty	129.7	103.8	162.8
condition	Full	74.4	91.4	142.5
	F	11.51	.66	.44
	p	.001	n.s.	n.s.

[a]Based on nondieting overweight subjects only.

"Yes," while only 2 of 14 skinny subjects and 1 of 14 overweight subjects did so. These data are consistent with, though hardly overwhelming in support of this speculation. However, if it is correct that it is ice cream that has artifactually obscured this relationship for normal subjects, it should be expected that, within this experiment, comparisons not involving ice cream will demonstrate the expected effects.

In his original writeup of this study Nisbett (1966) presents several tests of the hypothesis of differential sensitivity to internal cues that have nothing to do with ice cream. For example, he finds a significant correlation between the number of hours since he last ate and a normal subject's self-report of hunger. The greater the number of hours of deprivation, the hungrier the normal subject. There is no such relationship for obese subjects. These results are typical. In every analysis that Nisbett attempted, outside of the ice cream context, to test the hypothesis of differential internal sensitivity (e.g., number of sandwiches eaten as related to hours of deprivation; the extent to which subjects fortify themselves by eating heartily before their fast period begins; etc.), the results are the same—normals prove more sensitive to internal cues than do the obese. It seems reasonable, then, to conclude that the exception in Nisbett's data is due to the use of ice cream as the experimental food, and to interpret this body of data as, first, consistent with previous findings and, second, supportive of the hypothesis that there is a continuum of sensitivity to internal cues so that very skinny subjects are maximally sensitive and very fat subjects minimally sensitive.

The Effect of Quantity of Food

So far it has been demonstrated that manipulated time, purely a cognitive sort of cue, and taste, a peripheral, sensory cue, have markedly different effects on the eating behavior of obese, normal, and skinny subjects. Let us examine next the effects of manipulating the sheer quantity of food placed before a subject by considering an experiment designed by Nisbett (1968b). Nisbett suggests, ingeniously, that the simple act of eating is, in these external-internal terms, an engrossing behavior, for it involves the literal consumption and elimination of external cues. One may eat until there are no more immediate cues. When this happens will the eater still be hungry and attempt to get more food? Obviously, this will depend first upon the amount he has already eaten and, second, in present terms, upon the extent to which he is under external or internal control. If only a small quantity of food has been made available, the deprived, internally controlled person should eat what is before him and then rummage about for more food. If a large quantity of food has been placed before him, he should eat until sated and then no more. Making a logical extension of these ideas about the control of eating, the externally controlled person presents a fascinating contrast. With only a small amount of food available, he should eat what's there and, having consumed all immediate external cues, make no attempt to get more food. Presented with a small quantity of food and the opportunity to get more, obese subjects should, then, eat less than normal subjects. Presented with a large quantity of food, the obese should eat more.

To test these ideas, Nisbett asked subjects to serve in a study involving the measurements of such physiological variables as EKG, GSR, etc. In order to obtain accurate baselines for these variables, it was essential, they were told, that they not eat after 9:00 a.m. on the day of the experiment. Appointments were made for the early afternoon so that the minimum period of deprivation for any subject was 4 hours.

The experiment was run in conjunction with another study whose details are irrelevant for present purposes. Bogus recording electrodes were attached to the subject and for 30 minutes he performed a monitoring sort of task. At this point, the electrodes were removed, the experiment was declared officially over, and the subject was taken to another, less technical-looking room where he was asked to answer a few questionnaires. This room contained a refrigerator, a chair, and a table with a bottle of soda and either one or three roast beef sandwiches, each wrapped in white paper. The subject was asked to sit at the table and the experimenter casually said, "Since you skipped lunch for the experiment, we'd like to give you lunch now. You can fill out the questionnaires while you eat. There are dozens more sandwiches in the refrigerator, by the way. Have as many as you want." The experimenter then left the room asking the subject to check by his office on the way out.

The sole manipulation of this study, then, involved placing either one or three roast beef sandwiches directly in front of the subject while providing him with the opportunity to walk across the room to the refrigerator, open it, and remove more sandwiches if he chose to do so. There were three groups of subjects—underweight, overweight, and normal. These were 69 males, all 25 years old or younger, and students in Columbia University's summer school. Their physical characteristics are quite similar to those of the subjects in Nisbett's experiment on taste.

Given this experimental format, it should follow from this general schema that the one and three-sandwich manipulation will have the greatest effect on obese subjects and the least effect on skinny subjects. The relevant data are presented in Table 36, which records the mean number of sandwiches eaten in each of the conditions.

It is clear that the manipulation has had a marked effect on the amounts eaten by fat subjects, for they eat almost one sandwich more in the three– than in the one-sandwich condition. For underweight and normal subjects, the manipulation has had no effects at all, for both groups eat just about the same amounts in the two conditions. Obviously there is one discrepancy from strict expectations. To be completely consistent with this general framework, normal subjects should have eaten somewhat more in the three–than in the one-sandwich condition, and this is not the case.

Comparison of the absolute amounts eaten by the three groups of subjects is particularly striking. Presented with three sandwiches, obese subjects eat far more than either normal or skinny subjects (for either comparison $p < .05$). Presented with only one sandwich, however, the obese eat just as little as do skinny subjects, and significantly less than normal subjects ($p < .05$).

To further test implications of the notion that eating is the consumption of external cues, Nisbett (1968b) inserted the question, "Are you a 'clean-your-plate' type, or are you likely to leave something?" in a questionnaire concerned

TABLE 36 THE EFFECT OF QUANTITY OF FOOD ON THE AMOUNTS EATEN BY SKINNY, NORMAL AND OBESE SUBJECTS

Subjects	Number of sandwiches eaten when offered	
	One	Three
Underweight	1.50	1.62
Normal	1.96	1.88
Overweight	1.48	2.32

Analysis of Variance

Source	df	MS	F
Weight (W)	2	.90	3.48^a
Numbered offered (N)	1	1.42	5.46^a
W × N	2	1.29	4.97^b
Error	63	.26	

$^a p < .05$
$^b p = .01$

with eating habits that was administered to 260 male students at Columbia and Yale. Subjects could check one of the following three alternatives in answering the question:

_____ I nearly always clean my plate.

_____ I sometimes clean my plate and sometimes leave something.

_____ I nearly always leave something.

It should be expected, of course, that the obese, whose eating is triggered by external cues, will be the plate cleaners, eating until there are no more cues. The underweight, on the other hand, should be the leavers, eating only enough to eliminate the internal cues that initiate eating. The data are presented in Table 37. It is clear that the data conform exactly to expectations. Obese subjects are by far the most likely to call themselves "plate cleaners" and the least likely to describe themselves as "leavers". Skinny subjects are quite the reverse.

Let us turn next to one crucial detail of Nisbett's experiment which to this point has been ignored. Even if a subject consumes his sandwich or sandwiches and licks his plate clean of crumbs, there are still external, food-relevant cues impinging. There is a refrigerator in the room; the subject knows that it is full of sandwiches. Certainly this sight and this bit of knowledge are food-relevant cues; why, then, does the obese subject in the one-sandwich condition not eat more? There are many possible reasons. At this point, however, I should like to consider just three of them.

First, the fat person is self-conscious and, not wanting to seem a pig, will not eat in circumstances where it is possible for someone to check on him. In this experiment specifically, self-consciousness might have inhibited the subject from helping himself to more than had been laid out on the table. Though possible, it must be conceded that Nisbett's experiment was deliberately designed so as to minimize this possibility. Subjects ate in complete privacy; eating, as far as the subjects were concerned, had nothing to do with the experiment, and the refrigerator really was stuffed with sandwiches so as to make it unlikely that the

TABLE 37 RESPONSES TO THE "CLEAN YOUR PLATE" QUESTION

Weight	N	Nearly always clean my plate (%)	Sometimes clean, sometimes leave (%)	Nearly always leave something(%)
Underweight	82	26.8	50.0	23.2
Normal	83	39.8	45.8	14.5
Overweight	95	53.7	36.8	9.5

experimenter could keep track of how much had been eaten. In any case, self-consciousness as a general explanation, seems unlikely, for it demands that in virtually any experimental circumstances obese subjects eat very little. The fact is, however, that in a variety of experiments we have, by now, been able to specify and demonstrate the circumstances in which fat subjects will eat a great deal, far more, than presumably nonself-conscious normal subjects.

Second, the stereotype is correct and the fat person really is lazy—too lazy to cross the room to get a sandwich from the refrigerator.

Third, an external cue to trigger eating must be immediate, compelling, and potent. The sight of a hot dog, savory with mustard and steaming sauerkraut, may compel eating. The sight of a hot dog stand half a block away may not. In these experimental circumstances, roast beef sandwiches directly in front of the obese subject are sufficient to trigger eating; the knowledge that there are more of such sandwiches in the icebox is not.

It does seem to me to be essential,' eventually, to theoretically and experimentally spell out some such dimension as the "immediacy" of the cue, if for no other reason than to attempt to account for the facts that fat people do not by any means eat all of the time, even in the presence of cues, and, when they are eating, do eventually stop eating. The logical extension of the ideas offered so far requires that, in the presence of external cues, the fat person continue eating until he grows ill or dies. Though there are medical case-histories of fat people who die of an eating bout, certainly these are wild exceptions. Within my general framework, I can conceive of two notions that may help us account for the fact that fat people do stop eating. First, it may be that the obese are just as insensitive to the internal signals of satiety as they have proven to be to the signals of deprivation, in which case it may simply require more food for them to sense these signals, but they will eventually stop. Though this may be the case, this mechanism cannot, of itself, cope with such facts as that the obese subjects in Nisbett's one-sandwich condition eat considerably less than normal subjects. Second, the "immediacy" notion alluded to above suggests that an external cue must be particularly potent if it is to trigger eating among obese subjects. Compelling evidence that this is the case has recently been collected by Lee Ross (1970) in an experiment ostensibly concerned with thinking. In one set of conditions, the subject does his thinking in a normally lit room. In a second set of conditions, the subject thinks in a very dimly lit room. In both conditions, a bowl of shelled nuts is beside the subject. Obese subjects eat far more nuts in the brightly lit (36.9 gm) than in the dimly lit room (18.8 gm). For normals, the degree of illumination makes no difference; they eat no more in the bright (20.1 gm) than in the dim condition (24.9 gm).

Whether any, all, or none of these explanations is correct is still, of course, a completely open question, but the phenomenon is a solid fact and one which has an astonishing analogue in research on the hyperphagic rat. Numerous studies have shown that a bilateral lesion in the region of the ventromedial nuclei of the hypothalamus causes rats to overeat until they become extremely fat. Miller, Bailey, and Stevenson (1950) have demonstrated that though such rats eat far more ad libitum than do control rats, they eat far less when required to press a bar or lift a weighted lid to obtain food. Similarly, the experimental animals ran more slowly down an alley to food than did the control animals, pulled less hard when restrained by a harness, and were stopped by lower levels of electric shock at the goal. Though Miller *et al.* interpret these results entirely in motivational terms, it does seem to me that the immediacy of cue is an alternative explanation not ruled out by this design. Both obese subjects and hyperphagic rats eat more than do their controls when food is immediately available and easily accessible. They eat less when the food is either remote or requires effort to obtain.

There are still other parallels between research on the hyperphagic rat and these experiments on the obese human. Teitelbaum (1955), among others, has demonstrated that the taste of food has a marked effect on the amounts eaten by such animals. When fed a standard palatable diet, obese hyperphagic rats eat more than do normal rats. When fed a particularly palatable diet of their standard food mixed with 50% dextrose, such rats eat far more than do their controls. When fed the unpleasant mixture of a standard diet blended with quinine, these animals eat far less than do their controls. The similarity of these findings to those of the Hashim and Van Itallie (1965) study, and the Nisbett (1968a) and Decke taste experiments are striking.

Eventually we may learn much about human and rat obesity from such parallels. At this point, however, there is little more that one can do than point with bemusement at the comparability of these two sets of data.

Externality-Internality as a Dimension

One of the purposes of Nisbett's experiments was to extend the range of subject weight deviations so as to examine the hypothesis that the relative reliance on external versus internal cues is a dimension co-varying with weight deviation so that eating by the obese is triggered largely by external cues and eating by the underweight is controlled largely by internal cues. Normals presumably lie midway between these extremes, relying on both sets of cues. Examining the entire body of data so far presented, the evidence in support of such a formulation is, on the whole, reasonably good, though there are inconsistencies here and there.

Relevant to the effects of internal cues, the major facts are the following:

1. Normals describe themselves as hungry when their stomachs contract, the obese do not (Stunkard and Koch, 1964).

2. Manipulated food deprivation and fear have marked effects on the amounts eaten by normal subjects and no effects at all on obese subjects (Schachter, Goldman, and Gordon, 1968).

3. Deprived skinny subjects eat more ice cream than do skinny subjects who have just eaten. Manipulated deprivation has no effect on the amounts of ice cream eaten by obese or normal subjects. The results for obese subjects are consistent with expectations; the results for normal subjects are not. There is some independent support for the explanation that normal subjects, hungry or not, refused to make a meal of ice cream, and analysis of data not involving ice cream supports the general hypothesis (Nisbett, 1968a).

Relevant to the effects of external cues, the major facts are the following:

1. Obese subjects placed on a long-time, unappetizing diet markedly decrease caloric intake. Normal subjects do not. (Hashim and Van Itallie, 1965).

2. Manipulated time has stimulating effects on the amounts eaten by obese subjects and no such effect on normal subjects (Schachter and Gross, 1968).

3. Manipulated taste has a greater differential effect on the amounts eaten by obese subjects than on normal subjects than on skinny subjects (Nisbett, 1968a; Decke, unpublished).

4. The quantity of food made available has a marked effect on obese subjects and no effect at all on skinny or normal subjects. These results for skinny subjects are consistent with the idea of a continuum; the results for normal subjects are not. However, in an independent test of the same hypothesis, obese subjects are far more likely to describe themselves as "plate cleaners" than are normal than are underweight subjects (Nisbett, 1968b).

Given this body of data it does seem reasonable to conclude that there is support for the hypothesis. The apparent fact that underweight and overweight persons differ so markedly in their reliance on internal and external cues is particularly intriguing, for it suggests the beginnings of a plausible explanation of why the skinny are skinny and the fat are fat. We know from work such as that of Carlson (1916) that gastric contractions cease after the introduction of only a small amount of food into the stomach. To the extent that such contractions are directly related to the hunger "experience," to the extent that a person is under internal control, he should literally "eat like a bird," eating only enough to stop the contractions. Eating beyond this point should be a function of external cues—the taste, sight, and smell of food, perhaps the sheer joy of chewing. Externally controlled individuals, then, should have difficulty in stopping eating—a suggestion that may account for the notorious "binge" eating of the obese (Stunkard, 1961) or the monumental meals lovingly detailed by students (e.g., Beebe, 1966) of the great, fat, gastronomic magnificos.

Implicit in this line of speculation is the assumption that relative reliance on internal or external cues is a cause of obesity or skinniness—a matter which, to this point, I have meticulously avoided, for, from the experimental data, certainly, there is no more reason to assume that externality causes obesity than that the reverse is true. We have, to date, only one pertinent datum. At the end of Nisbett's experiment on taste, his subjects answered a questionnaire on their weight history. Some 37% of the normal subjects indicated that at some point in their lives they had been overweight. In Table 38, a comparison is made of the amounts of good and bad ice cream eaten by such subjects and by normal subjects who, by self-report, had never been overweight. It is evident that normals with a history of overweight eat considerably more of the good ice cream and less of the bad ice cream than do normals who have never been overweight (interaction $p = .02$). Once-fat subjects appear to behave as do currently obese subjects, for they are considerably more sensitive to the external cue, taste, than are normal subjects who have never been fat—an indication that the degree of reliance on external versus internal cues is an abiding characteristic and not necessarily a product of the condition of obesity.

These first indications that externality may be a cause of obesity do in themselves raise the intriguing question—Does the external control of eating behavior inevitably lead to obesity? I assume it is evident that logically this need not be so. Such a link is not inevitable, and the condition of external control of eating behavior can, under specifiable conditions, lead to the state of emaciation. An externally controlled person should eat and grow fat when food-related cues are abundant and when the person is fully aware of them. However, when such cues are absent or, for some reason, such as withdrawal or depression or total absorption in some engrossing activity, the person is unaware of these cues, the person under external control should not eat, and if the condition persists, grow concentration camp thin. Supporting this is a clinical literature which generally conveys the impression that there is an odd but distinct relationship between extreme obesity and extreme emaciation. For example, 11 of 21 case studies in Bliss and Branch's (1960) book on Anorexia Nervosa were at some point in their lives obese. For 8 of these 11 cases, anorexia was preceded and accompanied by

TABLE 38 AMOUNT OF ICE CREAM EATEN BY NORMAL
SUBJECTS AS A FUNCTION OF TASTE CONDITION
AND HISTORY OF OVERWEIGHT

Taste condition	History of overweight	No history of overweight
Good	198.3	136.9
N	12	16
Bad	18.1	38.6
N	9	19

either withdrawal or by depression. In contrast, attacks of anxiety or nervousness (states which the experiment by Schachter, Goldman, and Gordon, 1968, suggest would inhibit eating in normal subjects) seem to characterize the development of anorexia among most of the cases who were originally normal size.

If all of this is correct, we should expect to find in any experimental population of skinny subjects at least a few who behave as do obese subjects. We have as yet conducted no systematic study of this problem, but what data exist do support this guess. In both of Nisbett's studies, on any measure of eating behavior, the variance for underweight subjects is significantly larger than that for normal subjects—an indication that the underweight group is heterogeneous.

Obviously these last few pages have simply been idea-spinning—fun but ephemeral. Let us return to facts.

Chapter IX

Externality and Eating Habits

The gist of these several experiments is clear. The eating behavior of normal (and particularly skinny) subjects is closely tied to internal state. The eating behavior of the obese is relatively unrelated to visceral state, but is stimulated by food-relevant external cues. Though these facts have been demonstrated in experimental, relatively pure situations, they have implications for almost any area of human eating behavior. This and the following chapter describe studies designed to test these ideas in a variety of field settings.

These laboratory tests of externality have, of course, systematically manipulated the presence and the quality of food-relevant external cues. In real life, the presence or absence of such cues, their quality, and potency, depends on the individual's immediate surroundings. Should he be walking in the woods, it's unlikely that he will come into contact with any particularly potent food relevant cues. Should he be walking on a midtown street at noon, he will be bombarded by an onslaught of such cues. To the extent that one can anticipate where an individual will be and when, one can make fairly obvious guesses about his likelihood of chancing upon food-relevant cues. By consideration, then, of an individual's role and the routine and physical surroundings it imposes on him, one should, via this externality-internality schema, be able to make accurate surmises about his eating habits. As an illustration, I shall consider the lives of our college student subjects, and in the following discussion will make a series of more or less common-sense assumptions about three environmental or "psycho-ecological" attributes which seem cogent to present concerns:

1. The abundance and distribution of food-related cues.

2. The routine or scheduling of daily activities operating so as to systematize contact with food cues.

3. The existence of competing alternatives which decrease the salience of food-related cues or involve the individual in activities irrelevant to food or eating.

To examine the impact of these environmental attributes on everyday eating habits, two studies were conducted:

1. A questionnaire study which required the subjects to make a detailed report of their eating behavior on the two days prior to answering the questionnaire. This questionnaire was administered to all of the pretest and experimental subjects in the time manipulation study at the end of the experiment. These make a total of 54 male college student respondents—29 of them obese and 25 normal.

2. An eating diary study, conducted in collaboration with Lee Ross, Patricia Pliner, and Paul Nesbitt, which required subjects to keep a detailed daily record of what they had eaten and exactly when and where they had eaten it. They kept these records for a total of 13 successive days beginning on a Thursday and ending on a Tuesday. There were a total of 76 male college student diarists, all volunteers from the Introductory Psychology class at Columbia College. This group composed roughly 50% of the class membership. In return for their services, all volunteers were excused from two hours of a compulsory five-hour subject pool course requirement.

Fourteen of this group of 76 volunteers were more than 15.0% overweight (range 17.5%–59.2%), and were considered obese. The remaining subjects, all considered normal, ranged from 27.3% underweight to 14.9% overweight. Relevant to sampling problems, the distributions of weight, height, and weight deviation were virtually identical for volunteers and nonvolunteers.

These two studies provide the data which permit testing some of our guesses about the routine eating habits of obese and normal college students. In the following section, I shall develop a series of ideas about differential breakfast, lunch, and dinner habits of obese and normal subjects. A reader, accustomed to precision, will find this a remarkably loose performance, for at many points alternative explanations of the data will seem at least as cogent as the explanation offered. I would simply ask the reader to withhold judgment on these attempts to apply this external-internal schema to field settings until he has read the following two chapters.

Eating Breakfast

Though, culturally, one of the standard times to eat, for students breakfast is probably the meal least involved with external cues and most confounded by competing alternatives–the pleasant possibilities of sleeping late, dozing, daydreaming, or taking one's ease at shaving and washing. If one accepts this depiction of the factors affecting the decision of whether or not to have breakfast, it follows that the obese should be less prone to eat breakfast than normals.

The relevant data are presented in Table 39, which for the questionnaire study records answers to the question, "What time do you usually eat breakfast?" Some subjects listed a specific time and others checked the alternative, "I never eat it." It is immediately evident that normals are far more likely to eat breakfast than are the obese. While 44% of normal subjects report that they never eat breakfast, 79% of obese subjects do so.

In the eating diary study, the subjects each day answered the question, "Did you eat breakfast today?" and, if they answered "Yes," noted what time, where, and what. Since only 2 of the 76 subjects deny eating breakfast on all 13 days, it seems likely that the questionnaire study subjects have exaggerated their distaste for breakfast. However, the trends are in precisely the same direction in the two studies, for while 57% of obese subjects report skipping breakfast on more than half of the 13-day period, only 34% of normal subjects do so.

An obvious alternative explanation of these results is that the obese are dieting and therefore willing to dispense with breakfast. The data, however, belie this alternative. In the questionnaire study, of the 19 obese subjects who answered, "Yes" to the question, "Have you ever been on a diet to lose weight?" 26% eat breakfast; of the 10 obese subjects who answered, "No" to this question, only 10% eat breakfast. Irrespective of dieting, then, normals are far more prone to eat breakfast than are the obese.[1]

Eating Lunch: Weekdays versus Weekends

For college students, as for almost everyone, weekdays are highly routinized with tightly scheduled sets of restricted activities. Classes are held at regular hours, laboratory and gym periods are at designated times, libraries are open only at particular hours, athletic practice and club meetings are at specified times, and so on. This degree of routinization of daily life inevitably imposes a

---

[1] In considering this result as well as other results in this series of studies on obesity and eating habits, the reader may well have wondered if there are any differences in the physiological state characteristic of obese and normal subjects. For gastric motility, at least, the Stunkard and Koch (1964) study indicates no differences between these two groups in this respect. This finding is particularly applicable to these "breakfast" results, for they recorded gastric motility from 9:00 a.m. to 1:00 p.m. on subjects who had been instructed not to eat breakfast.

TABLE 39 OBESITY AND BREAKFAST

| | % Ss who: | |
| | Questionnaire study: | Eating diary: |
	"Never eat breakfast"	Skip breakfast on more than ½ of 13 days
Obese	79.3	57.1
Normal	44.0	33.9
p value	$< .01$	$< .20$
combined p	$< .01$	

very limited range of physical paths along which the individual repeatedly travels, a restricted number of places he visits, and a relatively small number of people, all also tightly scheduled, whom, during the week, he sees over and over again in much the same circumstances. Translating this routine into its relevance for food-related cues, it inevitably follows that the presence or absence of such cues must be as routinized and repetitive during the week as the presence or absence of any other sort of physical or social stimuli.

In distinct contrast, the weekend is a time of unpredictability. No classes, no schedule. The student may do anything from taking a trip home to exploring the city, having a date, going to a party, or anchorite-like staying in his room studying and sleeping. From Saturday to Sunday, from weekend to weekend, the degree of routine and repeated activity is simply lower than on weekdays. Inevitably, contact with food-related cues on weekends is relatively unsystematic and unpredictable.

Extending this characterization of weekday routine and weekend freedom to eating habits, it should follow that for the obese on weekdays, eating times should be very regular, meals being taken at much the same time each day. On weekends, however, mealtimes should be highly irregular, subject to all of the vagaries of an unpredictable round of activities. For normals, on the other hand, there should be relatively little difference between weekday and weekend regularity of eating. Less responsive to external cues, more responsive to internal state, the normal is inclined to eat when his stomach tells him to, rather than when circumstances dictate.

Let us consider the implications of this line of thought for the eating of lunch. During weekdays, virtually all undergraduates have morning classes. Come noontime, all students are up and about, surrounded by hordes of colleagues on their way to lunch, inevitably passing lunch counters, delicatessens, and dining halls. Whether for internal or external reasons, under such circumstances all students should be equally likely to eat lunch. On weekends, however, things are different. With no classes, the student may choose to stay in his room and study, go to the library, visit a museum, or indulge in countless activities that remove him from food-related cues. We should then anticipate that on weekends fat subjects are more likely to forego lunch than are normals.

The relevant data are reported in Table 40. In the questionnaire study, all subjects answered questions about when and if they had eaten lunch during the two previous days. The questionnaire was answered by all subjects in the time manipulation experiment which was run only on weekdays. Thus, if a student was a subject on a Wednesday, Thursday, or Friday, his answer referred to weekday lunches. If he was a subject on a Monday or Tuesday his answers referred to lunch on one or both days of the weekend. The left half of Table 40 records for the questionnaire study the proportion of students who skipped lunch on one or both days.[2] It is evident that on weekdays, there is no difference in the lunch-eating proclivities of normal and obese subjects. Some 21% of obese subjects skipped lunch on one or both weekdays, and 25% of normal subjects did so. On weekends, in sharp contrast, the two groups differ distinctly. Where only 11% of normals missed at least one lunch on the weekend, 53% of the obese did so.

The right half of Table 40 reports data gathered in the eating diary study and precisely the same trends are evident. There is no significant difference in the lunch eating proclivities of fat and normal subjects on weekdays, but on weekends fat subjects are far more likely to skip lunch.[3] In both studies, then, normals and obese prove equally likely to eat lunch on weekdays, whereas on weekends, the obese are far less likely to do so.

TABLE 40 OBESITY AND LUNCH

| | % Ss who miss one or more lunches on: | | | |
| | Questionnaire study | | Eating diary study | |
	Weekdays	Weekends	Weekdays	Weekends
Obese	21.4	53.3	57.1	92.9
Normal	25.0	11.1	33.9	58.1
p value	n.s.	$<.05$	n.s.	$<.05$

[2] If a student was a Tuesday subject, his data are coded only for Sunday lunch. Since eight of the Tuesday subjects were obese and five were normal, this coding rule should work against the hypothesis.

[3] The fact that the proportion of subjects skipping one or more lunches is consistently higher in the eating diary than in the questionnaire study is simply explained. Subjects in the eating diary study report their behavior over a 13-day period (including two weekends). Subjects in the questionnaire study report their behavior for a two-day period.

Dinnertime Regularity: Weekdays versus Weekends

Let us examine next the impact of weekday routine and weekend freedom on the regularity of eating, i.e., the day-to-day variation in the precise time of eating meals. It seems unnecessary to belabor what at this point must be a totally obvious prediction. If indeed the timing of food-related cues is irregular and unpredictable on weekends and systematic on weekdays, the obese should be far more irregular about mealtimes on weekends than on weekdays. For normals, this difference, if any, should be considerably smaller.

Since so few fat subjects eat breakfast regularly, and since the majority of fat subjects skip at least one lunch on weekends, this analysis is restricted to the time of eating dinner—a meal which most subjects, obese or normal, on weekends or weekdays, do eat.[4] In the questionnaire study, the answers to the following two questions provide the basic data:

> What time did you eat dinner last night?
> What time did you eat dinner the night before last?

Table 41 plots the mean discrepancy in minutes between the two times listed for all subjects who ate dinner on both nights.[5] It is immediately evident that there is a dramatic difference for the obese between weekends and weekdays. While on weekends, their two dinner times differ by an average of one and a half hours, on weekdays the discrepancy is only twelve and a half minutes. For normals, there is no such relationship—if anything there is a trivial and nonsignificant trend in the opposite direction.

[4] Following this general line of reasoning, one might anticipate similar, though considerably weaker, trends for dinner than for lunch. As can be seen in the following tabulation of data from the questionnaire study, there are no such trends and no differences that even approach tangential significance. Following this general weekend theme, one could conjecture that on weekends, libraries and museums close before dinner time, matinees end late in the afternoon, and even the thorniest college recluse is likely to come of his room by five or six in the afternoon—all events destined to expose the student to food-related cues.

	Weekday No. of Ss who ate:		Weekend No. of Ss who ate:	
	Dinner	No dinner	Dinner	No dinner
Obese	12	2	13	2
Normal	15	1	7	2

Similarly, in the eating diary study, there are no differences between weekends and weekdays. Both obese and normal subjects report eating an average of roughly 12.5 dinners over the 13-day period.

[5] The data for subjects run on Mondays and Tuesdays are again combined under the "weekend" heading. The data for the Saturday-Sunday dinner time discrepancy are quite similar to those for the Sunday-Monday discrepancy.

TABLE 41 THE DISCREPANCY BETWEEN DINNERTIMES ON WEEKENDS AND WEEKDAYS IN THE QUESTIONNAIRE STUDY

	Discrepancy (in minutes) between dinnertimes on:	
	Weekdays	Weekends
Obese	12.5	90.0
Normal	83.9	68.6

Interaction $p < .01$.

TABLE 42 THE VARIABILITY OF DINNERTIMES ON WEEKENDS AND WEEKDAYS IN THE EATING DIARY STUDY

	Average standard deviation of dinnertimes during:	
	Weekdays	Weekends
Obese	56.2	93.8
Normal	47.4	48.9

Interaction $p < .02$.

In the eating diary study, precisely the same relationships are evident. Table 42 presents the average standard deviation of supper times during the four weekend days of this 13-day study in contrast to the standard deviation for the weekdays during this period. It is evident that once again the obese are far more variable on weekends than on weekdays, while for normals the weekday-weekend dichotomy has no relationship to dinnertime variability.

These consistent indications of the irregularity of obese eating habits on weekends do constitute a caveat against any temptation to generalize the results of the time manipulation experiment described in Chapter VII. It does appear that the effects of time on the eating behavior of the obese are considerably more complex in real life than these experimental results would indicate. In the laboratory situation where, other than crackers which no one either particularly likes or dislikes, the passage of time is the only food-relevant cue, time is indeed a potent cue. In real life, where time is but one of a host of food-relevant cues and where competing alternatives to eating abound, the impact of time seems mediated by the weekday-weekend dimension of routinization. On weekdays, when life is routine, indications are that the eating schedule of the obese is relatively rigid and time bound. On weekends, when competing alternatives to eating are abundant, the effects of time seem slight and the obese person seems even more variable in his eating times than the normal.

Chapter X

Yom Kippur, Air France, Dormitory Food, and the Eating Behavior of Obese and Normal Persons

Continuing investigation of the generalizability of the experimentally-derived findings, Goldman, Jaffa, and Schachter (1968) examined implications of this internal-external formulation of eating behavior in a variety of nonlaboratory settings—specifically, religious fasting, tolerance of institutional food, and the effects of time zone changes on eating behavior.

Who Fasts on Yom Kippur?

Evidence indicates that for obese subjects the impulse to eat is triggered by an external, food-relevant cue. In contrast, the impulse to eat for normal individuals appears to be stimulated by the set of physiological cues consequent on food deprivation. If we assume that blocking this impulse by doing without food is an irritating or painful state, it should follow that in circumstances where food-relevant external cues are sparse or, where the individual can successfully distract himself from such external cues, the obese person will have a considerably easier time fasting or doing without food than will normally sized persons. The findings that the obese rarely eat breakfast or, on weekends, lunch, can be construed as consistent with this expectation.

In order to test directly this expectation and some of its corollaries, the relation of overweight to fasting on Yom Kippur was studied. Yom Kippur, the Jewish Day of Atonement, is the most sacred of Jewish Holy Days. It is also the only day of the Jewish year for which fasting is commanded by Biblical Law.

The traditional Jew begins his fast on Yom Kippur eve and does without food or water for 24 hours. Save for sleeping, he spends virtually all of his time in prayer in synagogue, a physical environment notoriously barren of graven images, let alone food-related cues, observing a ritual conducted in Aramaic and Hebrew whose chief direct reference to food is passing mention of a scapegoat. Almost certainly, informal conversations within the synagogue at this time must to some degree be concerned with the fast, but the ritual proper and the physical surroundings are virtually devoid of food-relevant cues.

Among contemporary Jews, observance of Yom Kippur ranges from those who meticulously adhere to every detail described, to those who are only vaguely aware that there is such a day. Between these extremes lies every variation of token or partial observance—people who will spend only an hour or two in synagogue, Jews who do without regular meals but sneak half a sandwich, and so on.

Given this characterization of Yom Kippur, if these speculations about obesity and fasting are correct, it should follow among Jews for whom the day has any meaning that:

1. Fat Jews will be more likely to fast than normally built Jews.

2. The difficulty of fasting will, for obese Jews, depend upon the abundance and prominence of food-related cues in their immediate environment, while for normal Jews these two variables will be unrelated. Thus it should be anticipated that fat, fasting Jews who spend a great deal of time in synagogue will suffer less from fasting than fat, fasting Jews who spend little time in synagogue, and there will be no such relationship for normal, fasting Jews. Plausibly, there will be far fewer food-related cues in the synagogue than on the street or at home. The likelihood, therefore, that the impulse to eat will be triggered is greater out of synagogue than in. For normal Jews, this distinction is of less importance. In or out of synagogue, stomach pangs are stomach pangs.

In order to test these expectations, a few days after Yom Kippur, 1965, Goldman, Jaffa, and Schachter (1968) administered a questionnaire to all of the students in several classes in introductory social science and psychology at the City University of New York and at New York University. The questionnaire was anonymous and designed to learn from Jewish respondents their sex, height, weight, whether or not they had fasted on Yom Kippur, how unpleasant they had found the fast, and a variety of other pieces of information relevant to how religious they were and their experiences during Yom Kippur.

Since these hypotheses are irrelevant to Jews who are totally irreligious and only dimly aware of the holiday and its proscriptions, the sample for analysis is limited to those Jews who gave some indication of being religious. The criterion is simple and derives from answers to the question "Approximately how many times have you been to synagogue in the last year?" Any Jew who had been to synagogue at least once during the past year, for some reason other than a wedding or a bar mitzvah, was considered a religious Jew. Of a total of 748 questionaires, 456 were from Jewish respondents (247 men; 209 women). Of these, 296 respondents (160 men; 136 women) are, by this criterion, religious Jews.[1]

The basic data on obesity and fasting are presented in Table 45. Whether or not a subject fasted was determined by his answer to the question, "Did you attempt to fast last Wednesday for the Yom Kippur holiday?" Anyone who answered "Yes" is classified as a faster. For the height and weight data, the Metropolitan Life Insurance Company (1959) norms were used to calculate weight deviations. Subjects were classified as obese if their weight deviations fell among the top 20% of all subjects of their own sex, a cutoff point used in the three studies described in this chapter. In this sample any male who was 15.4% overweight or more is classified as obese. For females, a 20% cutoff point includes girls who, from their answers to the questions about weight and height, are as little as 4.8% overweight. Despite the fact that one would hardly consider a woman, truly of this slight weight deviation, to be obese, for consistency's sake, we employed the 20% cutoff point for both males and females in all of the studies described in this chapter. Not wishing to debate the pros and cons of this procedure, I note simply that in the two studies involving females, employing a higher cutoff point for females strengthens the main effects.

The data in Table 43 are clearly consistent with expectations. Among fat religious Jews 83.1% fasted on Yom Kippur. In comparsion, 68.8% of normal Jews fasted. Obesity does play a part in determining who fasts on Yom Kippur.[2]

Let us examine next the impact of those factors presumed to differentially affect the difficulty of fasting for normal and obese subjects. As a measure of fasting difficulty, the following question was asked:

[1] Included in this group of religious Jews are 25 respondents who had not been to synagogue during the past year but who had fasted on Yom Kippur. In puzzling over just how to classify such respondents, it seemed to us that undertaking the Yom Kippur fast was, at least, as good an indication of religiousness as attending synagogue once or twice during the year. These nonsynagogue-going fasters are, then, classified as religious. It should be noted, however, that the main effects of the study (and the statistical levels of confidence involved) remain much the same whether or not this sub-group is treated as religious.

[2] There is a tendency for obese respondents to be slightly more religious than normal subjects, i.e., to attend synagogue slightly more during the year. Though this is a nonsignificant difference, it is troubling, for obviously the more religious are more likely to fast. In order to check on this alternative interpretation, the proportion of fasters among obese and normal respondents of various degrees of religiosity (as measured by the amount of synagogue going) was compared. At every point of comparison from slightly religious (1 or 2 visits to synagogue) to extremely religious (20 or more visits), the obese are more likely to fast.

Insofar as you did fast this Yom Kippur, how unpleasant an experience was it?

| Extremely unpleasant (5) | Very unpleasant (4) | Quite unpleasant (3) | Somewhat unpleasant (2) | Slightly unpleasant (1) | Not at all unpleasant (0) |

I note, in passing, that, in general, fat, fasting Jews tend to find the Yom Kippur fast somewhat less unpleasant than do normal, fasting Jews. The average rating on this scale for the obese is 0.78 and for normals 1.02 ($t = 1.44, p = .20$). If it is assumed that most Jews religious enough to undertake the fast are likely to spend at least some of their time in surroundings devoid of food-related cues, such a difference seems reasonable. It is clear though that crucial to the argument is the differential effect of such surroundings on obese and normal Jews. In keeping with this general scheme, it is assumed that the presence or absence of food-relevant cues directly affects the ease with which an obese person fasts and has relatively little impact on a normal person. If one accepts the characterization of the synagogue on Yom Kippur as devoid of food-related cues, it should be anticipated that for obese fasters answers to the question, "For how many hours did you attend religious services this Yom Kippur?" will be negatively related to ratings of fasting unpleasantness. The more hours in synagogue, the less exposure to food-relevant cues and the less unpleasant should fasting be for the externally controlled obese person. For the normal faster, attuned to his viscera, there should be little relationship.

The data are consistent with these expectations. For the obese, the correlation between hours in synagogue and unpleasantness is $-.50$. For normals, the correlation is only $-.18$. Testing the difference between these correlations, $z = 2.19$, which is significant at the .03 level. For the obese, the more time in synagogue the less of an ordeal is fasting. In contrast, for normals, hours in synagogue have little to do with the difficulty of the fast.

TABLE 43 OBESITY AND FASTING ON YOM KIPPUR

	Obese Jews	Normal Jews
Fasters	49	163
Nonfasters	10	74

$\chi^2 = 4.74; p < .05.$

Who Eats Domitory Food?

Considering the taste or quality of food as an external determinant of eating behavior, Nisbett (1968a) and Decke (Chapter 8) found that the taste of food had greater impact on the eating behavior of obese than of normal subjects. Generalizing from these findings, it seems reasonable to assume that taste will not only have an effect on how much fat, as compared with normal, subjects eat, but on where they eat. It seems a plausible guess that the obese will be more drawn to good restaurants and more repelled by bad ones than will normal subjects.

At Columbia, students have the option of eating in the university dining halls or in any of the swarm of more or less exotic restaurants, lunch counters, and delicatessens that surround this metropolitan campus. It is probably small surprise to the reader to learn that typical campus opinion of dormitory food is quite unfavorable. Several student-conducted surveys document widespread dissatisfaction with the university dining halls, enumerating complaints about cold food, poor service, stale desserts, etc. (University Dormitory Council, 1964).

If an undergraduate elects to eat in a dormitory dining hall, he may if he chooses join a pre-pay food plan at the beginning of the school year. For $500 he purchases a meal contract which entitles him to a weekly meal ticket worth $16.25 with which he can pay for the meals and snacks he enjoys at the university dining hall and snack bar. Anytime after November 1, the student may cancel his food contract by paying a penalty of $15.00 and the remainder of his money is refunded. If general campus opinion of dormitory food is at all realistically based, those for whom taste or food quality is most important should be most likely to discontinue their food contracts. Obese students, then, should be more likely to drop out of the food plan than normal students.

The sample for this study is the entire body of freshmen entering Columbia in 1965 who signed up for the food plan on first entering the college. There were 698 students in this freshman class of whom 211 signed food contracts for their first semester. This sample is limited to freshmen first because they constitute the bulk of meal plan subscribers and second because the noncommuters among them are required to live in dormitories during their entire first academic year. Thus, their decision to leave the plan could not be affected by moving out of the dormitories as it could for upperclassmen.

Weight deviations were computed from records in the Dean of Students' office using the Metropolitan Life Insurance Company (1959) norms.[3] As in the

---

[3]For 25 of the 211 freshmen who signed food contracts, the existing records were incomplete or unavailable so that it was impossible to determine weight deviation. Table 44 includes the 186 cases for whom the data are complete.

TABLE 44 THE RELATIONSHIP OF OBESITY
TO RENEWING MEAL CONTRACTS

	Obese	Normal
Dropped meal contract	32	100
Renewed meal contract	5	49

$\chi^2 = 5.40; p < .05.$

other studies in this chapter, the top 20% of the weight deviation distribution is classified as obese. For this sample, this includes all students who were 11.3% overweight or more.

The basic data are presented in Table 44 where it can be seen that expectations are confirmed. Some 86.5% of fat freshmen let their contracts expire as compared with the 67.1% of normal students who dropped out of the meal plan. Obesity does, to some extent, predict who chooses to subsist on institutional food.

Adjusting to Time Zone Changes

There are occasions when there is a marked discrepancy or opposition between external cues relevant to eating and the internal, physiological correlates of food deprivation or satiation. Examples of such a condition would be the presentation of a gorgeous dessert after consumption of a mammoth meal or being faced with some nauseating, rudely prepared concoction after a period of starvation. In such cases, this general line of thought leads to the expectation that the obese will be relatively more affected by the external cue than will the normal subject, i.e., he will eat more of the dessert and less of the mess. The studies by Hashim and van Itallie (1965), Nisbett (1968a) and Decke do, in good part, support these expectations.

A more subtle instance of this opposition of cues is represented by the Schachter and Gross (Chapter VII) study in which, by means of doctored clocks, subjects were manipulated into believing that the time was later or earlier than the true time. If we assume that the intensity of gastric motility, etc., is a function of true time (i.e., hours since last meal), then this clock manipulation can create circumstances in which external and internal cues are, to some degree, in opposition. For example, a subject may be under the clock-produced impression that it is after his usual dinner time while in actuality it is before this time. In such circumstances, Schachter and Gross found that the manipulated external cue almost entirely determined how much obese subjects ate and did not similarly affect normal subjects.

Long distance East-West travel creates a state which, in a way, is a real life analog of this time manipulation experiment. Given time zone changes, the traveler, biologically more than ready to eat, may arrive at his destination at a local time still hours away from routine eating times and from the barrage of food-related external cues invariably synchronized with culturally routinized meal times. For example, a jet flight leaving Paris at 12:00 noon requires eight hours to reach New York where, on arrival, the local time is 2:00 p.m. If the passenger has eaten an early lunch on the plane and no dinner, he is, on arrival, physiologically more than ready for a full meal but still four or five hours away from local dinner hours. Whatever mode he chooses of coping with his situation, eating a full meal on arrival, snacking, or putting off a meal until local dinner time, his situation is, for a time, an uncomfortable one, characterized by a marked discrepancy between his physiological state and locally acceptable eating hours and he must, in short order, adjust to an entirely new eating schedule. Though a prediction is by no means unequivocal, it seems an intuitively sound guess that the obese will have an easier time in this situation than will normal travelers. We know that the obese can fast more easily than normals; we know from a variety of experiments that eating by the obese is virtually independent of internal state; we know that the obese are sensitive to external cues and, particularly, that when faced with an experimentally produced discrepancy between the actual time and manipulated time, eating by fat subjects is determined almost wholly by manipulated rather than true time. Given this mélange of interrelated facts, it seems only a small step to suppose that the obese international traveler will have a considerably easier time adjusting to local eating schedules than will the normal-sized traveler.

Thanks to the good offices of the Medical Department of Air France, Goldman, Jaffa, and Schachter (1968) had access to data which, to some extent, permitted an evaluation of the hypothesis. Concerned with biological, psychological, and medical effects of time zone changes, Air France studied a sizeable sample of flight crew members regularly assigned to trans-Atlantic routes (Lavernhe, Lafontaine, and Laplane, 1965). The subjects of this inquiry were 194 male and 42 female personnel regularly flying the Paris-New York and Paris-Montreal routes. On the East to West journey these flights are scheduled to leave Paris roughly around noon, French time, fly for approximately eight hours and land in North America sometime in the early afternoon, Eastern time. Flight crew members all eat lunch shortly after takeoff and, being occupied with landing preparations and servicing passenger needs, are not served another meal during the flight. They land in North America, then, some seven hours after their last meal, at a time that is generally past the local lunch hour and well before local dinner time.

The Air France study was not directly concerned with reports of hunger or eating behavior, but the investigators systematically noted all individuals who volunteered that they "suffered from the discordance between their physiological state and meal time in America."[4] The interpretation of this coding is not completely clear cut, but it appears to apply chiefly to fliers who complain about the fact that they either do without food or make do with a snack until local dinner time. Possibly some complainers are those who eat a full dinner on landing, are then satiated at local dinner time, and are again physiologically hungry at a time long past local dinner time. In either case, it should be anticipated that the fatter fliers, sensitive to external rather than internal cues, should most readily adapt to local eating schedules and be least likely to complain of the discrepancy between American meal times and their physiologi‚ cal states.

The basic data are presented in Fig. 8 which plots the proportion of complainers at each quintile of the weight deviation distribution of this group of flying personnel. Because of the stringent physical requirements involved in air crew selection, there are, of course, relatively few really obese people in this sample. Despite this fact, it is evident that there is a consistent relation between the degree of weight deviation and the likelihood of spontaneously mentioning difficulties in adjusting to the discrepancy between physiological state and local meal times. The more overweight the French flier the less likely he is to be troubled by this discrepancy. The linear nature of the relationship is consistent with the results of Nisbett's (1968a) experiment. Comparing groups of extremely skinny, fat, and normal subjects, Nisbett demonstrated that the impact of the external cue, taste, on eating behavior was a direct function of the degree of overweight.

Testing the significance of the differences in this body of data by the same procedure as that employed in the two previous studies, we find $\chi^2 = 2.93$ ($p < .10$) for the heaviest quintile of French fliers, as compared with the remainder of the sample. If we compare all of those flying personnel who are overweight (0.1%–29.9% overweight) with all of those who are not overweight (0%–21.5% underweight), the data distribute as in Table 45 where it can be seen that 11.9% of the overweight complain as compared to 25.2% of the nonoverweight ($\chi^2 = 6.52, p < .02$). It does appear that fatter, flying Frenchmen are less likely to be troubled by the effects of time changes on eating.

TABLE 45 THE RELATIONSHIP OF WEIGHT DEVIATION
TO COMPLAINING ABOUT THE EFFECTS OF TIME ZONE
CHANGES ON EATING BEHAVIOR[a]

Subjects who:	Subjects who are:	
	Overweight	Not overweight
Complain	12	34
Don't complain	89	101

$\chi^2 = 6.52; p < .02.$

[4] J. Lavernhe and E. Lafontain, personal communication, 1966.

Discussion

From these three studies we know the following facts:

1. Fat Jews are more likely to fast on Yom Kippur than normal Jews.

2. For fat, fasting Jews, there is an inverse relation between the unpleasantness of fasting and the number of hours spent in synagogue on Yom Kippur. There is no such relation for normally built Jews who fast.

3. Fat freshmen are more likely to drop university meal plan contracts than are normal freshmen.

4. Fatter French fliers are less likely to be troubled by the effects of time zone changes on eating routine than are thinner French fliers.

Goldman, Jaffa, and I chose to interpret these facts in terms of our theory about the relation between weight deviation and the relative potency of external and internal stimulants to eating. These three studies were designed to test specific implications of this schema in appropriate field settings. As with any

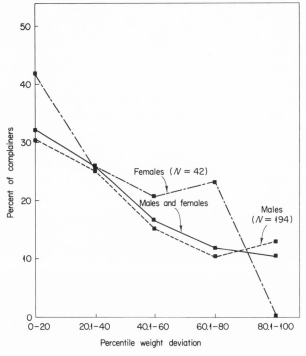

Fig. 8. The relationship of weight deviation to complaining about the effects of time-zone changes on eating.

field research, alternative explanations of these findings are legion and, within the context of any specific study, impossible to overrule. Except for the most obvious alternatives, we chose to avoid the tedium of listing and feebly feuding with more or less plausible alternative interpretations—a procedure whose chief virtue would be the demonstration that we were at least aware of our interpretive problems even if we could do nothing about them.

There is, however, one alternative interpretation cogent not only to the present studies but to some of the findings in the various laboratory experiments. Two of these field studies, Yom Kippur and Air France, are concerned with some aspect of fasting behavior and the ease with which the obese can do without food[5]—a finding deriving from and related to the laboratory demonstration that manipulated food deprivation has no effect on eating by the obese. Rather than the interpretation we have elected, which rests on the assumption that the obese do not label the physiological correlates of food deprivation as hunger, one could suggest that the obese are, after all, overweight, that they have large stores of body fat and, within the time limits of these studies, that they actually do not experience such states as gastric motility and hypoglycemia. Though a plausible hypothesis, the available evidence suggests that for gastric motility, at least, the hypothesis is not correct. The Stunkard and Koch (1964) study of gastric contractions and self-reports of hunger was in essence conducted under fasting conditons. Subjects ate their regular dinners, ate no breakfast, and came to the laboratory at 9:00 a.m. where, having swallowed a gastric balloon, they remained for four hours. During this period the extent of gastric motility was much the same for obese and normal subjects. The obese simply did not coordinate the statement "I feel hungry" with periods of gastric motility while normal subjects did.[6]

One final point in defense of this general schema. It is the case that nonobvious derivations do plausibly follow from this formulation of the inter-

[5] Other investigators who have noted this phenomenon in various contexts are Brown and Pulsifer (1965) and Duncan, *et al.*, (1962).

[6] One final datum from our own studies also suggests that this alternative interpretation is incorrect. If it is correct that the intensity of the physiological correlates of food deprivation is, within time limits, less for the obese than for normal subjects, it should follow that, under any conditions, obese subjects will find it easier to fast. The data on the relation of hours in synagogue to self-ratings of fasting difficulty in the Yom Kippur study indicate, however, that this is not the case. Obese subjects who spend most of the day in synagogue (eight or more hours) do suffer considerably less from fasting than do normal subjects who spend the same amount of time in synagogue. However, among those who spend little time in synagogue (two hours or less), the obese report more difficulty with the fast than do normals. It would appear that the obese have an easier time doing without food than do normals in the absence of external, food-relevant cues, but a more difficult time in the presence of such cues.

relationships of external and internal determinants of eating behavior. In these two chapters, we have "derived" from this set of ideas, as varied and exotic a set of relationships as the irregular eating habits of the obese on weekends and the negative correlation between hours in synagogue and the unpleasantness of fasting for the obese on Yom Kippur. I simply cannot conceive of an alternative conceptualization of this entire body of data, experimental and field, which would lead to such predictions. In any case, whatever the eventual interpretation of these field studies, if one permutes the facts, the implications are unassailable: fasting, fat, French freshmen fly farther for fine food—particularly on weekends.

Chapter XI

Field Dependence, Drinking, and Urination

The sporadic, irascible concern with alternative explanations that peppers the previous two chapters is an inevitable product of this freewheeling theoretical marriage of speculation about daily routine and customs with hypotheses and facts about obesity and eating. Though this schema has the charm of leading to some totally unexpected findings, it is obvious that, as applied to field settings, this is the loosest sort of semi-literary, conceptual scheme. For any single one of these findings about real-life eating, alternative explanations are abundant. Though I rather doubt that any seriously different theoretical scheme can incorporate quite this variety of findings, there is an alternative way of thinking of this entire body of data, experimental and field, which must be considered. It is conceivable that these various findings about eating behavior are simply a special case of a much broader phenomenon. Possibly all of the bodily processes or biological drive states of the obese are more vulnerable to environmental influences than are those of normal subjects. More broadly still, these findings may be a manifestation of a generalized sensitivity to external cues, biologically relevant or not. The psychologically knowledgeable reader has undoubtedly noted a resemblance between these notions of external and internal control and Witkin *et al.*'s (1954) schema of field dependence and independence. Generalizing from their experiments on perceptual style to a wide realm of personality characteristics, Witkin and his colleagues have identified a dimension they call field dependence by which they refer to the extent to which an individual relies on field or, in the present sense, external cues. Field independent persons are characterized by "activity and independence in relation to the environment; by closer communication with, and better control of, their own impulses." Field dependent persons are characterized by "passivity in dealing with the environment; by unfamiliarity with and fear of their own impulses" (Witkin *et al.*, 1954, p. 469). The language is more exotic, the ideas seem similar.

If these findings on obesity and eating behavior are to be subsumed under this or some other more general formulation, it should be anticipated, first, that obese subjects will be more field dependent than normal subjects and, second, that for other biologically based states such as thirst, micturition, sex, etc., the obese will prove less sensitive to internal cues and more vulnerable to external cues than normal subjects.

Are the Obese Field Dependent?

A study by Karp and Pardes (1965) indicates that the obese are relatively field dependent. These investigators studied a group of "34 white female volunteers, all attending a nutrition clinic for treatment of obesity problems." These ladies ranged in age from 15–56 years, with a mean of 41.8 years. The percentage of overweight of the group ranged from 24%–134% with a mean of 48%. A control group of 34 nonobese ladies was chosen from a large pool of volunteers, so as to match the obese group in age and education. Control subjects were paid $5.00 for participating in the experiment; obese subjects were not paid.

Both groups were tested on the rod-and-frame test, the body-adjustment test, and the short (12 card) form of the embedded-figures test—the three most widely used measures of field dependence. The results of this study are presented in Table 46. It can be seen that on all measures the obese tend to greater field dependence than do normal subjects. Differences between the groups are significant on two of the three measures, and the results of the embedded-figures test are particularly impressive with obese subjects requiring considerably more time to complete the test than do normals. Though certainly these data support the conclusion that the obese are relatively field dependent, unpublished studies conducted in my own laboratory on male, Columbia University undergraduates simply do not replicate these findings.

In one study Patricia Pliner and Harriet Kay administered the group form of the embedded-figures test to 65 subjects, roughly equally divided into groups of obese and normal subjects. The obese ranged from 20.7%–86.4% overweight, and averaged 40.7% overweight. On this test, the obese scored an average of 11.7 and normals an average of 12.9 correct responses. This is a nonsignificant difference indicating, if anything, a slight tendency for normals to be more field dependent.

In a second study, John Maher, Patricia Mayhew, and Miriam Zellner administered the long form (24 cards) of the embedded-figures test to 22 normal

TABLE 46   FIELD DEPENDENCE AND OBESITY (ADAPTED FROM KARP AND
PARDES, 1965)

Test[a]	Subject		*t*	*p*
	Obese	Control		
Bodily-adjustment	95.59	75.29	1.59	<.20
Rod-and-frame	139.94	102.12	2.29	<.05
Embedded figure	33'47"	21'25"	4.29	<.01

[a]Data for the bodily-adjustment and rod-and-frame tests are presented in degrees of deviation from the vertical; embedded-figure scores are in minutes and seconds of elapsed time. For the three tests, the higher the score the greater the field dependence.

and 21 fat subjects. Normals averaged 6'45" and the obese 9'08". This difference is in the direction of greater field dependence in the obese group, but it is a nonsignificant difference ($t = 1.10, p > .20$).

Since the results of the embedded-figures test provide the chief support for the conclusions of the Karp and Pardes study, these failures to find any differences between obese and normal subjects do cast doubt on a conclusion of differential field dependence. Just how to account for these varying results is an open question. Obviously the subject population of the two Columbia studies could hardly be more different from the group of middle-aged, Southern ladies who were the subjects for Karp and Pardes. Certainly this difference could account for the failure to replicate. However, it must be remembered that students from this same Columbia population served as subjects in most of the eating experiments described in this volume. Obese and normal students differ markedly in eating behavior; they do not differ in performance on the embedded-figures test—a pair of facts which casts serious doubt on the hypothesis that these differences in eating behavior can be considered a special case of differential field dependence.

My suspicion is that the explanation for these disparate results lies in the fact that there were differences between the Karp and Pardes experimental and control groups other than the degree of obesity. Their obese subjects were out-patients, people who had come to a nutrition clinic for help. Control subjects were nonpatient, paid volunteers. It requires only a modest extension of the conception of field dependence to assume that field dependent people, obese or not, are more likely to seek outside help than are field independent people. If correct, it should be anticipated that nonpatient obese subjects would be no more or less field dependent than a similar group of normally-sized subjects. Whatever the outcome of such a comparison, it does seem at the moment that the results of these several experiments on eating behavior cannot be accounted for in terms of differential field dependence.

Obesity, Thirst, and Urination

Whatever the ultimate status of the field dependence-obesity hypothesis, it is an empirical question as to whether or not these findings on obesity and eating are generalizable to other biologically derived drive states. Certainly, the distinction between external and internal controls seems applicable to almost any such drive state. Sex, of course, is a classic instance of a drive state under joint external and internal control. Less obvious, perhaps, is thirst. As with eating, we are so accustomed to relate drinking to water deprivation and tissue dehydration that it seems far-fetched to assume that there is not necessarily a one-to-one relationship between dehydration and drinking. Again, however, there is no compelling reason for assuming that the label "thirst" and consequent drinking inevitably accompanies tissue dehydration. At the very least, almost everyone has sometime stopped to drink as he passed a water fountain, or sipped at a glass of water placed before him in a restaurant, even though he was in no way dehydrated.

Still another state for which, on a common-sense basis, it seems particularly implausible to suggest any radical dissociation between bodily state and label is that of urination. Yet in Chapter V, several studies have been described which do indicate that the feeling state associated with the volume of fluid in the urinary bladder is remarkably manipulable by essentially cognitive procedures.

Both drinking and urinating, then, appear to be states to which one can apply this external-internal control formulation. If the individual differences manifested in the studies of eating behavior are generalizable to these states, it should be anticipated that the drinking and urinating behaviors of normal subjects will correspond closely to internal state while for obese subjects these behaviors will be more closely related to external cues.

In order to test this possibility Maher, Mayhew, and Zellner conducted an experiment in which they attempted to manipulate the bodily correlates of water deprivation and urination by the simple expedient of requiring subjects to drink either very large or small quantities of water. This experiment was couched as a study of the effects of a vitamin compound on visual processes. It required of a subject that, with the assistance of either two or twenty ounces of water, he swallow a vitamin pill (placebo), wait 20 minutes for the pill to be absorbed, spend 30 minutes taking a variety of perceptual tests, and about 5 more minutes answering a questionnaire about bodily state. The questionnaire answered, a measure was taken of Palmar Skin Response, "a measure of palmar sweating which has been found to be a good indicator of the general level of physiological arousal." This measure required simply that the subject place his hand deep in a tray of powdered graphite and then leave a palm print on a specially prepared sheet of paper—a bit of fol-de-rol designed only to get the subject's hand so dirty that he had to wash up in the men's room where an observer noted whether or not the subject used the urinal. Returned from the washroom, the subject was taken to a large room and was seated at a desk to fill out a final questionnaire. Next to the desk stood a large water cooler. An observer seated at a desk in a distant part of the room noted whether or not the subject drank and, if he did, how many cups.

This experiment, then, manipulated the amount of water a subject drank and measured the extent to which external cues—a urinal and a water cooler—evoked the appropriate responses. The subjects were all male undergraduates at Columbia. The obese group ranged from 20%–79% overweight. Normal subjects varied from 7% underweight to 10% overweight.

The Effects of Water Preloading on Urination

It is reasonable to assume that one hour after drinking 20 ounces (2 large glasses) of water, the intensity of the physiological correlates associated with the need to urinate will be greater than they will be one hour after drinking 2 ounces of water. If our findings on the external and internal control of eating generalize to the bodily state associated with the concentration of urine in the bladder, it should be anticipated that there will be an interaction between weight deviation and urination. Preloading should have relatively little effect on obese subjects while normal subjects should be more likely to urinate after drinking 20 ounces than after drinking 2 ounces of water. Further, in the presence of the host of external cues associated with a men's room, fat subjects should generally be more likely to urinate than normal subjects.

The data are presented in Table 47, where it can be seen that the preloading manipulation has no differential effect on the two groups of subjects. Both groups urinate about the same amount and both groups are slightly more likely to urinate after drinking 20 ounces than after drinking 2 ounces of water. There are flatly no indications that urination parallels the findings on eating.

The relatively low frequency of urination for any of the experimental groups is rather surprising, but is probably explained by the fact that the experimental

TABLE 47   THE EFFECTS OF WATER PRELOADING ON URINATION

Subjects	Preloading	N	Percent Ss who urinate
Obese	2 ounces	12	8.3
Obese	20 ounces	10	20.0
Normal	2 ounces	12	16.7
Normal	20 ounces	10	20.0

procedure virtually forced a subject to wash his hands before urinating—certainly a reversal of the customary sequence. It is conceivable that this may have so inhibited urination as to obscure differences between the two groups of subjects. With this one qualification, a conclusion of no difference between obese and normal subjects seems reasonable.

The Effects of Preloading on Drinking

If drinking parallels eating behavior, we should again anticipate an interaction between weight deviation, relative deprivation, and drinking. The data are reported in Table 48, which presents the proportion of subjects in each condition who helped themselves when in the presence of the water cooler. It is evident that the pattern of findings do not yield any indications that the obese are more sensitive to external water-related cues and normals to internal cues. Indeed there is a distinct trend in the opposite direction, for 50% of the obese subjects who preloaded on 2 ounces of water drank from the cooler, while not a single one of the 20-ounce obese subjects did so ($p < .05$). There is no such trend for normal subjects.

Though I doubt that this is, by any means, the last word on the subject, the evidence so far indicates that the relative reliance on external rather than internal cues that characterizes the eating behavior of the obese is specific to eating behavior. There are no indications that this differential sensitivity generalizes to either drinking or urination.

TABLE 48   THE EFFECTS OF WATER PRELOADING ON DRINKING

Subjects	Preloading	N	Percent Ss who drank
Obese	2 ounces	12	50.0
Obese	20 ounces	10	0.0
Normal	2 ounces	12	16.7
Normal	20 ounces	10	20.0

Part III

Crime and the Autonomic Nervous System

The experiments reported in the next two chapters were first described several years ago by Schachter and Latané (1964). These studies examine implications, for criminal behavior, of the proposition offered in Chapter I that under specified cognitive circumstances, "the individual will react emotionally or describe his feelings as emotions only to the extent that he experiences a state of physiological arousal." From my present point of view, these are maddening studies—the results are fascinating and potentially of social importance. The results are also, in many spots, tentative, and the analyses sometimes suffer the imprint of someone convinced that he's right and willing to force his data to prove it. These experiments should have been the beginning of a program of research. They are, instead, the beginning and the end.

I suppose that anyone stupid enough to attempt to go through the routine channels of New York City's bureaucracy deserves little sympathy. In any case, when I moved from the University of Minnesota, where this research began, to Columbia University, I intended to continue this work in the local prisons and petitioned the city's Department of Correction for permission to do so. This amiable organization, devoted to the idea, if not, as it developed, to the execution of research, could hardly have been more helpful and encouraging, and for eight months my assistants and I worked in the prisons selecting subjects, pretesting experimental designs, and generally preparing for a program of research on the biological and psychological correlates of criminal psychopathy. Meanwhile, our proposal had apparently been travelling casually through the upper levels of the Department of Correction, where a lawyer, overwhelmed by the possibility of municipal liability, vetoed the project and that was that. Disgusted by the loss of time and labor, and reluctant to repeat these preliminary efforts in another city's prison system, I simply dropped the project.

Chapter XII

Chlorpromazine and Cheating

The study of crime is an immensely complex affair involving the combined armament of law, sociology, economics, psychology, and psychiatry, but the act of committing a crime can itself be reduced to the simplest of terms. Owing to some specific set of circumstances, an impulse to some antisocial act is generated. Driven by hunger, a pauper considers stealing; a desire for revenge leads to thoughts of murder; a boy's dare may lead to a broken store window. Whether or not such an antisocial impulse will be inhibited or will result in a crime depends, of course, on a multitude of factors—some situational, some psychological. Of the battery of restraints which can inhibit such an impulse, I shall focus on a single source of restraint—fear. Other things constant, the greater the fear or anxiety, the less the likelihood that an antisocial impulse will be acted on. In and of itself, this proposition is banal and self-evident. Let us, however, consider the implications of recent work on emotion and fear for the study of the criminal act.

In the series of studies described earlier, exploring the interaction of cognitive and physiological determinants of emotional state, it has been proposed that an emotion be considered a function of a state of physiological arousal and of cognitions appropriate to this state of arousal. Given specified cognitive conditions, an individual will react emotionally or describe his feelings as emotions only to the extent that he experiences a state of physiological arousal. In order to test this proposition, the experiments described in the first three chapters of this book manipulated arousal by the use of autonomic drugs—a class of pharmacological agents whose actions either mimic or, to some extent, block the action of components of the autonomic nervous system. In one of these studies, Schachter and Singer (Chapter I) demonstrated that in experimental situations designed to make subjects euphoric, those subjects who were injected with epinephrine were more euphoric than were subjects injected with placebo. Similarly, in situations designed to make subjects angry, those who received epinephrine were angrier than subjects who received placebo. Schachter and Wheeler (Chapter II), testing reactions to a slapstick movie, extended the range of manipulated activation by use of epinephrine, placebo, and the mildly sympatholytic drug chlorpromazine. Laughter at the movie was the dependent variable, and the evidence is good that amusement is a direct function of manipulated sympathetic arousal.

In tests of the relationship of activation to fear (Chapter III) Singer demonstrated that under fear-inducing conditions, manipulated by simultaneous presentation of a buzzer, a bell, and a flashing light, rats injected with epinephrine were considerably more frightened than were placebo-injected rats who, in turn, were more frightened than rats injected with chlorpromazine. In nonfear control conditions there were no differences among the three drug conditions. In another study related to fear, Latané and Schachter (1962) showed that rats injected with small doses of epinephrine were markedly more capable of avoidance learning than were rats injected with placebo.

It is clear from this body of studies that fear, as well as a variety of other emotions, can be manipulated in both rats and human subjects by the manipulation of physiological arousal. Returning now to consideration of the criminal act, the implications of these studies of emotion are straightforward. Given a criminal impulse, given the existence of restraining, fear-inducing conditions, the likelihood that a crime will occur can be manipulated by the manipulation of sympathetic activation. If this reasoning is correct, it should be possible experimentally to encourage crime by the use of sympatholytic drugs and to discourage it with sympathomimetic agents.

This chapter and the next will be devoted to a description of studies designed to test these notions; first, an experiment on the effects of chlorpromazine on cheating and, second, a study of the effects of epinephrine on the criminal sociopath.

Chlorpromazine and Cheating

Though hardly a major crime, that prevalent academic offense—cheating—is an excellent example of an act involving all of the elements of crime outlined above. In an atmosphere where grades and examinations are heavily stressed it is likely that cheating is a virtually omnipresent temptation. It is held in check, in part, by the severity of the penalties imposed on a cheater who is caught. At best, he faces an official reprimand and warning; at worst, he is expelled.

Whether or not a specific individual will cheat and when depends, of course, on a collage of factors such as his moral code, the importance of the examination, the closeness of proctoring, and the like. Granting the importance of all such factors, if we assume that they are held constant or, in an experimental situation, effectively randomized, we can hypothesize that cheating will vary inversely with the fear of being caught. If, then, we can manipulate the physiological component of fear, we should at the same time manipulate the likelihood of cheating. To test this expectation, Hiroshi Ono and I conducted the following study.

Procedure

The general sequence of the experiment involved having subjects first take a brief but important examination; second, undergo manipulation of physiological arousal under the guise of a presumed study of the effects of vitamins (chlorpromazine or placebo) on perception and, finally, while under the influence of the drug, have the opportunity to cheat by themselves grading the examination they had taken. This chain of events was staged in the following fashion. When a group of 6–8 subjects, girls enrolled in the second semester of an introductory psychology course, had gathered, the experimenter began:

> Today we are going to be doing two short experiments which together will take a little over an hour. One of these will be a study of perception and the other will be a special study that the psychology department is conducting as a means of evaluating their course material, the text used, and the method of lecturing. As you know, it's a common stereotype that what you learn in a course at college you forget rather quickly. "In one ear and out the other," or at least "out the other" once the final is over. Now no one is really sure that this is true, but to the extent that it is true, it is obviously a rather disturbing thing for a department, for, believe it or not, your professors really do work hard at their courses.

> The Psychology Department wants to find out how well the material it teaches is remembered once the heat is off and you no longer have to worry about a final. All of you here today have taken Psychology 1, you've taken the exam, you've passed it, and the course is by now a couple of months behind you. One of the questions we are interested in is, "How well do you remember the material from Psychology 1?"

> Now, obviously, how well you remember the material will depend on many factors—how well you prepared originally, how long a time since you took the course, and, possibly most important, how motivated you are to remember.

The experimenter then explained that this study was concerned with the effects of motivation on memory, that this group was fortunate enough to be in the high motivation condition, and that,

> If you, as highly motivated subjects, do well on this exam, you will have extra points added to the grade you get on your final exam in Psychology 2. The

number of points added to the grade you get on your final exam will depend on how well you do on this exam.

He then went on to describe a scoring procedure whereby, depending on how well they did, they could have as many as six extra points (sufficient to change a high C to an A grade) added to their final grade. The subjects then took the examination; the experimenter collected their answer sheets, laid them aside, and continued:

> The second experiment we are doing today is concerned with perception. We have been working on a long-range study to find out the exact effects of the new vitamin called Suproxin. Today, we are studying the effect of Suproxin on perception. We are now interested in the question, " Does this vitamin actually help us perceive better and more accurately?"
>
> For you to take part in this experiment, you have to take a Suproxin pill. It is perfectly harmless—we have given it to many people with no harmful results. Of course, we can't force it down your throat—so it is up to you whether or not to participate in this experiment. If you are willing to go ahead, here is some water and the pills. (All subjects agreed to take part.)

Having taken the pills, the subjects then were exposed to fifty-five minutes of invented scientific-appearing activity designed only to fill the minimum time that pretests had indicated was necessary for orally administered chlorpromazine to take effect. During this portion of the experiment, which required darkening the experimental room, an assistant, unseen by the subjects, quietly removed the answer sheets, made copies, and returned them.

In the last ten minutes of the pseudo-experimental session, the experimenter handed round questionnaires designed, in part, to assess the effects of chlorpromazine, and took the subjects' pulses. Then, in order to set up the opportunity to cheat, he said:

> I would like to thank you for participating in this experiment. But before I leave, I would like to ask a small favor. I have an appointment and must run, but I am giving that Psychology 1 test you took to about 300 students—and it's not that I have anything against the Psychology Department or anything—but I'm afraid that I might get stuck with scoring 300 of them. So could you help me out and mark your own paper?

While handing back the exam sheets, the experimenter explained the scoring key which he had written on the blackboard and told the subjects, "When you are through with scoring your own exam, please put the number of correct answers on the top of your answer sheet." He continued with a plea to subjects not to talk about the examination to students who had not yet been in the experiment. Then saying, "When you are finished with scoring the test, leave it in your booth. I'll pick them up later," the experimenter left the room.

Inducing Cheating

The examination that all subjects took was a 30-item multiple-choice test consisting entirely of questions taken from the text used in the first semester of the two-semester course in which these students were enrolled. The students were each provided with a copy of the examination and a separate answer sheet on which they circled in pencil the correct alternative for each item. Two precautions were taken to insure that each subject would have ample opportunity to cheat should she choose to do so. First, the test was too long for most of the subjects to complete within the eleven-minute time interval. Only 34.9% of the subjects managed to answer all 30 items. Second, 6 of the 30 items on the scoring key that the experimenter provided were miskeyed so that one of the wrong answers to a question was scored as correct. Using this key, subjects' scores on the examination ranged from 5–18 "correct" answers.

Throughout the entire course of the experiment, the subjects were seated in a row of individual booths partitioned so that no subject would see any other subject. Thus, each subject both took and scored her examination in complete privacy.

Manipulating and Measuring Sympathetic Activation

Immediately after taking the examination, half of the subjects in each group took a 35 mg oral dose of chlorpromazine, and half took a 35 mg placebo pill. The sympatholytic effects of chlorpromazine have been described in Chapter II. Relevant to the present experiment is the fact that previous work with animals (e.g., Singer, 1963; Verhave, Owen, & Slater, 1958) has demonstrated that it is an effective fear-reducing agent.

In order to determine for each subject whether or not chlorpromazine was having a physiological effect, two sorts of measures were taken immediately before the announcement about grading examinations. First, subjects answered the two questions on dehydration which, in Schachter and Wheeler's study (Chapter II), had proven particularly effective in discriminating those injected with chlorpromazine from those injected with placebo. These questions were concerned with mouth dryness and nose stuffiness.

As the second measure of the effects of chlorpromazine, pulse was taken twice: first, immediately after the subjects had swallowed the pill and while they were filling out a brief questionnaire and, second, approximately 55 minutes after swallowing the pill and before the announcement about grading the examination.

Subjects

The subjects were all girls recruited from the subject pool of students enrolled in the second semester of the introductory course in psychology at the University of Minnesota. The records of all potential subjects were cleared with the Student Health Service in order to insure that no difficulties would result from the administration of chlorpromazine.

Results

Physiological Effects of Chlorpromazine

Before the experiment proper was run, a series of pretests was conducted on the effects of various dosages of orally administered chlorpromazine on blood pressure, pulse rate, and self-report of dehydration. The results of these pretests forced us to a compromise dose. Though larger doses than the 35 mg dose finally chosen had moderately strong effects, they also had the unfortunate delayed side effect of acting as intense soporifics. With doses of 100, or even 50 mg, several pretest subjects had grown extremely sleepy several hours after oral administration. Since we were unwilling to put up with recriminations from girls who had fallen asleep on dates, or to write excuses for those who had been unable to study for examinations, we were forced to adopt the smaller dose despite the fact that its effects on our several dependent measures were relatively weak. Indeed, for a few pretest subjects, there appeared to be no effects at all.

Given this background, let us examine the effects of chlorpromazine on our experimental subjects. Table 49 presents the basic data on the three indices of the effectiveness of chlorpromazine. It will be noted that the two groups do not differ on dryness of mouth, but do differ on self-report of nose stuffiness and pulse change.[1]

For comparison purposes, Table 50 reports the results on identical measures of a 25 mg intra-muscular injection of chlorpromazine. These figures are from the Schachter-Wheeler (1962) study in which the data were collected approximately

---

[1] Since the two groups differ in initial pulse rate, it should be noted that this alone cannot explain the pulse change differences. Controlling for this initial difference, we note that placebo subjects whose initial rate was 80 or more beats per minute decreased an average of 7.24 beats; similarly high chlorpromazine subjects decreased 5.28 beats, a difference significant by a median test at the .04 level. Placebo subjects whose initial rate was 79 or less decreased 4.06 beats per minute, while similar chlorpromazine subjects decreased 0.26 beats, a difference significant at the .03 level. For subjects with either high or low intitial pulse rate, chlorpromazine has had an effect.

TABLE 49 THE PHYSIOLOGICAL EFFECTS OF CHLORPROMAZINE

Condition	N	Mouth dry	Nose stuffy	Pulse		Pulse change
				First meas.	Second meas.	
Chlorpromazine	66	0.45	0.70	76.9	74.6	−2.3
Placebo	66	0.44	0.47	80.2	74.5	−5.7
p value		n.s.	.06			< .01

TABLE 50 THE EFFECTS OF CHLORPROMAZINE
IN THE SCHACHTER–WHEELER (1962) EXPERIMENT

Condition	N	Mouth dry	Nose stuffy	Pulse		Pulse change
				Preinjection	Postinjection	
Chlorpromazine	46	1.12	2.16	81.4	86.0	+4.6
Placebo	42	0.30	0.68	78.7	75.5	−3.2
p		< .001	< .001			< .001

one-half hour after the injection. Comparing the data for chlorpromazine in the two tables, it is immediately evident that the effects of the oral administration have been considerably weaker than those of the injection. Considering the absolute level of the scores on the several measures, it is quite clear that orally administered chlorpromazine has had only weak effects relative to placebo. This weak effect will compel us to examine separately the data on cheating for those subjects on whom the drug had physiological effects, and for those on whom it had no effect.

Chlorpromazine and Cheating

Cheating is defined as the deliberate changing of an examination so as to increase the score. As an unequivocal index, cheating refers to any instance of erasing or crossing out an answer and replacing it with the correct answer, or of answering a question that had been left blank when the examination was first taken. By these criteria 30.3% of all chlorpromazine subjects cheated, and 19.7% of placebo subjects cheated. By chi-square test this difference is significant at slightly better than the .20 level of confidence. The relationship, then, is in the predicted direction, but quite weak.

It has been noted, however, that the drug manipulation was weak, several of the subjects giving no indication that, within the time limits of the experiment, chlorpromazine had had any physiological effects at all. Let us then examine separately the cheating behavior of those subjects on whom chlorpromazine had an effect, for only these are the subjects for whom the manipulation worked. As indicators of the effectiveness of chlorpromazine, we relied on the two measures which discriminate between placebo and chlorpromazine subjects—the pulse change and stuffiness measures. If a chlorpromazine subject indicated that she felt any degree of stuffiness, this was accepted as one indication that the drug had an effect. For the pulse change data, the distribution of pulse changes of chlorpromazine subjects was split at the median. If the pulse rate increased, remained the same, or decreased by two or fewer beats per minute, this was considered an indication that chlorpromazine had an effect. Subjects who reported absolutely no stuffiness and whose pulse decreased by three or more beats per minute were considered cases on whom chlorpromazine had no effect at all. It should be noted that 24.2% of all chlorpromazine subjects were high on both criteria compared to only 7.6% of placebo subjects. Similarly 27.3% of all chlorpromazine subjects are low on both criteria as compared with 47.0% of placebo subjects. These criteria do distinguish between subjects who have taken chlorpromazine and those who have taken placebo.

In Table 51 are presented the data on cheating for the three groups of subjects—those on whom chlorpromazine had an effect, those on whom it had no effect, and placebo subjects. Twice the proportion of subjects on whom chlorpromazine had an effect cheat as compared with placebo subjects. Some 40% of the subjects on whom the drug works cheated; only 20% of placebo subjects did so—a difference significant, by chi-square test, at the .02 level of confidence.[2] The difference between those subjects on whom chlorpromazine had been effective and those on whom it had no effect is significant at the .03

TABLE 51   THE EFFECTS OF CHLORPROMAZINE
ON CHEATING

Condition	N	Percent cheaters
Chlorpromazine effective	48	39.6
Chlorpromazine ineffective	18	5.6
Placebo	66	19.7

[2] Since this effect has been demonstrated only by use of an internal analysis of the data, it is necessary to make a similar analysis of placebo subjects in order to determine if chlorpromazine is indeed responsible for cheating, or if these data simply reflect a tendency for subjects with high pulse rates and stuffy noses to cheat. Though, interestingly enough, in terms of data presented in the following chapter, there is a slight tendency in this direction, this factor cannot account for these trends. Placebo subjects with high pulse rates or stuffy noses cheat considerably less than similar chlorpromazine subjects.

level; the difference between placebo subjects and those for whom chlorpromazine was ineffective is not significant. It does appear that chlorpromazine, when
physiologically effective, facilitates cheating—a finding which opens new
interpretive possibilities for the frequent student observation that taking
tranquilizers improves performance on examinations.

Chapter XIII

Criminal Sociopathy, Epinephrine, and Avoidance Learning

Though cheating is a gentle crime, the principles involved in this demonstration of the manipulability of cheating are easily adaptable to more brutal and sinister areas. Let us extend our introductory consideration of the nature of the criminal act by making a distinction between crimes committed because motivation or passion reach overwhelming dimensions and those committed because the deterrents are feeble. Hate can reach such a festering pitch that no deterrent can contain it. Hunger can become such a consuming appetite that no fear of the consequences can prevent stealing. Alternatively, the deterrents, such as fear, may be so very weak that a crime will be committed whether the motivation is high or low. Following this rough distinction, one should find in the prisons, inmates who, at some point in their lives, driven by circumstances, have lost all control of their impulses, and other prisoners who are there because their anxiety about, or fear of, the consequences of being caught was low. If it is assumed that such lack of fear can be a chronic, abiding characteristic, we should find in this latter group the type known to the clinicians as the psychopath or the sociopath.

This type, the sociopath, is generally characterized by the psychiatrists as the classic bad boy. Incorrigible, the sociopath is presumed, from childhood on, to get into one antisocial scrape after another. This chronic antisocial behavior has been labeled by Prichard (1835) as "moral imbecility."

In probably the most extensive psychiatric treatment of this condition, Cleckley (1955) suggests general affective poverty as the chief characteristic of the sociopath. To quote Cleckley directly:

The opinion here maintained is that the psychopath fails to know all those more serious and deeply moving affective states which make up the tragedy and triumph of ordinary life, of life at the level of human personality ... no normal person is so unevolved, no ordinary criminal so generally unresponsive and distorted, but that he seems to experience satisfaction, love, hate, grief, a general participation in life at human personality levels, much more intense and more substantial than the affective reactions of the psychopath. (p. 427).

Though the sociopath experiences only "the ghostly facsimiles of emotion or pseudo-emotion" he does, following Cleckley, learn to mimic appropriate affective responses. " ... he will learn to reproduce appropriately all the pantomime of feeling but, as Sherrington said of the decerebrated animal, the feeling itself does not come to pass."

To convey some feel for this sort of person, I shall quote from the case of Roberta, one of the many case histories in Cleckley's book. Roberta, a young woman with an I.Q. of 135, was twenty years old when she first became one of Cleckley's patients. To set the stage, I quote first from one of Cleckley's discussions with the girl's father.

"I can't understand the girl, no matter how hard I try," said the father shaking his head in genuine perplexity. "It's not that she seems bad or exactly that she means to do wrong. She can lie with the straightest face, and after she's found in the most outlandish lies she still seems perfectly easy in her own mind."

Roberta was a frequent truant and during school hours she wandered

through shops stealing a few things for which she seemed to have neither need nor specific desire. She did not seem to be activated by any "compulsive" desire emerging against a struggle to resist. On the contrary, she proceeded calmly and casually in these acts. She experienced no great thrill or consummation in a theft nor found in it relief from uncomfortable stress.

The girl was apparently fond of animals. "Yet when her own dog was killed by an automobile she showed only the most fleeting and superficial signs of concern."

Her experiences with sex vividly convey the "ghostly facsimiles of emotion." In her initiation into sex, we find the girl sitting in a hotel lobby:

Soon she was approached by a middle-aged man. He was far from prepossessing, smelt of cheap liquor, and his manners were distinctly distasteful. He soon offered to pay for her overnight accommodations at the hotel. She realized that he meant to share the bed with her but made no objection. As well as one can tell by discussing this experience with Roberta, she was neither excited, frightened, repulsed nor attracted by a prospect that most carefully brought up virgins would certainly have regarded with anything but indifference .... Despite extensive promiscuity since that time she has never experienced a sharp and distinguishable orgasm or found sexual relations in any way a major pleasure or temptation. Nor has she felt any of the frustration and unrelieved tension so familiar in some women who are aroused but left unsatisfied. (pp. 75–76).

So much for Roberta. Her case is a typical one. It would appear, then, that the psychiatrists have identified a class of people who are characterized by chronic misbehavior and by marked emotional flatness. In terms of our previous reasoning the link between these characteristics seems clear-cut. If anxiety or fear is chronically low or absent, one of the major deterrents of antisocial behavior is absent.

In a brilliant study, Lykken (1955, 1957) first tested the relationship of anxiety to criminal sociopathy. Following Cleckley's general characterization, Lykken assumes that sociopaths are "defective in their ability to develop anxiety in the sense of an anticipatory emotional response to warning signals previously associated with nociceptive stimulation." (Lykken, 1955, p. 91.) They should, therefore, "show abnormally little manifest anxiety in circumstances ordinarily conducive to this response," and "be relatively incapable of avoidance learning where such learning can only be effected through the mediation of the anxiety response."

To test these hypotheses, Lykken selected matched groups of criminal sociopaths (a group he calls "primary sociopaths"), of nonsociopathic criminals (a group he calls "neurotic sociopaths"), and of normals. He ran his subjects through a series of test situations, some psychometric, some physiological, some experimental, and demonstrated convincingly that sociopaths are relatively anxiety free. Testing his hypothesis about avoidance learning, Lykken found that his criminal sociopaths were virtually incapable of learning to avoid a painful stimulus, while normals readily learned.

Let us, at this point, tie together the several lines of thought which have guided this chapter.

1. The psychiatrists have identified a class of persons who are characterized by their chronic misbehavior and marked emotional flatness. For the state of anxiety at least, Lykken has experimentally verified the relatively anxiety-free nature of the criminal sociopath.

2. A body of experimental studies has demonstrated that any of a variety of emotional states, including fear and anxiety, can be manipulated via the manipulation of sympathetic activation.

3. The experiment on chlorpromazine and cheating has demonstrated that even a weak sympatholytic agent facilitates cheating.

Given this assortment of facts, one begins to wonder about sympathetic activation and the sociopath, and an experiment immediately suggests itself—the replication of Lykken's work using the sympathomimetic agent, epinephrine.

Epinephrine, Sociopathy, and Avoidance Learning

This experiment is a replication, in part, of just one facet of Lykken's work—the experimental test of the ability of criminal subjects to avoid pain.

Lykken accepts the well-known proposition that anxiety reduction is a key mediator in learning to avoid pain and reasons that anxiety-free people should be relatively incapable of learning to avoid pain. The derivation is supported by his data.

In essence, Schachter and Latané (1964) repeated Lykken's comparison of sociopathic and nonsociopathic prisoners, and added only one new twist. Each subject was tested twice—once with an injection of placebo and once with an injection of epinephrine.

Procedure

The Selection of Subjects

The source of subjects for this study of criminals was the Minnesota State Prison at Stillwater and the Bordentown Reformatory of New Jersey. The Stillwater prison is the maximum security prison of the state of Minnesota and houses largely chronic criminals with long records, difficult cases promoted from lesser security jails, and first-time offenders guilty of particularly serious offenses such as murder. The Bordentown Reformatory services a similar segment of the younger criminal set of New Jersey. Given these potential populations of subjects, the attempt to distinguish sociopathic from nonsociopathic criminals was guided entirely by the line of thought developed by Cleckley and Lykken which focusses on chronic misbehavior and emotional flatness, or lack of affect, as the dominant characteristics of the sociopath.

Nomination by Prison Psychologists and Case Workers. As a first step in locating potential subjects we followed precisely the procedure employed by Lykken. Prison psychologists and case workers were each provided with a detailed description of a Cleckley-type sociopath and asked to nominate both prisoners who fit the description closely and prisoners who did not. The description was simply a listing of the major criteria suggested by Cleckley as characteristic of the sociopath. Each nominator received the following list of criteria with a brief elaboration appended to each:

1. Average or superior intelligence.
2. Free from irrationality and other commonly accepted symptoms of psychosis.
3. Free from any marked nervousness or other common symptoms of psychoneurosis.
4. No sense of responsibility.
5. Disregard for truth.

6. No sense of shame.
7. Antisocial behavior without apparent compunction.
8. Inability to learn from experience.
9. General poverty of affect.
10. Lack of genuine·insight.
11. Little response to special consideration or kindness.
12. No history of sincere attempts at suicide.
13. Sex life shows peculiarities (weak sex-craving, regard sex casually).
14. Onset of psychopathic characteristics no later than early twenties.

From the resulting list of nominees, all subjects were automatically eliminated whose health records were such that an injection of adrenaline might have been dangerous, or whose I.Q.'s were below 100. (Since the experimental task involved a rather complicated learning routine, a particularly obtuse subject might have been working away at the task long after the effects of adrenaline had worn off.) In order to select the most appropriate subjects from the remaining list of potential subjects, our next step was to go intensively through each nominee's case history searching for indications that the above description was or was not apt. The chief guidepost employed in studying these case histories was the search for indications of emotionality. Examples of such screening would be the following: a sociopathic nominee who was imprisoned because in a jealous rage he beat up his girl friend would be eliminated as a potential subject; a sociopathic nominee who on his entry interview is described as "crying and extremely anxious" would also be eliminated; a nominee for the normal group who was described by several interviewers as "cold-blooded" or "emotionless" would also be eliminated as a potential subject.

Our initial step, then, in the assignment of subjects to experimental groups, was the nomination of potential subjects by the people within the prison who knew the men best. It should be noted that though this was only a first step in this study, Lykken's original study was based entirely on this selection procedure. The reasons for this discrepancy in procedure are twofold. First, we were able to build on Lykken's work by using measurement devices which he demonstrated discriminated between nominated sociopaths and normals. Second, the prisons in which we worked were both considerably larger than those in which Lykken collected data. In one of our prisons, the prisoner-caseworker load was so heavy that a caseworker could see each prisoner for approximately one hour each nine months. Given such limited contact, neither we nor the nominators felt particularly confident about relying solely on the nomination technique, and multiple criteria were, therefore, used in assigning subjects to experimental groups. This initial step provided, first, a potential supply of subjects and, second, a screening along the dimension of emotional flatness. As a second criterion of emotional flatness we used a psychometric device developed by Lykken.

The Lykken Scale. As one of the tests of his hypothesis that sociopaths are relatively anxiety-free, Lykken designed a 33-item scale on which, for each item, the subject must choose between two activities or events, both of which are unpleasant. One of the activities is unpleasant because it is anxiety arousing (e.g., "Having an accident with a borrowed car," or "Knocking over a glass in a restaurant"), and the other because it is distasteful or tedious (e.g., "Cleaning out a cess-pool," or "Cleaning up a spilled bottle of syrup"). Presumably, the emotionally flat, anxiety-free sociopath should choose more of the anxiety-arousing alternatives. In both Lykken's study and in the two prisons of the present study, this scale discriminated between nominated sociopaths and normals.

These, then, were the procedures for selecting subjects along the dimension of emotional flatness. In order to select along the dimension of chronic misbehavior, two criteria were employed: the number of offenses, and the time in prison. F.B.I., police, and imprisonment records provide, of course, the obvious source for indices of incorrigibility. Presumably, the more sociopathic a prisoner, the longer will be his history of arrest and convictions, and the more time he will have spent in jail.

The Number of Offenses. Each offense for which an individual was arrested without having the charge dismissed was considered an indication of antisocial behavior. No attempt was made to distinguish the seriousness of the charge, and the total number of offenses is considered as an index of incorrigibility. Given this basic datum, it is possible, of course, to construct more elaborate indices which correct the number of offenses for age, opportunity, etc. It should be noted that all such indices we have attempted intercorrelate so highly that they make virtually no difference in the classification of subjects.

Imprisonment Time. Though sheer number of arrests would seem an ideally simple index, the records from which such an index was constructed seemed sufficiently unreliable and noncomparable from subject to subject (in part depending on a prisoner's self-report, in part on the idiosyncracies of a reporting agency, and in part on the compassions and malices of local police agencies) to warrant an additional index of incorrigibility. Such an index was constructed by computing the proportion of a prisoner's life since the age of nine (the youngest age at which any of our subjects had been imprisoned) spent in jail. These imprisonment records seem relatively trustworthy and comparable from prisoner to prisoner. Though we assume that the more time in jail, the greater the incorrigibility, to some extent the index weighs both frequency and seriousness of crime. The two indices of incorrigibility correlate with rho = +.54 in the Stillwater jail and +.28 in the Bordentown Reformatory.

We have, then, four indices which are coordinated to the two major characteristics of the Cleckley-Lykken sociopath—emotional flatness and incorrigibility. Subjects were classified for degree of sociopathy according to their positions on each of these indices. On the Lykken scale and the two indices of incorrigibility, a subject was considered high in sociopathy if his score fell above the median of the distribution of experimental subjects within his prison. Obviously, if a subject was nominated as a sociopath and this nomination was corroborated by the screening of his case study, he was considered, on this criterion, high in sociopathy. A prisoner who is high on three or four of these criteria was classified as a sociopathic subject; a prisoner who is high on none or one criteria was classified as a normal subject; and a prisoner who is high on two of these four criteria was considered a mixed subject.

It should be noted that this was, in part, an ad hoc assignment of subjects—a procedure necessitated by the routines of prison life and office procedure which in many cases made it flatly impossible to get all of the criterion data before the experiment proper was scheduled to run. Given this fact of life, our procedure was to make an initial assignment of subjects which was based on nominations, the screening of case histories, and on whatever other data were available for a particular prisoner. In this initial assignment we attempted to match the sociopathic and normal groups man for man on I.Q. and age (variables which conceivably could interact with the effect of adrenaline or the quickness of learning).

Once this initial assignment of subjects had been made, the experiment proper was run. Missing criterion data were gathered in the course of or on completion of the experiment and, on the basis of the completed body of criterion data, the subjects were finally assigned to their experimental classification. Though the initial plan of study called for only the two extreme classifications of subjects, this final classification inevitably yielded a number of subjects who were high on just two of the four criteria of sociopathy—a group destined to be labeled "Mixed." The characteristics of the three groups of subjects are presented in Table 52. On all criteria except the Lykken scale score, the three groups fall neatly along a "dimension" of sociopathy. On the characteristics for which we attempted to match the groups, age, and I.Q., the sociopathic and normal groups match quite closely, but the mixed group is considerably younger than either of the other groups. These discrepancies may account for the high Lykken scale score of the mixed group. In any case, the fact that the mixed group is so very much younger than either of the other groups does make its comparability somewhat tenuous. In later sections, although data will be presented for all three groups, we shall, because of these differences, concentrate on comparison of the sociopathic and normal groups.

The final column appended to Table 52—the proportion of subjects in each classification who have, at some time, attempted to escape from jail—can

TABLE 52 CHARACTERISTICS OF THE SUBJECTS

Group	N	Percent nominated as sociopath	Lykken scale score	Number of offenses	Percent of adult life in jail	Age	IQ (AGCT)	Percent attempting escapes
Sociopath	15	100	14.0	8.3	36.2	28.4	120.7	33.3
Mixed	10	40	14.8	6.4	21.2	21.4	115.4	20.0
Normal	15	0	10.3	3.3	18.1	29.2	117.5	0

possibly be interpreted, since no account was taken of this datum in the classification of subjects, as additional evidence for our characterization of the sociopath. If we make the reasonable assumption that attempting to escape from jail requires some degree of fearlessness, the fact that 33% of the sociopaths, 20% of the mixed group, and 0% of the normals have attempted escapes, could be interpreted as evidence that these groups do differ in the degree to which they are anxiety-free. Obviously this interpretation must be tempered by the fact that these groups differ in the amount of time they have spent in jail. It is the case, however, that most of these attempted escapes were made rather early in the subjects' careers, and differential opportunity cannot wholly account for these differences.

Measuring Avoidance Learning

The chief experimental problem involved in testing the relationship of anxiety to avoidance learning is that of restricting the effects of motivations other than anxiety. The demonstration that subjects can differentially learn to avoid painful stimuli is of little consequence for present concerns if such learning can be explained by higher order need satisfactions such as social approval or self-administered ego rewards. The proper test requires a situation in which anxiety is the only motive relevant to making an avoidance response. Lykken's solution to this problem was to make the avoidance task "incidental" to another simultaneous "manifest" task to which the subject could direct all his ego-serving needs. In essence, the subject was placed in an experimental situation where, at one and the same time, measures were taken of his ability to learn a reinforced task on which his attention was concentrated and an avoidance task which was structured so as to seem completely incidental to the learning of the reinforced task.

The test apparatus consisted of a metal cabinet on which was mounted a counter, two pilot lights, and four switches.[1] It was internally programed in such

[1] I wish to thank Dr. David Lykken for providing us with his original apparatus.

a way as to constitute a complicated mental maze. There were twenty choice-points in the maze; at each choice-point the subject could advance to the next choice-point only by pressing an arbitrarily correct switch. When the subject pressed the correct switch a green light flashed and with the sound of relays the machine moved to the next choice-point. If the subject pressed one of the three incorrect switches, the machine did not advance and an error accumulated on a counter that the subject could see. The subject was instructed to get through the maze with the fewest possible errors and was given twenty-one runs through the maze. The sequence of switches defined as correct was, of course, the same for each of these runs. At the end of each run the machine was reset to the starting point, and the number of errors was recorded as the score on the manifest task. The avoidance task was superimposed upon the manifest task by punishing certain errors with an electric shock. At each choice-point, one of the three incorrect switches was arbitrarily programed to deliver a moderately painful electric shock through a pair of electrodes attached to the fingers of the subject's left hand.[2] At the end of every run through the maze, the number of errors made by the subject and the number of shocks delivered to him were recorded. (The latter measure was recorded secretly.)

By judiciously selecting his errors, a subject could avoid the electric shock. No indication was given in the instructions, however, that this was desirable or even possible, as the use of the shock was justified as an additional and randomly administered stimulant to do well on the manifest task. During the instructions and administration of the test, the subject's attention was focused entirely on the manifest or positively reinforced task of learning the correct path through the maze. The experiment was set in the framework of a test of learning ability requiring intelligence. At the end of each run, unless it was completely ludicrous to do so, the subject was praised for his performance and generally encouraged.

Manipulating Sympathetic Activation

The degree of sympathetic arousal was manipulated by the injection, immediately before the subject started on the experimental apparatus, of

[2] The shock was a brief pulse of current (with a peak voltage during the pulse of 430 volts at about 10 mA) produced by a discharge of a high voltage condenser. During the course of an experimental session, the current was increased every five trials in order to minimize adaptation effects. A questionnaire answered by all subjects at the end of the experimental hour included two questions designed to learn how painful these shocks were. These questions were "How painful did the shocks seem to you?" and "How annoying did you find the shocks to be?" Both questions were accompanied by 5-point scales ranging from "Not at all" to "Extremely." On these two scales, the mean points checked by both the sociopathic and normal groups correspond closely to the "Somewhat painful" and "Somewhat annoying" points of these scales. By these measures, at least, there are no significant differences in the degree of pain experienced by the two groups of subjects.

placebo or of the sympathomimetic agent, epinephrine. In the placebo condition, each subject received a subcutaneous injection of ½ ml of physiological saline solution. In the epinephrine condition, subjects received an intra-muscular injection of ½ ml of a 1 : 1000 solution of Parke, Davis Adrenalin Chloride.

In order to check on the effectiveness of the manipulation of sympathetic activation, several measures were taken. In both prisons a physician took the subject's pulse immediately before giving the injection and again immediately after the subject had finished the mental maze. In the Bordentown Reformatory an attempt was made to get a continuous measure of heart rate by use of a telemetric EKG device. Finally, at the end of each session, each subject gave his own impression of his physiological state by answering the questions on palpitation and tremor used in our earlier studies. (Chapter I, p. 12).

That the injections were effective in manipulating sympathetic activity can be seen in Table 53, where, on all indicators, there is a marked difference between placebo and adrenaline conditions. I shall, in a later section, discuss differences between sociopathic and normal subjects on these measures. For the moment, it is quite clear that, in general, the manipulation has been effective.

The Experimental Session

Inmates who had been selected to be in the experiment received passes to report to the experimental room set up inside the walls of the institution. After being introduced to the two experimenters and the physician, they listened to an explanation of the experiment. Briefly, they were told that this was an experiment on the effects of Suproxin (a hormone) on learning ability, that it would require two hour-long sessions, and that they would be paid for participating ($5.00 in Stillwater, $7.50 in Bordentown). The use of prisoners as subjects was explained as owing to the fact that the study required subjects who lived under constant and known dietary and sleeping conditions and who, unlike the usual college student subject, were unable to spend their nights carousing. Finally, they were told that they particularly had been selected to be in the experiment because their I.Q. tests indicated that they could do well on the complicated learning task involved. After this buildup, they were asked to

TABLE 53 THE EFFECTIVENESS OF THE MANIPULATION OF SYMPATHETIC AROUSAL

Condition	N	Pulse		Tremor	Palpitation
		Preinjection	Postinjection		
Placebo	40	81.6	75.4	.58	.43
Adrenaline	40	83.6	87.9	1.43	.80
p value		n.s.	$< .001$	$< .001$	$< .02$

commit themselves as to whether they would take part in the experiment. Forty-three of the forty-eight inmates interviewed agreed to do so.

At this point, a subject was seated in front of the learning apparatus and shocking electrodes were taped to the fingers of one hand. He then received detailed instructions concerning the mental maze and was given a sample shock. When it was clear that the subject understood the task, the physician took his pulse and gave him an injection. In order to discourage the subject from using the injection as an alternative, nonemotional explanation of his physiological state (Schachter and Singer, 1962) he was told that "we have given this injection hundreds of times over the past several years and we know that it is perfectly safe and harmless. We even know that it has no noticeable side effects; that is, you won't feel any different as a result of the injection."

Immediately after the injection, the subject proceeded to work on the mental maze. His first several responses were carefully watched to make sure that he fully understood the task, and then he proceeded at his own pace through the maze for a total of 21 runs. At the end of the session his pulse was taken again, he filled out a short questionnaire, and after a reminder that we would return in two weeks, he left.

The second session followed exactly the same pattern. The instructions were briefly repeated and the subject was told that the task remained the same, although the particular maze had been changed; he received the injection, and went to work. At the second session, of course, the subject received a different form of Suproxin than he had at the first session. Half the subjects received placebo as first injection and epinephrine as second, and the other half received the injections in the reverse order.

Results

Learning the Manifest Task

The experimental device employed simultaneously measured the ability of subjects to learn a "manifest" positively reinforced task and to learn a "latent" pain-avoidance task. Before turning to our central concern—avoidance learning— let us examine the results on the manifest task in order to learn, first, if sociopaths and normals differ in learning ability on a task where emotionality should have little effect and, second, if adrenaline has any effect on the ability to learn the positively reinforced manifest task.

The basic data are presented in Fig. 9 which plots, over blocks of successive trials, the average number of errors, both shock and nonshock, made by the several groups of subjects. Concentrating first on the normal versus sociopathic curves, it will be noticed that the two groups are quite similar. Both groups learn the task at about the same rate. At no point along the curve do the differences between these groups even approach significance. In toto, normals averaged 262 errors and sociopaths 241 errors, a nonsignificant difference. Obviously the normal and sociopathic subjects did not differ in their ability to learn the manifest task. The mixed group of subjects make somewhat fewer errors than either of the purified groups throughout the course of the experiment, but at no point are the mean differences between the mixed and either of the other groups close to significance. These results replicate Lykken, for his groups of subjects, too, proved identical in their ability to learn the manifest task.

Comparing placebo and adrenaline curves, it will be noted that for each group of subjects the two curves are again quite similar, at no point during the course of the experiment differing significantly from one another. The average number of errors made by subjects on placebo is virtually identical with the number of errors made by these same subjects on adrenaline—239 for placebo, 232 for adrenaline. Adrenaline has had no effect on learning the manifest task.[3]

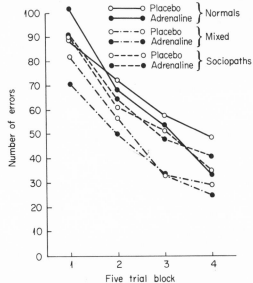

Fig. 9. Number of errors per five-trial block.

[3]This failure of adrenaline to affect positively reinforced learning is a phenomenon we have noted repeatedly in a series of unpublished studies (done in collaboration with Charles Clifton and Philip Rappaport) on rats. Using either food or water as a reinforcer for animals on various deprivation schedules, in three different experiments employing a Skinner box, a T maze, and a more complex maze, we have failed to find any differences in either acquisition or performance rates between animals injected with placebo and animals injected with any of a variety of dosages of adrenaline. These results stand in sharp contrast to the marked facilitating effects (Chapter III) that mild doses of adrenaline have on avoidance learning in rats.

It is clear, then, that sociopaths do not differ from normals in their ability to learn positively reinforced, nonemotional tasks, and that adrenaline has no effect on this sort of task. Any difference found in avoidance learning ability cannot, then, be attributed to overall differences in learning ability or to a generally facilitating effect of adrenaline.

Avoidance Learning

Let us review Lykken's findings on avoidance learning. Lykken employed three experimental groups—sociopathic prisoners, nonsociopathic prisoners, and a group of nonimprisoned normals who were matched with the prison groups for age and for intelligence. Lykken's nonimprisoned normals manifested avoidance learning by sharply decreasing their proportion of shocked errors during the course of the 20 trials of his experimental session. In distinct contrast, the sociopathic group gave almost no indication of avoidance learning, for they were shocked almost as frequently at the end of the experiment as they were during the first few trials. The group of nonsociopathic prisoners (who are comparable to the group called "normal" in the present study) are intermediate between the two extreme groups, manifesting better avoidance learning ability than the sociopaths but not doing as well as the nonimprisoned normals. The difference between Lykken's sociopathic and normal groups is significant with $p = .01$. The difference between sociopathic and nonsociopathic prisoners is only peripherally significant with $p < .20$.

Our own results on avoidance learning are presented in Fig. 10 for subjects on placebo, and Fig. 11 for adrenaline subjects. The ordinate of these figures represents an avoidance ratio calculated simply as the number of shocked errors to total errors. This ratio, then, is the percent of errors on which a subject is shocked. Obviously, as a subject learns to avoid the unpleasantness of being shocked the ratio decreases.

The avoidance ratio is plotted along the abscissa for each third of the total number of errors made by a subject during the course of the experiment. Rather than using blocks of trials as the obvious indicator of the course of the experiment, we have been forced to use blocks of errors because several subjects learned the reinforcement maze to perfection in less than the standard 21 trials. Obviously it is possible to compute an avoidance ratio only when a subject is making errors.

The correspondence between Lykken's results and ours can be noted in Fig. 10, which presents the avoidance learning curves for subjects injected with placebo. Normal subjects decrease their proportion of shocked errors steadily during the course of the experiment. In contrast, the sociopaths give only the slightest indication of learning, increasing their ratio at first and ending up only 1.4 percentage points lower than their beginning figure.

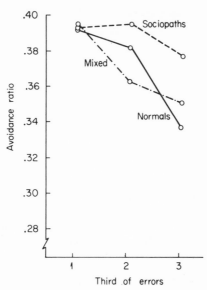

Fig. 10. Avoidance ratio under placebo by thirds of errors.

These basic data and the results of the necessary statistical comparisons are presented in Table 54. Comparing the first with the final third of errors, it can be seen that the decrease in the avoidance ratio is highly significant for normals and insignificant $(p > .50)$ for sociopaths. The normals are learning to avoid shock, the sociopaths are not.

Comparing these two groups during the final third of errors, the difference, as in Lykken's study, is only peripherally significant. It will be recalled that Lykken's major difference was between his groups of imprisoned sociopaths and nonimprisoned normals. Considering that in a maximum security prison most prisoners are likely to be somewhat sociopathic, the failure to find larger within-prison differences can scarcely be considered surprising. As a final check on Lykken's results, Latané and I ran 22 college students (not matched for age or intelligence with the prison groups) on this avoidance learning apparatus after giving them an injection of placebo. This group, too, significantly learned to avoid shock $(p < .05)$. The mean avoidance ratio for this group was .365 for the first period of errors and .309 for the third and final period. This latter figure differs from the corresponding figure for the sociopaths with $p = .07$. All in all, Lykken's data have replicated quite well.

The gist of Lykken's study and of this replication is clear. Normals and sociopaths are equally capable of learning a positively reinforced task. On avoidance learning, presumably mediated by anxiety, the two groups differ— normals learn well, sociopaths not at all.

TABLE 54 AVOIDANCE LEARNING UNDER PLACEBO AND ADRENALINE

	N	Avoidance ratio during:		p value
		First third of errors	Third third of errors	
Avoidance Learning under Placebo				
Normals	15	.392	.339	.01
Sociopaths	15	.393	.379	n.s.
p value		n.s.	.20	
Avoidance Learning under Adrenaline				
Normals	15	.375	.377	n.s.
Sociopaths	15	.369	.278	.03
p value		n.s.	.03	

Additional Statistical Comparisons

Comparison	p value for:	
	First third of errors	Third third of errors
Normals: placebo vs. adrenaline	n.s.	.20
Sociopaths: placebo vs. adrenaline	n.s.	.05

Turning now to the effects of adrenaline on avoidance learning, Fig. 11 and Table 54 present the relevant data. The contrast is immediately evident. Sociopaths who seemed virtually incapable of learning to avoid pain when injected with placebo learn dramatically well under the influence of adrenaline. Normals, on the other hand, appear to be adversely affected, for with adrenaline they do not learn at all. Obviously there is a marked interaction between degree of sociopathy and the effects of sympathetic arousal on avoidance learning ability. This interaction is vividly illustrated in Fig. 12, which plots the relationship of avoidance learning to sociopathy in the two drug conditions. The avoidance learning score along the ordinate is computed simply by subtracting the avoidance ratio during the final third of errors from the ratio during the first third of errors. The greater the difference, the greater the learning. Clearly the effects of the two injections are markedly different. Under placebo, avoidance learning decreases as sociopathy increases. Under adrenaline, avoidance learning increases as sociopathy increases. This interaction is significant at better than the .01 level of confidence.

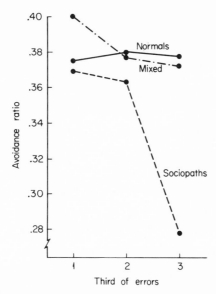

Fig. 11. Avoidance ratio under adrenaline by thirds of errors.

These then are the facts. Sociopaths and normals are equally capable of positively reinforced learning. In nondrug or placebo conditions, normals learn to avoid pain with facility, sociopaths do not. Under the influence of adrenaline, normals, if anything, perform more poorly than they do after an injection of placebo, while sociopaths show marked improvement in their avoidance learning, performing even better than did the normals under placebo.[4] The facts are dramatic and potentially of considerable social importance but how are they to be explained?

Autonomic Arousal and Avoidance Learning

If we reconstruct the rough, semi-intuitive line of thought that led to this replication, with a pharmacological twist, of Lykken's work, the simple-minded chain of reasoning would run something like this: emotional states, fear among them, can be manipulated by manipulation of sympathetic arousal; fear or anxiety is presumed to be a major deterrent of antisocial impulses; sociopaths,

---

[4] Despite the fact that normals do worse with adrenaline than with placebo, it is difficult to decide just how seriously to treat this reversal. In another study using male college students as subjects, we have found no difference in avoidance learning ability, as measured by Lykken's device, between subjects injected with adrenaline and those injected with placebo. Perhaps these two sets of data indicate something quite special about imprisoned "normals" or, more conservatively, perhaps the total body of data should be taken as an indication that adrenaline does not affect avoidance learning in normals.

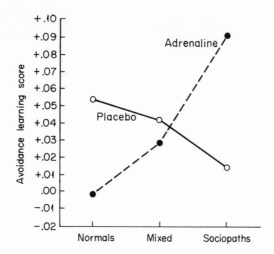

Fig. 12. Avoidance learning under placebo and adrenaline.

notoriously antisocial, are presumed by the clinicians, notably Cleckley and Lykken, to be emotionally flat and anxiety-free. Given this chain of speculation and fact, the next steps are virtually self-evident—perhaps there is something amiss in the sympathetic activity of the sociopath, and perhaps adrenaline can remedy the defect. At this point adrenaline does appear to be a remedy, but a remedy for what?

Undoubtedly, the simplest and most direct diagnostic guess is that sociopaths are simply less sympathetically responsive. Whatever the cause—endocrinological, neurological, or learning history—low autonomic responsiveness should, following a formulation of emotion as a joint function of cognitive and physiological states, lead to emotional flatness and low anxiety.

If this convenient and tidily integrating assumption of the nonreactivity of the sociopath is correct, one should, of course, expect to find independent supporting evidence for the assumption. The only direct measure of the autonomic activity of all subjects in the study of prisoners is the measure of pulse rate taken immediately before injection and again, roughly 30 minutes later, immediately after the subject had completed the maze learning task. Since anticipation of the injection is undoubtedly somewhat disturbing, one might expect that normals would have a higher initial pulse rate than sociopaths. Obviously, on the basis of a single reading, and with no knowledge of possible base rate differences, one can draw no unequivocal conclusions. At this point, however, let us simply examine the data in Fig. 13 and momentarily delay the question of differential responsivity versus differential resting level.

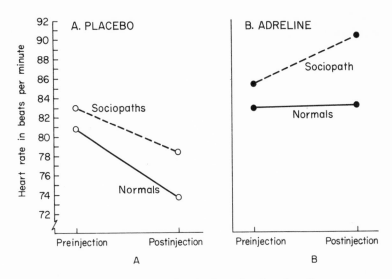

Fig. 13. Pulse rate under placebo and under adrenaline.

From Fig. 13 it is evident that the naive expectation of a pulse difference is wrong. If anything, the reverse of the expectation is true, for normals average 81.9 beats per minute in their two preinjection measurements and sociopaths average 84.3 beats. This is not a significant difference. It is of interest to note the suggestion of a differential sensitivity to adrenaline in the two groups of subjects. Following the injection of adrenaline, the pulse rate of the sociopathic group increases an average of 5.0 beats while the pulse rate of the normal group remains virtually unchanged, increasing only .3 beats per minute. A test of this difference yields $p = .15$.

Obviously the expectation about pulse rate generated by the assumption of differential sympathetic responsivity is flatly wrong. What trend there is, is in a direction opposite to immediate intuition. Rather than dismissing this trend as a chance fluctuation, let us pursue it, for pulse rate is, for the moment, our only toehold into a possible explanation of these differences between sociopaths and normals. Two tendencies are suggested in the data: first, sociopaths have a somewhat higher preinjection pulse rate than do normals. Second, adrenaline has a stronger effect on sociopaths than on normals. Is there other evidence relevant to these relationships?

Sociopathy and Heart Rate

During the course of the cheating experiment described earlier, all subjects took Lykken's scale, which it will be recalled was one of the criteria used for the assignment of subjects in these prison studies. For all subjects there is also a measure of pulse rate which was taken about one or two minutes after they had finished their examinations and immediately after they had swallowed their Suproxin pills. The relationship of pulse rate to scores on this measure of sociopathy is presented in Table 55.[5] On the basis of a median split (median = 10), the subjects were divided into groups high and low in sociopathy. It is clear in Table 55 that the relationship is consistent with that found in prisons. The greater the sociopathy, the higher the pulse rate.[6] The difference between the high and low sociopathic groups is significant at the .002 level of confidence. Given the statistical advantages of a large number of cases, the tendency, which manifested itself in the prisons, appears now to be a firm, well-established relationship.

With this additional confidence in the relationship, how is it to be interpreted—in terms of base rate differences or of differential sympathetic responsivity? In a study designed in part to illuminate this problem, Valins (1963) tested the physiological reactivity of groups of students selected by means of the Lykken scale as high or low in sociopathy. Valins introduced the experiment to his subjects as "an investigation of the physiological and intellectual concomitants of various activities." While explaining each piece of apparatus, he connected his subject to devices designed to measure heart rate and GSR. He then took a five-minute base reading of these autonomic indicators during which the subject simply sat quietly saying nothing. Following the base line period, the subject in sequence responded verbally to a word association test, looked at a series of grotesque photographs of facial injuries, answered a number of embarrassing questions, and finally was led to anticipate that a

TABLE 55 THE RELATIONSHIP OF SOCIOPATHY TO PULSE RATE IN THE CHEATING EXPERIMENT

Subjects scored as:	N	Pulse rate
High sociopaths	89	80.4
At the median	21	77.0
Low sociopaths	86	75.5
p value high vs. low		< .002

[5] This table includes the data for 64 girls who were run in an additional condition of this cheating experiment. Though this condition was irrelevant to the concerns of this book, it was run simultaneously with the other conditions and, to the point of taking pulse, the procedure was identical in every detail with that already described.

[6] It might be expected in the cheating experiment that cheaters would score higher on Lykken's scale of sociopathy than noncheaters. This satisfying result, which would tie together the strands of these two studies as prettily as a gift-wrapped package, is unfortunately not the case. In the placebo condition where the largest difference should be expected, cheaters score lower than do noncheaters. *Utinam vita imitet artem.*

sample of his blood would be taken. The effects of these procedures on heartrate are presented in Table 56. It will be noted first that at the resting state, base level pulse rates of these two groups of subjects are quite similar and, by t test, do not differ significantly. In terms of reactivity, however, the two groups do differ. The final column of this table presents the average deviation from base rate during the several test activities of the experiment. Subjects identified as high on sociopathy by means of the Lykken scale increase an average of 6.4 beats per minute; subjects low on sociopathy increase only 0.1 beats. This difference is significant by t test with $p < .05$. It should be noted, too, that this difference was maintained, at different levels, at each phase of the experimental procedure. Whether responding to a word association test or anticipating the withdrawal of blood, subjects high in sociopathy manifested greater cardiac reactivity than did subjects low in sociopathy. Valins' data on GSR fall in precisely the same pattern, though on this measure the differences between the two groups are not statistically significant.

Valins' study, then, may be taken as an indication that the consistent pulse differences found in the prison and cheating studies may be interpreted in terms of greater autonomic reactivity on the part of the sociopath. In three independent studies we have, then, noted precisely the same relationship—subjects identified as high in sociopathy exhibit greater autonomic reactivity than do those rated low in sociopathy. Though this finding was, for us, completely unexpected [and, indeed, appears to be contrary to much of the literature, to be considered in a later section of this chapter, on the relationship of anxiety states to autonomic arousal (Martin, 1961; Duffy, 1962)], subsequent search of the literature did yield a number of little-known studies with strongly supportive results. The earliest relevant study I have been able to locate is Landis' (1932) study of GSR reactivity in 100 juvenile delinquents. Landis ran all of his subjects through an intense 45-minute experimental session in which they worked steadily at an "unlearnable" pursuit rotor task. During this session, 19 of the subjects became markedly emotional, either growing frightened, or angry, or breaking into tears. Such emotional subjects averaged 18.9 PGR's during the experimental session, markedly less than the 35.1 average for nonemotional subjects. Landis confesses himself as puzzled by these results and writes,

TABLE 56 PULSE RATE IN THE VALINS (1963) STUDY OF SOCIOPATHY AND AUTONOMIC REACTIVITY

Subjects	N	Base level pulse rate (beats/minute)	Average deviation from base rate during experiment
High on sociopathy	9	81.6	+6.4
Low on sociopathy	9	83.4	+0.1
p value		n.s	< .05

> ... just exactly what this means is difficult to say, since it certainly runs contrary to all expectation. On the basis of current psychological theory one would expect that the frightened, angry, or tearful individual, that is, those giving all outward signs of an emotional condition, would give very frequent PGR's. Instead, we find that they are much less frequent than with the normal. (p. 285.)

Jones (1950), pursuing Landis' finding, reports somewhat similar results for subjects in the Adolescent Growth Study at the University of California. For all of these subjects there exist "ratings of personal expressiveness and of various social traits, made independently by at least three observers, on playgrounds and in many other free situations." One hundred of the subjects in this longitudinal study were run through a series of free association tests during which measures were taken of autonomic responsiveness. Arranging his subjects according to the average magnitude of GSR, Jones compares the ratings of high reactives (the upper 20% in GSR reactivity) with those of low reactives (the lower 20%). Low reactives are judged to be animated, assertive, somewhat tense, and "to be easily excited, irritable, impulsive, and to behave in ways that seem somewhat irresponsible to adult observers." High reactives, on the other hand, are rated as calm, deliberate, good-natured, and said "to have greater constancy of mood." Both Landis and Jones, then, find that GSR reactivity is greater for subjects who independently are characterized as nonemotional than for those characterized as emotional.

Closer to present concern with sociopathy is the finding by Learmonth, Ackerly, and Kaplan (1959) of a correlation of +.63 between scores on the psychopathic deviate scale of the MMPI and the magnitude of change in palmar skin potential during a procedure involving the unexpected firing of a gun, electric shock, and the cold stressor test. Also consistent with this emerging pattern of findings, these investigators report a negative correlation between a Rorschach index of emotionality and changes in skin potential.

Finally, Dykman, Ackerman, Galbrecht, and Reese (1963) note that subjects high on anxiety measures (such as the Taylor scale) are less reactive in heart rate during a somewhat stressful experimental session than are subjects low on anxiety measures. This finding, these authors note, has been replicated by Reese, Dykman, and Galbrecht (1961) on a population of psychiatric patients.

Lykken (1955, 1957), reports data that appear to be partly supportive and partly nonsupportive and, in either case, are somewhat difficult to interpret. Using GSR as an index of autonomic reactivity, he exposed his subjects to a variety of disturbing situations. A close examination of his data reveals that on most of his indices of electrical activity—basal resistance level, decrease in basal resistance during shock trials, mean GSR to a shock stimulus, and GSR conditioning—sociopaths showed somewhat, but not significantly, higher reactivity than did nonsociopathic prisoners. On most of these indices, however, his group of nonimprisoned normals showed considerably more reactivity than did the prisoners. As Lykken points out, however, (Lykken, 1955, p. 171) his group of normals were tested during midsummer heat and the prisoners during cooler seasons. Lykken accounts for the highly significant difference in basal level of skin resistance (normals being considerably higher than sociopaths) in terms of temperature differences. If one accepts the assumption of sweat gland involvement in GSR activity, it is conceivable that these seasonal differences may vitiate Lykken's sociopath-normal comparisons.

On the whole, the phenomenon appears to have substantial support. In at least eight independent studies concerned with some aspect of the relationship of the "characteristic" of emotionality with autonomic reactivity, the evidence is consistent and strong, for both heart rate and GSR, that nonemotional types are more reactive autonomically than are emotional subjects. Granted, then, that the phenomenon is a real one, we are, of course, faced with the engrossing problem of understanding the mechanism underlying the fact. A possible lead may lie in the tentative indication of differential sensitivity to adrenaline among the prisoners.

Sociopathy and Sensitivity to Adrenaline

Though the indications of differential cardiac sensitivity to adrenaline in the prison population were significant, at best, at peripheral levels of confidence, it must be remembered that the single postinjection reading of pulse was taken only after a subject had completed his trials on the avoidance learning apparatus—usually about 30 minutes after injection. Since adrenaline is a rapidly acting agent which is metabolized quickly, it is obvious that any differences between sociopathic and normal groups would have been considerably attenuated by the time the second measure of pulse was taken.

In an attempt to get a continuous record of heartrate, we employed, in the Bordentown prison, an experimental model of a telemetric EKG transmitter. This ingenious device, cigarette-pack size, was simply placed in a subject's shirt pocket and connected to two electrodes taped onto each side of a subject's chest. If the components of this device were in working order and the battery fresh, and if the local television station or prison diathermy machine was not broadcasting, it was possible to receive a clean signal on the FM receiver tuned to the transmitter's broadcast frequency. If the receiver did not drift it was possible to make a continuous recording of heartrate all through those portions of an experimental session when ink had not clogged the recorder pen or the drive sprocket fouled the recording paper. In the event that all of these contingencies were favorable for both of a subject's experimental sessions, it was possible to get comparable records of his continuous reaction to both adrenaline and placebo. We were able to get such records for four members (of a possible six) of the sociopathic group and four members (of a possible five) of the normal group. By good fortune, the preinjection and postinjection pulse readings of these subgroups of subjects were all quite close to the means (Fig. 13) of the larger groups of which they were members. Their data, then, may be considered representative.

The averaged records of these two subgroups of subjects are presented in Fig. 14. These curves cover the following sequence of experimental events. Approximately 10 minutes before he was to receive the injection, the subject was connected to the EKG device, which incidentally was explained to him "as a way of measuring the rate of blood flow so that we have an accurate idea of how fast the body is absorbing the Suproxin." While the experimenter was explaining the experiment, a technician, well in the background and out of the experiment, fiddled with the controls in order to obtain a clear signal. The curves in Fig. 14 begin at that point when good signals were recorded for all eight subjects in a drug condition. By this time the subject was seated in front of the avoidance learning apparatus receiving instructions in its use. About a minute or so before the injection, the doctor approached the subject, took his pulse, rolled up his sleeve, swabbed the upper arm with alcohol, and injected. Immediately after the injection (perhaps 15 seconds) the subject began work on the maze learning task. From this point on, he worked steadily and without interruption at the learning task until he had completed his 21st and final trial, at which point the doctor took his pulse again and the EKG device was removed from his person. In order to keep the two curves in a drug condition completely comparable, the curves in Fig. 14 end at that point when the fastest subject (in a drug condition) had completed his final trial.

Under placebo, Fig. 14A, we note, once again, the phenomenon documented in the previously presented studies of sociopathy and pulse rate—sociopaths are somewhat more reactive than are normals. During the preinjection period the sociopaths, averaging 93.1 beats per minute, are somewhat higher than are the normals who average 88.7 beats. In immediate reaction to being injected and beginning the experiment, the sociopaths increase 5.1 beats to an average of 98.4 during the first two postinjection minutes, while normals increase only 1.1 beats to an average of 89.8 beats. For the remainder of the experiment this difference decreases but the sociopaths remain steadily slightly higher, averaging 86.5 beats per minute to the normals' 84.5.

The effects of adrenaline, plotted in Fig. 14B, are dramatic and almost startling. As in the placebo condition, during the preinjection period sociopaths are slightly higher than are normals. Following the injection of adrenaline, the mean pulse rate of the sociopathic group jumps markedly and remains at very high levels for the duration of the experimental session. The normals also increase following injection, but quickly return to a steady level only slightly

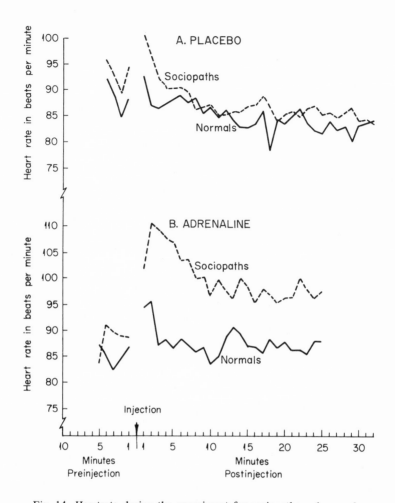

Fig. 14. Heartrate during the experiment for sociopaths and normals.

greater than preinjection rate. These effects are summarized in Table 57, where it will be noted that sociopaths increase an average of 17.3 beats during the first third of the postinjection period, in comparison with an increase of only 3.9 beats for normals. There is no overlap in the distribution of heartrate increases during this period. The highest normal increase is 6.7 beats and the lowest sociopath increase is 13.1 beats per minute. Testing the significance of the mean difference in heartrate increase, $t = 3.97$ which, with 6 degrees of freedom, yields $p < .01$. Obviously, in their initial reactions, this group of sociopaths appears to be markedly more sensitive to adrenaline than is a normal group.

TABLE 57 THE EFFECTS OF ADRENALINE ON THE HEART RATE OF NORMALS
AND SOCIOPATHS

	N	Preinjection heart rate	Heart rate during postinjection period		
			0–7 minutes	8–15 minutes	16–24 minutes
Normals	4	85.4	89.3	88.2	87.3
Sociopaths	4	88.2	105.5	98.1	97.2

Despite these striking differences, however, it seems evident that these data on sensitivity to adrenaline must be treated tentatively. Though the differences indicated in Fig. 14*B* and Table 57 are impressively large, the number of cases involved is distressingly small, and this must be considered as essentially case study material.

Granted the tentativeness of this data, if it is correct that sociopathy is directly related to sensitivity to adrenaline, it would be expected that those who react strongly to adrenaline will manifest sociopathic behavior. Failure to learn shock avoidance on Lykken's apparatus is not at all a bad analog for the real life situation of the sociopath who, chronic recidivist, seems unable to keep away from trouble or out of jail. The relationship of avoidance learning ability in the placebo condition of the present study to reactivity to adrenaline in the adrenaline condition should, then, test the suspicion that adrenaline-sensitives will behave sociopathically.

The relevant evidence is presented in Table 58.[7] Using a median split, strong reactors are classified as those above the median (an increase of two beats) on the distribution of pre-minus postinjection pulse readings in the adrenaline condition; weak reactions are those below the median. The criterion of aptitude for learning to avoid pain is, of course, performance on Lykken's apparatus in the placebo condition—very simply, a subject has learned to avoid pain if he reduces his proportion of shocked errors during the course of the experiment (i.e., his avoidance ratio has decreased from the first to the final third of total errors); if this proportion does not decrease, he has not learned. It can be seen in the table that 89% of weak reactors to adrenaline successfully learn to avoid the shock under placebo, while only 37% of strong reactors do so. Reactivity to adrenaline is a better predictor of avoidance learning ability than any single one of the criteria of sociopathy or, indeed, than any combination of these criteria. This astonishing relationship, significant at approximately the .005 level, would

---

[7]In considering these data, it should be remembered that the two experimental sessions for each subject were approximately two weeks apart. In addition, half of the subjects received the placebo treatment first. Obviously the possibility of some sort of artifactual causal connection between the violence of a subject's reaction to adrenaline and his ability to learn pain avoidance when injected with placebo, is, at best, remote.

TABLE 58 THE RELATIONSHIP OF ADRENALINE SENSITIVITY
TO AVOIDANCE LEARNING UNDER PLACEBO

	Learn to avoid	Do not learn to avoid
Strong reactors	7	12
Weak reactors	16	2

$\chi^2 = 8.55; p < .005.$

certainly seem to indicate that adrenaline sensitivity is involved in the sociopathic complex. Differential sensitivity to exogenously administered adrenaline
may be an excellent lead for understanding the reasonably well-supported
relationship of sociopathy to autonomic activity in nondrug or placebo circumstances, and, in turn, perhaps, to understanding the behavioral correlates of the
dimension, sociopathy.

Discussion

To recapitulate the major results of these studies of sociopathy; about
learning we know the following:

1. Sociopaths and normals are equally capable of learning positively reinforced behaviors.

2. In nondrug or placebo circumstances, normals learn to avoid pain with
facility; sociopaths do not.

3. When injected with the sympathomimetic agent adrenaline, sociopaths
show marked improvement in avoidance learning; normals do not.

About autonomic activity, we know the following:

1. Sociopaths are more autonomically responsive to a variety of more or less
stressful stimuli than are normals.

2. Sociopaths appear to be more sensitive to adrenaline than do normals.

How are these two sets of facts to be integrated? Do the data on autonomic
activity contain the key to the differential learning ability of these two groups of
subjects? In terms of the initial expectation that the emotionally flat, anxiety-
free nature of the sociopath could be explained by low autonomic reactivity, it
is clear that not only were we wrong, but that the reverse is true. Not only are
these findings incompatible with initial expectations, but they appear to be in
direct opposition to much of the work on the relationship of high anxiety states
to autonomic arousal summarized by Duffy (1962) and Martin (1961). Though
viewed en masse, the results of the numerous studies in this area are by no means

completely consistent, probably the majority of such studies do demonstrate that in experimental stress situations of one sort or another, subjects classified as psychoneurotic, or anxiety neurotic, or high on some dimension of anxiety, are more autonomically reactive than are comparison groups of normals. From the results of these studies, as well as from our own results, it would appear that high autonomic reactivity characterizes both those who are extremely high in anxiety and emotionality and those who are extremely low in anxiety and emotionality—a state of affairs noted in passing by Jones (1935), who reported that "children who give the largest galvanic deflections tend to receive either exceptionally high or exceptionally low ratings" of emotional responsiveness in an experimental situation.[8] Can these apparently incompatible trends be reconciled?

Let us return briefly to consideration of the cognitive-physiological formulation of emotion that prompted these studies of sociopathy. It will be recalled that, following this view, a state of physiological arousal is a necessary but not a sufficient condition for emotion. As Schachter and Singer (Chapter 1) demonstrated, it is possible to have subjects in a state of sympathetic arousal who give

[8]Obviously, this overview of the research in this area implies that there is a U-shaped relationship between emotionality, or anxiety, and autonomic reactivity. If this is the case, one may well ask why, other than Jones (1935), almost none of the numerous researchers in this domain have noted such a relationship. The reason, I suspect, is simple. If, as in our own work, one is basically interested in low anxiety, subject classification efforts are concentrated on the identification of extremely low anxious subjects and, given the usual difficulties of matching, one is willing for comparison group purposes to settle for subjects, who, though higher in anxiety, are not necessarily extremely anxious. Similarly, if the investigator is essentially interested in high anxiety, it seems likely that he will settle for comparison subjects who, though low in anxiety, are hardly sociopaths. Few investigators have described their selection procedures in sufficient detail to evaluate this point. The Bitterman & Holtzman (1952) study of anxiety and GSR conditioning, however, is an excellent example. On the basis of extensive testing, observation, and interviewing, these investigators classified their college student subjects as manifesting five degrees of anxiety. The distribution is presented in the following tabulation which is adapted from Table 1 of the Bitterman and Holtzman paper:

Degree of Anxiety	N
1 (low anxiety)	1
2	5
3	13
4	13
5 (high anxiety)	5
total	37

Subjects with overall anxiety ratings of 4 and 5 were designated as the high anxiety group, and subjects with ratings between 1 and 3 comprised the low anxiety group. It can be seen that 13 of the 19 "low anxiety" subjects were actually at the midpoint in rated anxiety.

no indication, in either behavior or introspective self-report, of emotion. Such subjects had been injected with adrenaline, given an accurate description of the physiological effects of this agent, and then thrust into an experimental situation calculated in one condition to induce euphoria and in another condition to induce anger. In neither condition did such subjects give any signs of emotion; indeed they were less emotional than subjects who had been injected with placebo. In marked contrast were those subjects who, also injected with adrenaline, had been told that the drug would have no side effects. Such subjects proved markedly emotional, depending on the condition, being either distinctly euphoric or quite angry. These differences were interpreted in terms of labeling—when a subject is in a state of sympathetic arousal and has no appropriate, experimentally provided explanation of why he feels this way, he labels this state in terms of his immediate situation and behaves accordingly. If, on the other hand, such a subject understands precisely what he feels and why (i.e., he has been told that he will feel this way because of the injection) he has an immediately appropriate explanation of his bodily state and he will not label his bodily feelings in terms of his situation. This experiment, then, demonstrates one point, crucial to an understanding of these findings on sociopathy—sympathetic arousal is not necessarily associated with an emotional state; cognitive and situational factors determine whether or not a state of physiological arousal will be labeled as an emotion.

The crucial problem then, appears to be one of labeling. How does the sociopath label his bodily feelings? The gist of the data on autonomic activity and sociopathy so far is this—sociopaths appear to be more responsive to virtually every titillating event, whether only mildly provoking or dangerously threatening. In the Valins study (1963), the heartrate of sociopathic subjects increases as much during word association as when they are anticipating giving blood. The sociopath reacts sympathetically to events that are labeled frightening by others, but he also reacts to events labeled as relatively harmless by others. Such generalized, relatively indiscriminate reactivity is, I would suggest, almost the equivalent of no reactivity at all. If almost every event provokes strong autonomic discharge, then, in terms of internal autonomic cues, the subject feels no differently during times of danger than during relatively tranquil times. Bodily conditions which for others are associated with emotionality are, for the sociopath, his "normal" state. It would appear from the data on the effects of adrenaline on avoidance learning that only intense states of autonomic reaction, presumably stronger than, and differentiable from, his normal reactions, acquire emotional attributes for the sociopathic subject. Given a chronic history of autonomic reactivity, only a marked increase in activation will be labeled as an emotional state, and perhaps even noticed.

I would be the first to concede that this attempt to reconcile these two lines of data has a vapid and vacuous quality. Ad hoc explanations do have the feel of eating Puffed Rice. Alternative explanations of this unexpected pattern of findings are, at this stage, so numerous[9] that, short of direct experimental attack, any attempt to fortify this particular interpretation seems gratuitous. There is, however, one implication of this line of thought which is sufficiently engrossing to warrant some elaboration. The gist of this viewpoint is the suggestion that sociopaths are individuals characterized by marked autonomic reactivity, who, over the course of their development, have learned not (or, have not learned) to apply emotional labels to their states of arousal. This interpretation does imply that the psychological state of sociopathy can be derived from the physiological condition of autonomic hyperreactivity rather than that the condition of autonomic hyperreactivity is to be derived from a series of assumptions about the cognitive and psychodynamic world of the sociopath. Obviously, there is no immediate supporting evidence for this suggestion. We have, however, been attracted to this interpretation by the very suggestive findings on the adrenaline sensitivity and sociopathy which do, at least, hint at a purely physiological or biochemical mechanism to account for autonomic hyperreactivity.

Clearly, this line of thought imposes a heavy theoretical weight on the still flimsy supposition of differential adrenaline sensitivity. However, the results of an experiment conducted by Rappaport, Gordon, and Schachter (unpublished) suggest that there is more to this line of thought than pure enchantment with the possibility of deriving an extremely complex human condition from a simple physiological mechanism. In this study adrenaline sensitivity in rats is related to avoidance learning ability. To determine adrenaline sensitivity, over a period of 14 days each rat received three intraperitoneal injections of epinephrine (.008 mg of epinephrine per 100 gm) in a saline solution. Heartrate recordings were made for the 25 minutes before and 45 minutes after each injection. Using an adaptation of Lacey's (1956) method of correcting for base line differences, reactivity is calculated for each of the three injections and then averaged to provide an index of adrenaline sensitivity. On the day following the last injection, each rat was run for 50 trials in a Miller—Mowrer shuttlebox. There were three experimental conditions—extremely high shock (1.0 mA), mild shock (0.2 mA), and very light shock (0.1 mA). The assumption is made that the release of adrenaline, and the consequent deviation from base line reactivity, will be a direct function of the intensity of shock. If this assumption and this general line of reasoning are correct, it could be anticipated that the sociopath-normal differences will be paralleled in this animal study; that is, in the very low shock condition, there will be a negative relationship between adrenaline sensitivity and avoidance learning, while in the high shock condition there will be a positive

[9]The most prominent alternative is probably the suggestion made in one form or another, by Jones (1950), by Block (1957), and by Learmonth, Ackerly, and Kaplan (1959) that autonomic reactivity is inversely related to the degree of overt expression of emotionality.

relationship. The data are presented in Fig. 15, which plots, for the three conditions, the magnitude of tau between adrenaline sensitivity and the total number of avoidances the animals make in the 50-trial experimental session. It can be seen that the results parallel expectation. In the light shock condition the adrenaline sensitive animals made fewer avoidances than did the relatively insensitive animals, while in the high shock condition this relationship is reversed. The difference in the values of tau in the high and low shock conditions is significant with $p < .05$. If these results are confirmed in further experiments, it would certainly appear that the notion of adrenaline sensitivity merits further exploration.

What about the emotionally volatile subject such as the anxiety neurotic who, as demonstrated in studies discussed earlier, also appears to be autonomically hyperreactive? The simplest explanation is one consistent with the original expectations and line of thought—the cognitive system and personality structure of this sort of individual is such that he constantly interprets his world in threatening or emotional terms—an interpretation that triggers autonomic activity. Viewed in this manner, the autonomic hyperreactivity of the anxiety neurotic and of the sociopath arise from entirely different causes. Where the autonomic reactivity of the sociopath is caused by an innate sensitivity to adrenaline, the reactivity of the anxiety neurotic is cognitively determined and unrelated to adrenaline sensitivity.

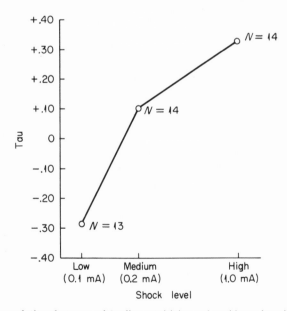

Fig. 15. Tau correlations between adrenaline sensitivity and avoidance learning as related to the level of shock administered in a shuttle box.

Though this is a reasonable and conservative beginning interpretation of the U-shaped relationship between autonomic arousal and emotionality, it would, at least, be intriguing to test the anxiety neurotic for adrenaline sensitivity for, fanciful though it may seem, it is just conceivable that these two conditions may both be derived from a common state of adrenaline sensitivity. If an individual can learn not to apply emotional labels to his bodily feelings in situations that customary social usage defines as emotional, it seems equally possible that the opposite will hold; that is, that an autonomically hyperreactive individual can learn to apply emotional labels to his bodily feelings in situations that would customarily be defined as nonemotional. One can conceive of unusual circumstances (e.g., a child raised by a hysterical mother) that would lead to the development of superemotionality in an autonomically hyperreactive person. If this general line of thought is correct, it should be anticipated that anxiety neurotics will prove as sensitive to adrenaline as are sociopaths.

Cognitive Factors and Criminality

The formulation of the criminal act that prompted this series of studies is based on the relative magnitudes of the impulse to commit a crime and the restraints against doing so. In Lewinian terms, if the magnitude of the driving force is greater than the magnitude of restraining forces a crime will be committed. If the reverse relationship holds, it will not. Obviously the two experiments that have been described in this paper have been deliberately designed to manipulate the magnitude of the restraints. The circumstances of both studies have been so structured that the manipulation of sympathetic arousal has served to manipulate the state of anxiety. What about the impulse to commit a crime? Should it be similarly manipulable? Indeed it should. In studies described earlier, it has proven simple to manipulate such states as anger, euphoria, and fear by the manipulation, in proper cognitive circumstances, of sympathetic activation. There seems to be no reason that such states as hate, rage, lust, and jealousy could not be similarly manipulated. Conceive of an experiment in which a subject is injected with either adrenaline or a sympatholytic agent, a gun is shoved into his hand, and he is taken by the arm and thrust into a room where he finds his wife in bed with a stooge. Undoubtedly the reader will agree that under such circumstances a subject whose heart suddenly starts pounding, face flushing, and body trembling, will be more likely to shoot than will a subject who contemplates this disturbing scene in a state of manipulated physiological quiescence. Why such an outcome rather than, as in the cheating experiment, the reverse? Because the situation has been so structured as to virtually force the immediate cognitive-emotive sequence: "I have been betrayed, I hate them, I could kill them," and the intensity of the state will be a function of the degree of physiological arousal.

It is possible, then, to conceive of situations in which the manipulation of physiological arousal will, depending on cognitive factors, serve to manipulate either the impulse to commit a crime or the restraints against doing so. Given this analysis, one may ask why the sociopath is a chronic troublemaker. His presumed emotional flatness should dampen both the restraints against committing a crime and the intensity of the impulse to commit one. If he is indeed emotionally flat, he should be as free of the emotional flareups that can precipitate a crime as of the anxiety that can inhibit it, and his reputation as a troublemaker should be no more serious than any normal person's. This should, of course, be the case if the impulses to criminal activity were purely emotionally generated, but such is obviously not true. Crimes are committed not only out of passion but to satisfy simple needs for necessities and comforts, and there is certainly no reason to assume that sociopaths feel any less hungry, cold, or covetous than do normals. If these considerations are correct, one should, however, anticipate different patterns of crime for normals and sociopaths. Sociopaths should be responsible for predominantly "cool" crimes such as burglary, forgery, con games, and the like, whereas normals should tend to be involved in such activities as manslaughter, assault, and sex crimes. That this is very much the case is indicated by the fact that only 40% of the 45 nominated[10] sociopaths, compared with 69% of the 35 nominated normals, had, at any point during their criminal careers, committed a crime that by any stretch of legal categorization might include elements of passion (e.g., assault, manslaughter, rape, etc.)—and this despite the fact that nominated sociopaths averaged almost twice as many crimes as did normals. On the whole, the sociopaths were chronic burglars and con men, and even their presumed crimes of passion have an entirely different cast than do similarly categorized crimes of normals. Where the normal subject who was a murderer had killed the high school principal who was sleeping with his wife, the sole sociopathic murderer had killed in a well-calculated attempt to collect insurance.

[10]Since type of crime was one of the considerations entering into the final selection of subjects, these figures are calculated for the total group of subjects initially nominated by prison personnel as prospective subjects for this study. In making these nominations, the prison personnel relied almost entirely on their personal acquaintance with the men and did not refer to prison records.

Bibliography

Ambler, E. *Background to danger.* New York: Dell Publishing Co., 1958.

Ax, A. F. The physiological differentiation between fear and anger in humans. *Psychosomatic Medicine,* 1953, **15**, 433-42.

Ayrapetyants, E. S., Labanova, L. V., & Cherkasova, L. S. Materials on the physiology of the internal analyzer in man. *Trud. Inst. Fiziol. Pavlova,* 1952, **1**, 3-20.

Becker, H. S. Becoming a marijuana user. *American Journal of Sociology,* 1953, **59**, 235-242.

Beebe, L. *The big spenders.* New York: Doubleday, 1966.

Bitterman, M. E. & Holtzman, W. H. Conditioning and extinction of the galvanic skin response as a function of anxiety. *Journal of Abnormal and Social Psychology,* 1952, **47**, 615-623.

Bliss, E. L. & Branch, C. H. *Anorexia nervosa.* New York: Hoeber Co., 1960.

Block, J. A study of affective responsiveness in a lie-detection situation. *Journal of Abnormal and Social Psychology,* 1957, **55**, 11-15.

Brown, J. D. & Pulsifer, D. H. Outpatient starvation in normal and obese subjects. *Aerospace Medicine,* March, 1965, 267-269.

Bruch, H. Transformation of oral impulses in eating disorders: A conceptual approach. *Psychiatric Quarterly,* 1961, **35**, 458-481.

Bykov, K. M. New data on the physiology and pathology of the cerebral cortex. Communication cited by H. Gwynne Jones, The application of conditioning and learning techniques to the treatment of a psychiatric patient. *Journal of Abnormal and Social Psychology,* 1956, **52**, 414-419.

Cannon, W. B. The James–Lange theory of emotions: a critical examination and an alternative theory. *American Journal of Psychology,* 1927, **39**, 106-124.

Cannon, W. B. *Bodily changes in pain, hunger, fear and rage.* (2nd ed.) New York: Appleton, 1929.

Cannon, W. B., Lewis, J. T., & Britton, S. W. The dispensability of the sympathetic division of the autonomic nervous system. *Boston Medical and Surgical Journal,* 1927, **197**, 514-515.

Carlson, A. J. *The control of hunger in health and disease.* Chicago: University of Chicago Press, 1916.

Cleckley, H. *The mask of sanity.* (3rd ed.) St. Louis: C. V. Mosby, 1955.

Dana, C. L. The anatomic seat of the emotions: a discussion of the James–Lange theory. *American Medical Association Archives of Neurological Psychiatrics,* 1921, **6**, 634-639.

Duffy, Elizabeth. *Activation and behavior.* New York: Wiley, 1962.

Duncan, C. G., Jenson, W. K., Fraser, R. I., & Christofori, F. C. Correction and control of intractible obesity. *Journal of the American Medical Association,* 1962, **181**, 309-312.

Dykman, R. A., Ackerman, P. T., Galbrecht, C. R., & Reese, W. G. Physiological reactivity to different stressors and methods of evaluation. *Psychosomatic Medicine,* 1963, **25**, 37-59.

Festinger, L. A theory of social comparison processes. *Human Relations,* 1954, **7**, 114-140.

Goldman, R., Jaffa, M., & Schachter, S. Yom Kippur, Air France, dormitory food, and the eating behavior of obese and normal persons. *Journal of Personality and Social Psychology,* 1968, **10**, 117-123.

Griggs, R. C. & Stunkard, A. J. The interpretation of gastric motility: II. Sensitivity and bias in the perception of gastric motility. *Archives of General Psychiatry,* 1964, **11**, 82-89.

Gwynne Jones, H. The application of conditioning and learning techniques to the treatment of a psychiatric patient. *Journal of Abnormal and Social Psychology,* 1956, **52,** 414-419.

Hall, C. S. Emotional behavior in the rat: I. Defecation and urination as measures of individual differences in emotionality. *Journal of Comparative and Physiological Psychology,* 1934, **18,** 385-403.

Hashim, S. A. & Van Itallie, T. B. Studies in normal and obese subjects with a monitored food dispensing device. *Annals of the New York Academy of Sciences,* 1965, **131,** 654-661.

Hohmann, G. W. The effect of dysfunctions of the autonomic nervous system on experienced feelings and emotions. Paper presented at the Conference on Emotions and Feelings at the New School for Social Research, New York, October, 1962.

Hohmann, G. W. Some effects of spinal cord lesions on experienced emotional feelings. *Psychophysiology,* 1966, **3,** 143-156.

Hunt J. McV., Cole, M. W., & Reis, E. S. Situational cues distinguishing anger, fear, and sorrow. *American Journal of Psychology,* 1958, **71,** 136-151.

Hutchinson, R. R. & Renfrew, J. W. Stalking attack and eating behavior elicited from the same sites in the hypothalamus. *Journal of Comparative and Physiological Psychology,* 1966, **61,** 360-367.

James, W. *The principles of psychology.* New York: Henry Holt, 1890, p. 449.

Jones, H. E. The galvanic skin reflex as related to overt emotional expression. *American Journal of Psychology,* 1935, **47,** 241-251.

Jones, H. E. The study of patterns of emotional expression. In M. L. Reymert (Ed.), *Feelings and emotions.* New York: McGraw-Hill, 1950, pp. 161-168.

Kaplan, H. I. & Kaplan, H. S. The psychosomatic concept of obesity. *Journal of Nervous and Mental Diseases,*1957, **125** (2), 181-201.

Karp, S. A. & Pardes, H. Psychological differentiation (field dependence) in obese women. *Psychosomatic Medicine,* 1965, **27,** 238-244.

Killam, Eva K. The pharmacological aspects of certain drugs useful in psychiatry. In J. O. Cole and R. W. Gerard (Eds.), *Psychopharmacology: Problems in evaluation.* National Academy of Sciences, National Research Council Publication 583, 1959, pp. 20-45.

Kosman, M. E. & Gerard, R. W. The effect of adrenalin on a conditioned avoidance response. *Journal of Comparative and Physiological Psychology,* 1955, **48,** 506-508.

Lacey, J. I. The evaluation of autonomic responses: toward a general solution. *Annals of the New York Academy of Science,* 1956, **67,** 123-164.

Landis, C. An attempt to measure emotional traits in juvenile delinquency. In K. S. Lashley (Ed.), C. P. Stone, C. W. Darrow, C. Landis, & Lena L. Heath, *Studies in the dynamics of behavior.* Chicago: The University of Chicago Press, 1932,

Latané, B. & Schachter, S. Adrenalin and avoidance learning. *Journal of Comparative and Physiological Psychology,* 1962, **65,** 369-372.

Lavernhe, J., LaFontaine, E., & Laplane, R. An investigation on the subjective effects of time changes on flying staff in civil aviation. Air France Medical Department paper presented before the Aerospace Medical Association, April, 1965. (Mimeo)

Learmonth, G. J., Ackerly, W., & Kaplan, M. Relationships between palmar skin potential during stress and personality variables. *Psychosomatic Medicine,* 1959, **21,** 150-157.

Levine, S. & Soliday, S. An effect of adrenal demedullation on the acquisition of a conditioned avoidance response. *Journal of Comparative and Physiological Psychology,* 1962, **55,** 214-216.

Lykken, D. T. A study of anxiety in the sociopathic personality. Unpublished doctoral dissertation, University of Minnesota, 1955.

Lykken, D. T. A study of anxiety in the sociopathic personality. *Journal of Abnormal and Social Psychology*, 1957, **55**, 6-10.

Mandler, G. Emotion. In R. Brown, *et al., New directions in Psychology*. New York: Holt, Rinehart and Winston, 1962, pp. 267-343.

Marañon, G. Contribution à l'étude de l'action émotive de l'adrénaline. *Revue française d'Endocrinologie*, 1924, **2**, 301-325.

Martin, B. The assessment of anxiety by physiological behavioral measures. *Psychological Bulletin*, 1961, **58**, 234-255.

Metropolitan Life Insurance Company. New weight standards for men and women. Statistical Bulletin, 1959, **40**, 1-4.

Miller, N. E., Bailey, C. J., & Stevenson, J. A. F. Decreased "hunger" but increased food intake resulting from hypothalamic lesions. *Science*, 1950, **112**, 256-259.

Moran, G., Ahmad, S. S., & Meagher, R. B., Jr. Adrenalin and avoidance learning: Partial replications. *Journal of Experimental Research in Personality*, 1970, **4**, 84-89.

Moyer, K. E. Effect of adrenalectomy on anxiety-motivated behavior. *Journal of Genetic Psychology*, 1958a, **92**, 11-16.

Moyer, K. E. & Bunnell, B. N. Effect of injected adrenalin on an avoidance response in the rat. *Journal of Genetic Psychology*, 1958, **92**, 247-251.

Moyer, K. E. & Bunnell, B. N. Effect of adrenal demedullation on an avoidance response in the rat. *Journal of Comparative and Physiological Psychology*, 1959, **52**, 215-216.

Moyer, K. E & Bunnell, B. N. Effects of adrenal demedullation on the startle response in the rat. *Journal of Genetic Psychology*, 1960a, **97**, 341-344.

Moyer, K. E. & Bunnell, B. N. Effect of adrenal demedullation, operative stress, and noise stress on emotional elimination. *Journal of Genetic Psychology*, 1960b, **96**, 375-382.

Nisbett, R. E. Taste, deprivation, and weight determinants of eating behavior. *Journal of Personality and Social Psychology*, 1968, **10**, 107-116.

Nisbett, R. E. Determinants of food intake in obesity. *Science*, 1968, **159**, 1254-1255.

Nisbett, R. E. & Schachter, S. The cognitive manipulation of pain. *Journal of Experimental Social Psychology*, 1966, **2**, 227-236.

Plutchik, R. & Ax, A. F. A Critique of "determinants of emotional state" by Schachter and Singer, 1962. *Psychophysiology*, 1967, **4**, 79-82.

Prichard, J. C. *Treatise on insanity and other disorders affecting the mind*. London: Sherwood, Gilbert, and Piper, 1835.

Razran, G. The observable unconscious and the inferable conscious in current Soviet psychophysiology: Interoceptive conditioning, semantic conditioning, and the orienting reflex. *Psychological Review*, 1961, **68**, 81-147.

Reese, W. G., Dykman, R. A., & Galbrecht, C. R. Psychophysiological reactions of "normals" and psychiatric patients: Methods of quantification. *Psychiatric Research Reports*, 1961, **14**, 91-103.

Rosenweig, M. R. The mechanisms of hunger and thirst. In L. Postman (Ed.), *Psychology in the making*. New York: Alfred A. Knopf, 1962, pp. 73-143.

Ross, L. D. Cue- and cognition-controlled eating among obese and normal subjects. Unpublished doctoral dissertation, Columbia University, 1970.

Ross, L. D., Pliner, P., Nesbitt, P., & Schachter, S. Patterns of externality and internality in the eating behavior of obese and normal college students. Unpublished manuscript, Columbia University, New York, 1969.

Ross, L. D., Rodin, J., & Zimbardo, P. G. Toward an attribution therapy: The reduction of fear through induced cognitive-emotional misattribution. *Journal of Personality and Social Psychology*, 1969, **12**, 279-288.

Ruckmick, C. A. *The psychology of feeling and emotion.* New York: McGraw-Hill, 1936.

Schachter, J. Pain, fear, and anger in hypertensives and normotensives: A psychophysiologic study. *Psychosomatic Medicine,* 1957, **19,** 17-29.

Schachter, S. *The psychology of affiliation.* Stanford, California: Stanford University Press, 1959.

Schachter, S. The interaction of cognitive and physiological determinants of emotional state. In L. Berkowitz (Ed.), *Advances in experimental social psychology,* Vol. 1, New York: Academic Press, 1964.

Schachter, S. The assumption of identity and peripheralist-centralist controversies in motivation and emotion. In M. Arnold (Ed.), *Feelings and emotions.* New York: Academic Press, 1970.

Schachter, S., Goldman, R., & Gordon, A. The effects of fear, food deprivation, and obesity on eating. *Journal of Personality and Social Psychology,* 1968, **10,** 91-97.

Schachter, S. & Gross, L. Manipulated time and eating behavior. *Journal of Personality and Social Psychology,* 1968, **10,** 98-106.

Schachter, S. & Latané, B. Crime, cognition and the autonomic nervous system. *Nebraska Symposium on Motivation,* 1964, **12,** 221-273.

Schachter, S. & Singer, J. E. Cognitive, social, and physiological determinants of emotional state. *Psychological Review,* 1962, **69,** 379-399.

Schachter, S. & Wheeler, L. Epinephrine, chlorpromazine, and amusement. *Journal of Abnormal and Social Psychology,* 1962, **65,** 121-128.

Sherrington, C. S. Experiments on the value of vascular and visceral factors for the genesis of emotion. *Proceedings of the Royal Society of London,* 1900, **66,** 390-403.

Sieling, R. J. & Benson, W. M. Effect of catecholamines on the conditioned emotional response in the rat. Paper presented at the Federation of American Societies for Experimental Biology, Atlantic City, April, 1959.

Singer, J. The effects of epinephrine, chlorpromazine, and Dibenzyline upon the fright responses of rats under stress and nonstress conditions. Unpublished doctoral dissertation, University of Minnesota, 1961.

Singer, J. E. Sympathetic activation, drugs and fright. *Journal of Comparative and Physiological Psychology,* 1963, **56,** 612-615.

Stein, M. Some physiological considerations of the relationship between the autonomic nervous system and behavior. In D. C. Glass (Ed.), *Neurophysiology and Emotion,* New York: Rockefeller University Press, 1967.

Storms, M. D. and Nisbett, R. E. Insomnia and the attribution process. Unpublished manuscript, Yale University, New Haven, 1970.

Stunkard, A. J. Obesity and the denial of hunger. *Psychosomatic Medicine,* 1959, **21,** 281-289.

Stunkard, A. J. Hunger and satiety. *American Journal of Psychiatry,* 1961, **118** (3), 212-217.

Stunkard, A. J. The perception of hunger. In D. A. Hamburg, K. Pribram, and A. J. Stunkard (Eds.), *Disorders of perception.* Baltimore: Williams and Wilkins (in press).

Stunkard, A. J. & Koch, C. The interpretation of gastric motility: I. Apparent bias in the reports of hunger by obese persons. *Archives of Genetic Psychiatry,* 1964, **11,** 74-82.

Teitelbaum, P. Sensory control of hypothalamic hyperphagia. *Journal of Comparative and Physiological Psychology,* 1955, **43,** 156-163.

University Dormitory Council. Report on food services at Columbia University. *Columbia Spectator,* March 9, 1964, p. 1.

Valins, S. Psychopathy and physiological reactivity under stress. Unpublished masters thesis, Columbia University, New York, 1963.

Valins, S. Cognitive effects of false heart-rate feedback. *Journal of Personality and Social Psychology,* 1966, **4**, 400-408.

Valins, S. Emotionality and autonomic reactivity. *Journal of Experimental Research in Personality,* 1967, **2**, 41-48.

Valins, S. & Ray, A. A. Effects of cognitive desensitization on avoidance behavior. *Journal of Personality and Social Psychology,* 1967, **7**, 345-350.

Von Holst, E. & Von Saint Paul, U. Electrically controlled behavior. *Scientific American,* March, 1962, 50-59.

Verhave, T., Owen, J. E., Jr., & Slater, O. H. Effects of various drugs on escape and avoidance behavior. In H. H. Pennes (Ed.), *Psychopharmacology: pharmacologic effects on behavior.* New York: Hoeber-Harper, 1958, pp. 267-279.

Welhem, W. C. & Behnke, A. R. The specific gravity of healthy men. *Journal of the American Medical Association,* 1942, **118**, 498-501.

Wenger, M. A. Emotion as visceral action: An extension of Lange's theory. In M. L. Reymert (Ed.), *Feelings and emotions: the moosehart symposium.* New York: McGraw-Hill, 1950, pp. 3-10.

Wikler, A. The relation of psychiatry to pharmacology. Published for the American Society for Pharmacology and Experimental Therapeutics. Baltimore: Williams and Wilkins, 1957.

Witkin, H. A., Lewis, H. B., Hertzman, M., Machover, K., Meissner, P. B. & Wapner, S. *Personality through perception.* New York: Harper & Brothers, 1954.

Wolf, S. & Wolff, H. G. *Human gastric function.* New York: Oxford University Press, 1943.

Woodworth, R. S. & Schlosberg, H. *Experimental psychology.* New York: Holt, 1954.

Wrightsman, L. S. Effects of waiting with others on changes in level of felt anxiety. *Journal of Abnormal and Social Psychology,* 1960, **61**, 216-220.

Wynne, L. C. & Solomon, R. L. Traumatic avoidance learning: Acquisition and extinction in dogs deprived of normal peripheral autonomic function. *Genetic Psychology Monographs,* 1955, **52**, 241-284.

Subject Index